Probation and Re-Education

Elizabeth Glover had a wide knowledge of Club work, to which she gave seven years' service at the beginning of her career. This was followed by a period of voluntary work in the Metropolitan Juvenile Courts. She joined the Probation Service in 1931 and remained in it until 1946, working at first in the London Courts, and later as a member of the Probation Training Board and an Inspector.

While *Probation and Re-Education*, originally published in 1949, was primarily written for all who had to do with delinquent children, it was addressed not only to specialists, but to the wider public who were beginning to feel some concern about post-war moral standards. It was revised in 1956 in the light of changes brought about by the Criminal Justice Act of 1948.

What is probation? What happens to the person put on probation? What good is it supposed to do to him or to society? These are the questions which this book sets out to answer. Today it can be read and enjoyed in its historical context.

I0028285

Probation and Re-Education

Elizabeth R. Glover

Routledge
Taylor & Francis Group

First published in 1949
Second edition (revised) 1956
by Routledge & Kegan Paul Ltd

This edition first published in 2024 by Routledge
4 Park Square, Milton Park, Abingdon, Oxon, OX14 4RN

and by Routledge
605 Third Avenue, New York, NY 10017

Routledge is an imprint of the Taylor & Francis Group, an informa business

Publisher's Note
The publisher has gone to great lengths to ensure the quality of this reprint but points out that some imperfections in the original copies may be apparent.

Disclaimer
The publisher has made every effort to trace copyright holders and welcomes correspondence from those they have been unable to contact.

A Library of Congress record exists under LCCN: 56002520

ISBN: 978-1-032-80472-9 (hbk)
ISBN: 978-1-003-49702-8 (ebk)
ISBN: 978-1-032-80476-7 (pbk)

Book DOI 10.4324/9781003497028

PROBATION
AND RE-EDUCATION

by

ELIZABETH R. GLOVER, M.A.

*Sometime Deputy Principal Probation Officer for London,
and Joint Secretary of the Probation Training Board*

With a Foreword by
CONSTANCE REAVELEY

ROUTLEDGE & KEGAN PAUL LIMITED
Broadway House, 68-74 Carter Lane
London, E.C.4

First published 1949
Second edition (revised) 1956

To

Alice E. C. Glover

PRINTED IN GREAT BRITAIN BY
LUND HUMPHRIES
LONDON · BRADFORD

TABLE OF CONTENTS

Contents

Foreword

by Constance Reaveley

This book is written primarily for those who are directly concerned in making a success of Probation, especially magistrates and probation officers, and also the police, those in charge of Approved Schools and Homes, employers, teachers, foster-parents (and indeed parents) and any who may find themselves in contact with probationers and want to help them.

But the book is designed also for a wider public, and this for several reasons. During the last decades we have as a people felt increasingly a sense of obligation towards those who for one reason or another cannot help themselves—the aged, children deprived of normal home life, the disabled, the mentally afflicted, the refugees. All the great political parties have responded to the growing weight of desire that real help should be given by the community as a whole to those whose own resources are not sufficient to save them from wretchedness of one kind or another. The provision for probation in the Act of 1907 was one of the earliest manifestations of this spirit : part of the great programme of humanitarian legislation carried by the Liberal Government of 1906.

In the case of certain kinds of handicap, blindness for instance, or bereavement, there is no question of attaching blame either to the sufferers or to the community, and the sense of obligation rests simply on the recognition of human need, on the obscure yet strong conviction, which expresses itself in deeds rather than in words, that indifference towards those who need help is a disgrace to a nation. The probationer, on the other hand, has committed offences for which, not long ago, the severest penalties were thought proper.

And the community, by the laws which it has made, the institutions and way of life which it has developed, the education which it has imposed, has created an environment in which it seems that offences must needs come. We have never settled the question who is most to blame, we have never cleared our minds on the ethics of punishment nor found out whether or how punishment really deters. We simply enacted that in certain cases at the magistrates' discretion not retribution but cure should be attempted. That experiment was begun over forty years ago, and subsequent legislation has not abandoned but supplemented it.

As a result of this experiment of nearly half a century, probation officers are reaching conclusions which bear directly on the wider problems of public life. It is coming to be recognized that in human affairs very much depends on a factor which we have for long neglected, from lack of skill in handling it. This factor is human personality itself. In almost every sphere of life great efforts have been made, in the modern era, to build up institutions and procedures which will of themselves mould human nature into desired habits of behaviour. In diplomacy, in industrial relations, even in the nursing of the sick and the education of the young, and in a hundred other spheres, we have done our best to elaborate formal rules and routines for dealing with people in the mass, with the minimum of attention to individuality. The immense increase of population during the nineteenth century did much to necessitate these methods. But they do not suffice ; and to-day we are experimenting with more personal techniques. Modern methods of building military morale, the introduction of personnel officers into industry, the growth of psychiatric clinics and matrimonial advice bureaux are instances of this new conception. These and many other innovations rest on the recognition that the individual human mind, its thoughts and feelings, is the source from which conduct springs.

This lesson probation officers have been learning for a long time : they have been compelled by the nature of their work to become sensitive to human individuality, and to rely on no mass methods or stereotyped routines. And their experience has brought them to conclusions, which provide practical confirmation for some of those reached by psychiatrists and psychoanalysts along other routes ; and which reaffirm the essential teaching of the Christian religion.

Finally, at a time when we are coming to grips with the problems of our recently nationalized industries and services, it is of no little interest that the Probation Act, introduced so many years ago, has within the framework of its provisions, given great freedom to its officers to work out their own experimental and creative methods, based on sensitive insight into the needs of individuals. From this it would appear that there is in the nature of things no necessity for public servants, acting for the community, to work in any rigid or inhuman way, or to be shackled by such regulations as rule out tenderness and wisdom in dealing with people. A study of the work of probation officers has therefore a certain timeliness at this juncture.

Preface

In offering to the public this theory of probation I must first present my credentials, the experience upon which it is founded.

I was trained for social work at the Time and Talents Settlement in Bermondsey, and served my apprenticeship, for seven years, in club work. I worked in girls' clubs, in boys' clubs, in mixed clubs, and in adult clubs. I worked in the kind of club where the youngsters were liable to lock themselves up in the lavatories to drink intoxicants, and in those where play readings and musical appreciation programmes were the order of the day.

I joined the probation service in 1931 under the aegis of the London Police Court Mission, after some months of voluntary work in the Metropolitan Juvenile Courts. I worked in petty sessional divisions, in the stipendiary courts, and in the County of London Sessions. When I became Deputy Principal Probation Officer for London it was part of my duty to attend Case Committees and to discuss the progress of individual probationers with men and women probation officers all over London. I was also responsible for building up a register of Approved Lodgings for young delinquents bound over to London probation officers. I visited innumerable potential foster-mothers and landladies, registered those thought suitable, and visited them again after they had had some experience of mothering probationers. This was at the beginning of the scheme for Approved Lodgings, and all lodging cases both in the juvenile and adult courts in London were my special concern. During this time, too, I served on the Committees of two Approved Probation Hostels and one Approved Probation Home. I lived in one of the Hostels myself for six months. As a Temporary Inspector of the

Probation Branch of the Home Office I had opportunity to
visit, and stay in, many Approved Homes, Hostels and Schools
up and down the country.   During the war I had a very
precious year's experience in two residential schools for
evacuated children in the country, which brought me into
far closer contact with a child's mind and a child's reactions
than anything I had had before.

As one of the Joint Secretaries of the Probation Training
Board my experience was further widened.   Here my duty
took me all over the country to men and women probation
officers in both town and rural areas with whom Home Office
trainees were placed for part of their practical training.
I discussed the principles of probation, the organization of
the work and the training of students with these officers,
chosen for their wisdom and experience.   I also organized
training courses for student probation officers, lectured to
them on the principles of probation case work, and discussed
with them the application of their theoretical knowledge to
the delinquents whom they had already met.

It is not possible to name or to thank personally all who have
contributed to my thought, for they are too many.   Those
of them who read these pages will meet themselves here and
there and recognize their contributions, sometimes perhaps
with another's interpretation.   While acknowledging my
debt and offering my thanks to them all I must express my
special gratitude to Miss O. K. I. deBerry, Miss J. E. Channell,
Miss M. F. Griffiths and Mr W. G. Minn, with whom it was
my privilege to work in close contact for several years.   Insofar
as there is wisdom in the following pages it is gathered
wisdom, learnt from all these men and women colleagues of
mine in our official and unofficial talks, but the final interpretation and assessment here presented is mine.

Of the people whose stories are here quoted as examples,
some were personally known to me, some to my colleagues ;
the circumstances of others were told me by students in case

discussions. In every case fictitious names have been given, and only those facts which seemed relevant to the point at issue. I hope that neither they nor any of their friends or relatives will be pained by anything recorded in this book, if they should chance to read it, or feel that their confidences have been abused.

This book would never have been written or seen the light of day without my sisters Mary and Janet, who over the course of years have continually read and re-read it, helped with its typing, corrected, edited, challenged and discussed it. I am very grateful, too, to Mrs Barbara Wootton who read most of the chapters in typescript and gave me valued criticism, much of which has been acted upon. Miss Eileen Young-husband, M.B.E., J.P., Miss G. M. Stafford, Mr W. Matthews and Mr W. G. Minn have also helped me by reading critically certain chapters and offering suggestions, and I am grateful for their help. Finally, I have to thank Miss Constance Reaveley for her encouragement and the Foreword.

Preface to the Second Edition

Since this book was written there have been many changes in matters affecting probation. The Criminal Justice Act of 1948 has superseded the old Probation Act of 1907. Poverty and unemployment are now no longer major problems in this country. Our statutory social services have been re-modelled and renamed. Hence the need for some revision. But the principles of treatment and ways of approach which I put forward earlier still hold good, and I still believe that the main causes of delinquency and the factors making for recovery alike, are emotional rather than economic. I have not therefore attempted to substitute new examples of cases for my original ones.

I am deeply indebted to Mr C. J. Collinge, Chief Clerk to the Metropolitan Juvenile Courts, for assisting me in this task of revision on the legal side, and I have greatly valued his generous help, wide knowledge and infinite patience.

March, 1955   E. R. G.

I

The Law

"John Smith, in view of all the circumstances the Court has decided to give you one more chance if you agree to take it. We are going to put you on probation. . . ."

"What happened to old Johnny down at the court, Chum?"

"Put on probation." . . .

". . . And do you know, after all the damage that boy's done, they've gone and put him on probation."

Snatches of conversation like this, with this refrain, are not uncommon to those who are interested in news of the courts. But there the matter generally ends. What happens to John after he's been put there? What is this probation? And what good does it do to him, or to injured society? These are the questions which this book sets out to answer.

Time was when the offender was put, not on probation, but out of the way. He was hanged, or deported, and society was rid of him without more ado. But this was inhumane, and men revolted from the policy. Sooner than condemn their fellows to penalties of this sort jurymen were prepared to perjure their oaths and bring in verdicts of Not Guilty. To do nothing at all about the offence, however, though more humane than exacting the supreme penalty, is still not effective. People came to see that if they did not get rid of the offender they must continue to live with him, and it was therefore in their own interests to do something to reform his character. All these men, women and children who offend against society now continue to be members of it. Somehow or another we have got to get on with them, employ them, or else pay for their upkeep in prisons or institutions of some sort.

The treatment of the offender is thus an economic problem as well as an ethical one. How can he be turned into a social asset instead of a liability?

The Probation of Offenders Act came into being in this country in 1907. This method of treatment has therefore now had half a century of official practice, time to develop, and time to prove itself. The provisions relating to it were somewhat modified in the Criminal Justice Act of 1948, and it may be useful to begin our study of the system by looking at these, and at the law as it now stands in relation to probation.

There is nothing in the Criminal Justice Act which limits the use of probation to first offenders or trivial offences. Its provisions may be applied to anyone, man, woman or child, who is convicted of an offence (unless it is one for which, as in the case of murder, the sentence is fixed by law). Thus persons found guilty of arson, bigamy, burglary, sexual assaults, frauds, as well as of many lesser offences, can be "put on probation". The court has to be satisfied that "having regard to the circumstances, including the nature of the offence and the character of the offender", it is expedient to make a probation order. Hence persons with many previous convictions, who have already served sentences of imprisonment or preventive detention can be, have been, and are, "put on probation" when the court is satisfied that this is the best course to take in the interests of the public.

It will be noted that the attention of the court is directed to certain relevant aspects of the case, which must be considered before coming to the decision to use probation. The character of the offender must be considered, that is to say, his antecedents, the background of his life up to the present, the influences to which he has so far been subjected, and the factors, social and personal, which have moulded his character.

Age is no longer specifically mentioned as a factor—perhaps in order to make it clear that probation is not, as was sometimes thought, something meant for young offenders only.

Age, nevertheless, is one of the circumstances which the court must take into account. Young children sometimes do a great deal of damage simply through inexperience, ignorance, or lack of supervision. Adolescents have well recognized difficulties of their own. Men and women in later life are known to pass through a disturbing phase of physical change, which may have its effect for a while on their behaviour.

Health, too, though no longer named as a ground for using probation, is clearly among the relevant circumstances. Ill health or different stages of incipient disease may make a person unusually irritable, indolent or anxious, sometimes desperate. Health affects mentality, and hence reformation of character may depend to a large degree on recovery of health.

The reference in the Act to the nature of the offence directs the attention of the court to the immediate occasion of the offender's appearance before it. This in itself may make it more likely, or less likely, that probation will be a suitable way of dealing with the offender. In the case of those road traffic offences which involve automatic disqualification for driving, for instance, the High Court has pronounced that probation is not suitable, and there are many other offences under modern statutes to which the purpose and method of probation are inappropriate.

Finally, the court must decide what is most expedient in all the circumstances. It is the function of the court to safeguard the interests and welfare of society as a whole. Crime is a dead, impersonal thing ; it has happened ; nothing can undo it. Punishment will not alter the past, though it may have a material effect on the future. For instance, if it aroused resentment or desperation in the offender it might do more ultimate harm to society than good. The criminal is a living person, endowed still with the same potentialities of good and ill. His gifts of intelligence, imagination, physical endurance, courage, manipulative skill—whatever they may be—are still there, and can be used for society's benefit or the reverse. The court has to decide how, in all the circumstances, society's interests can best be served in relation to this individual, how best to ensure that this offence is not repeated, and that he becomes an asset to society rather than a liability.

If, bearing all these things in mind, the court decides on probation, it may make a probation order. But the Act gives the offender the last word, because the order cannot be made (except in the case of a child under 14) without his consent. He can decline to be "put on probation", and refuse to accept the "requirements" entailed, and if he does so, no probation "order" can be made. This does occasionally happen. Some offenders prefer the prospect of six months imprisonment and then freedom, to a year or more of supervision by a probation officer. (Six months is the maximum sentence which a magistrates' court in England can normally impose for any one offence.) But there is more in it than this. The Act is here founded upon profoundest truth. No power on earth can compel another to be good. One can forcibly restrain another from actively doing wrong; if you lock a man up in irons, for instance, in a padded cell, he will not be able to "do" much harm; but no one can similarly constrain another to "be" good. Probation then is founded on the free will and assent of the offender.

If the offender agrees to probation he has to undertake to fulfil or abide by certain "requirements", or in other words agree to certain conditions. He is required, first and foremost, to be under the supervision of a probation officer, for a named period. This may be anything from one to three years in the first instance. It may subsequently be reduced, or extended, but never beyond the maximum of 3 years for any one offence.

He is further usually required "to be of good behaviour and to lead an industrious life". No definition of this somewhat tall order is given, but it is of course commonly taken to mean that he must engage not to commit another legal offence or breach of the peace. If he does, he can be dealt with for the original offence as well as the new one. An industrious life means in the case of an adult going to work regularly, and in the case of a child attending school regularly.

Further stipulations are that he must notify the probation officer of any change of address or employment, keep in touch with him as instructed, and receive visits from him. Clearly there can be no effective supervision without regular contact and intimate knowledge.

Additional requirements may be included to deal with particular circumstances. Where a youngster, for instance, needs stricter discipline than he is getting at home, the companionship of others of his own age, or a greater measure of sympathy and understanding, it may be necessary to get him away from his own home, to some place that will cater for these needs. The offender may therefore be asked to go and live at some specified place for a stated length of time as a condition of his release. This is called "a requirement as to residence", and can be a valuable factor. Its possibilities are described in greater detail in subsequent chapters. There is now also a specific power to include a "requirement as to mental treatment", where the court finds, on the evidence of a doctor experienced in mental disorders, that the offender is not certifiable but might respond to treatment at a child guidance clinic, for instance, or as a voluntary patient in a mental hospital. Or, in other types of case, he may be asked to abstain from certain things, such as drinking, going to the cinema, frequenting named places of shady reputation, or associating with persons of known bad character. Such requirements sound plausible enough, but in actual fact it is usually impossible to secure their observance. No probation officer can follow any one probationer around every hour of the day or night, watching where he goes and whom he meets as he pursues his business or pleasure. It is a pity to have

B

stipulations in the order which cannot be enforced. Or he may be required to do certain things—he must promise to go to Church or Sunday School regularly, to be indoors by a stated time each night, or to join a youth organization. The same objection applies to some of these. But apart from the practical difficulty of enforcement, most probation officers feel it is a mistake to make specific details of such a kind as these the requirements of a probation order. The offender's recovery depends upon the degree to which he can, of his own preference, turn away from evil influences to good ones, and it is the officer's job to direct his attention and whet his appetite for the latter. Since the basis of the probation system lies in free will, it is a pity to insert requirements such as these, which certainly take the flavour of coercion, and thereby partly defeat their own purpose.

The Act further makes provision for the payment of damages or compensation by the offender. It is strange from the point of view of logic and ethics that these provisions are so rarely used. It would appear to most lay minds to be a matter of common justice that where one person has caused damage or loss to another he should at any rate make an effort to pay back the monetary value. And how can the offender be allowed to feel that he is " being of good behaviour " if he does not do his utmost to make good the harm done ? This is what we commonly try to teach children in the nursery. Yet compensation is comparatively rarely ordered. Sometimes, of course, the damage runs into some hundreds of pounds, and it is quite beyond the means of a couple of errand boys or a jobbing gardener, for instance, to make good such a loss. On the other hand a large number of probationers who have defrauded their fellows of smaller sums, or stolen their valued personal possessions, are "put on probation" with never a word said as to the duty or propriety of paying compensation.

The Act lays down that before making a probation order

the court must explain to the offender in ordinary language the effects of its provisions, and all his obligations in regard to it, and make clear that if he disregards these he will be liable to be dealt with. Some courts take great pains to carry out this duty, but the offender does not always hear or take it in. For one thing there is in some courts a great distance between the bench and the dock, and many officials coming and going and conducting their business in whispers in the intervening space—and this is distracting. If he does hear, he does not always understand or follow. His mind is in a whirl of nervous confusion. And some magistrates address the offender in public school language, with which in most cases, he is unfamiliar. Some courts, too, take less care than others to explain what is involved, and what is "ordinary language" to the legal mind may be far from simple to the lay and a complete enigma to the unlettered. Hence the first question which some of these offenders ask on leaving the court, after "it has all been explained" is "What is the sentence?"

The court is supposed to give copies of the order forthwith to the probation officer, who in turn is supposed to give one to the probationer. But many courts do not manage to get the orders drawn up at once, so that the offender is apparently allowed to go home without more ado. A few days later the probation officer arrives with a printed paper couched in legalistic language. This, it is now explained, is what the probationer promised the court to observe. In other areas on leaving the court room he is told to go with the probation officer who will tell him all about it. Thus in many cases full explanation and discussion follows rather than precedes the making of the order. This inverted procedure naturally brings its own difficulties to the officer concerned.

The duties of the probation officer are defined in a Schedule to the Act, and in Statutory Rules. He is to keep in touch with the probationer, see that he understands and observes the order, report upon his progress to the magistrates, and generally "advise, assist and befriend him". He must seek to find him suitable work where this is necessary, and encourage him to use the available statutory and voluntary agencies for his welfare. The trilogy "advise, assist and befriend" is interesting. There is no note here of coercion. The officer has no authority to order the offender about. The latter is released by the court to go about his business and direct his affairs as seems to him right or desirable. It is clearly the intention of the Act that the offender should be a free man, undertaking full responsibility for his actions, but with the obligation of keeping in touch with his probation officer so that the latter may both assist him if desired, and satisfy the court as to his conduct. Here again the Act is sound. This offender has failed in responsibility; the way to teach responsibility is to give it. Every public school and up-to-date youth club knows this. You cannot help irresponsible people to be responsible by depriving them of responsibility.

The Act (Schedule I) makes provision for the probation order to be amended, if this is later deemed to be desirable. This may be done on the application of the probation officer, or the probationer himself, to the court for the area in which the probationer lives, which is called the supervising court. If the officer applies, the probationer must (except in a few cases) be summoned to attend, so that he can hear what is now proposed and have a chance to dispute it or disagree. Unless he is under 14 the order can only be amended with his consent. If he does agree the duration of the order can be extended (never beyond the total maximum of three years) or diminished: old conditions can be deleted, or new ones inserted. The order can in fact be discharged completely, but only by the court which originally made it. Application for this must be made, and is occasionally made, by the probation officer or the probationer, usually on the grounds that further supervision is deemed to be no longer either expedient or necessary.

Provision is made in the Act (Section 6) for what is known as "breach of probation". It is this clause which gives the probation officer such authority as he has, but it proves in practice to be very little. If the offender breaks his promise, the officer must first satisfy the court that there are sufficient grounds upon which to issue a summons. " Elsie has not been to see me for three weeks, though I made her clearly understand she was to come weekly." " Ronald has missed Sunday School twice running. It was a requirement of the order that he should attend regularly." "Mr Smith was seen leaving the White Swan public House at 10 p.m. last night. He undertook not to frequent this house and to abstain from taking alcoholic liquor." These things sound trivial in a court of law, and the same magistrates who made them a binding requirement of the probation order sometimes find themselves very loath to take action on them. " Sent to Prison because he had a Pint with his Pals " or because " He Cut his Club " would not make pleasant reading in the headlines of the sensational press. Probation officers have sometimes been advised in the circumstances not to take too harsh a view ; that these things do not constitute a criminal offence ; and, even, that the court can take no action unless a new offence has definitely been committed. If, therefore, the officer was unwise enough to begin the probation on a basis of authority and threats, he may find himself deflated, and have to begin ignominiously climbing down in his relations with a now triumphant offender, who no longer respects or believes him.

But the court may feel the report is sufficiently serious to warrant a hearing, so the offender is summoned to court. He may admit the breach, but if he does not the officer has to prove in the witness box on oath under cross examination that a breach of the order has been committed. The most vital condition of any order is that which binds the offender to keep in close touch with the officer, and to visit him or be at home at times arranged by him.   If there is no contact there can be no probation.

This is the commonest breach of probation, but it is difficult to prove.   The officer states perhaps that the arrangement was for William to visit him at the office on Wednesday evenings at 6 p.m. on his way home from work.   In fact he has failed to do so for the last six consecutive weeks, in spite of reminders by post.   William contests this.   He maintains that he could not come last week, he had to work late ; and the week before he set out to come but got a puncture and arrived just too late, finding the door closed ; the week before that his mother was taken ill, and he had had to hurry home with a bottle of medicine for her.   Or he mistook the day, and called on a Thursday by mistake.   Could he not have intimated some of this to the officer to avoid all this bother ? " Yes," maintains William, " I did, sir ; I got on the telephone three times, but could get no reply.   And my mother wrote a letter to explain."   No one has received the letter.   Who can confute all this ?   The probation officer is not in a position to do so, so the case is dismissed, William cockier than ever, and the officer in a difficulty.

Although it is not uncommon for courts to hesitate, or even to decline to take action in breach cases of this kind, a great many courts take alleged breach of probation seriously. The probationer is summoned, and if he gives evidence cross-questioned about the matter.   This in itself may provide a jolt for an irresponsible person, unaccustomed to having to answer for his actions.   Even if the case is not proved, and has to be dismissed, the incident in many cases acts as a pull-up.   It is often accompanied by a serious talk or a warning from the magistrates.   If a breach is proved it is not necessary to cancel the order, or to commit the offender to prison or to an Approved School, or even to fine him.   Such severity is usually quite unnecessary.   The case may be adjourned for a week or two to see if the probationer mends his ways.   This sometimes has quite a sobering effect. The probation order may be extended. This is a logical thing to do if weeks of probation have been wasted through loss of contact. In some cases new requirements may be added—as to residence, for instance. A summons for breach of probation therefore may be a salutary experience for the offender.

The court is bound to weigh the evidence in breach cases as meticulously as in any other charge, and to presume that the offender is innocent until the probation officer proves him guilty. It is right that probationers should be protected from too great a measure of authority on the part of the officers. It is alien to British law to put one person into the unrestrained power of another. Two considerations emerge from a survey of the working of this clause of the Act. First, when imposing the conditions of any probation order, an eye should be cast on the possibility of a breach. How would any sentence passed on proof of a breach of this condition be viewed by an appeal court, for instance? All but the absolutely basic fundamentals of probation should in this light be cut out. These are that the offender must agree (i) to endeavour to be of good behaviour and (ii) to maintain close contact with the officer. A requirement as to residence or mental treatment, or an order for compensation may further sometimes be invaluable. If the conditions are cut down to a minimum in this way courts might be readier to uphold them—even the appeal courts, and if a breach is proved, appropriate action taken. It is quite clear from the wording of Section 6 of the Act that an offender can be dealt with for the original offence if he disregards or flouts any of the requirements of his probation order. He can be fined up to £10 if a breach is proved, or, in appropriate cases, sent to an attendance centre, without ending probation. Nevertheless some courts are still reluctant to exercise their powers unless a fresh offence is committed, and the results of this attitude may be disastrous. Every time an offender gets away with a flagrant breach of his probation his immediate neighbours are mystified by what seems to them the inefficiency of the law, while any confederates are emboldened in their contempt for it.

The second consideration concerns probation officers themselves. To begin probation on the basis of authority and to conduct it by means of threats and menaces is not only to court disaster, but to travesty the Act. The position should be made perfectly clear from the start to the probationer, so that there is no misconception in his mind at all as to the role each has to play. " I am not in authority over you, Daisy ; let there be no mistake about that. You are responsible, not me. You have given the court a promise to be of good behaviour ; I can't make you behave well. Only you can do that. My job is to help you if I can ; to back you up, not to order you about. I shall tell you if I think you are making a mistake or going the wrong way about things, and make suggestions sometimes if I think they would be helpful. But it is you who are responsible. You must do what you think is right, I have to report to the court how you are getting on. If the court does not like what they hear from me about you, they will send for you and ask you about it. And if they think when they have heard what you have to say that you have not kept your promise, they may cancel this probation, release you from your promise, and think what to do instead about your stealing that money."

If the probation officer explains the procedure in this way, a summons to court later, if things go wrong, appears reasonable. "The arrangement you made with the court, Daisy, is not working. You promised the court you would keep in touch with me, and you haven't. There may be very good reasons why you haven't, but you haven't. I must report this to the court. This was part of the bargain. And, as I told you, they will probably want to see you and ask you about it." And if the court thereafter decide to do nothing, the officer's position and attitude remain exactly the same ; he has done

what was clearly his duty ; he was always interested in the
probationer and he remains so, even though the order has
broken down. The officer should always discuss with the
probationer the reports he proposes to make to the court, or if
there is no personal contact through failure of the probationer
to carry out agreed arrangements, tell him by post. Not
infrequently the serious talk which results causes the probationer to think again and take the matter more seriously.
It cannot be too often or too stringently impressed upon the
probationer that he is responsible, and that if the probation
breaks down, and is finally cancelled by a sentence of imprisonment, a fine or an approved school order, such an approach
as is here described (suitable with modifications for any age)
does not necessarily involve a breach of good relations
between the officer and the offender and his family. In
some cases the offender has been rational enough to take the
view, " Oh, well, you couldn't help yourself ; you had to ;
my fault I suppose ". Naturally not all probationers could
take this line. Many offenders are neurotic people whose
reasoning apparatus is out of order. Such folk will take the
view that the court, the officer, everyone, and life itself, have
treated them unfairly. But if the officer has proceeded from
the false basis of authority, " Now, Daisy, do that once more
and I shall report you to the court, and you know what that
means ", the natural reaction is, " The probation officer had
me put away". That is, this calamity was due to the probation
officer, (not me). The merit of the probation system
properly used is that it is a means of inculcating that supremely
important principle of life, personal responsibility.

These, then, are the main provisions for the probation of
offenders in this country. The basis of the system as laid
down by the Act is founded on sound philosophy. It is
built on the free will and personal responsibility of the
offender and on the friendship and help of the officer, not on
compulsion, restraint or authority. The interpretation

within this framework is left with very wide discretion to the magistrates and the probation officers who work it.

II

Probation as Treatment

Probation has now been available to the English courts for half a century, so it is possible to draw some conclusions from experience as to the value of the various interpretations given to it, and its potentialities.

It was undoubtedly first devised as a means of saving people from the degradation of a prison sentence. (Even yet a prison sentence is rarely regarded as anything other than disastrous from the point of view of the prisoner.) That is to say, it was a " let off ". It was assumed that the more decent type of offender would naturally realize that he had merited punishment, and be deeply moved by gratitude and penitence if instead of condemning him to this, society gave him the chance to make amends. It was assumed, too, that he could do this, if he wanted to. Nearly fifty years' experience of probation have now shown us that these assumptions may be in some respects over-confident.

First, offenders cannot be classed into black and white, depraved and decent. Offenders, like everybody else, are a mixture of good and bad qualities. They can be generous and unreliable, loyal and unscrupulous, competent and self-seeking, well-intentioned and impulsive, all at one and the same time, making them admirable people in some respects, unsatisfactory in others.

Secondly, experience has shown that very few offenders are humble enough to believe that they have merited the humiliation and exposure of arrest and charge, and the condemnation of public opinion. Very few people take this view of other disastrous happenings in life, such as being dismissed from a job, failing in business, losing a friend. Offenders are no

exception. " I'm no worse than anyone else. Why pick on
me ? " " Stealing a rotten old pair of shoes is not so bad as
stealing somebody's husband. Why don't they run after
Mrs So-and-So and arrest her for stealing my husband ? "
" They ought to look after their stuff better." Most people,
they think, are out for Number One ; most people placed as
they were would have done the same ; life has always been
hard ; it's unfair ; some people have all the luck. The new
probationer leaves the court relieved—yes, certainly relieved—
but neither penitent nor grateful ; full of self-pity, angry
humiliation and suspicious apprehension about the supervision
he has let himself in for.

Thirdly, we have come to see that for the very reason that
people are such a mixture of conflicting traits of good and ill
they are not always—on the contrary they are rarely—able
to change their nature by an act of will. Human nature is
not as simple as this. Though we all like to think we act by
our own freely determined choice, we do not. What we
choose to do to-day depends upon the disposition of our minds,
and that depends on our past habits of living and thinking.
A person habitually attuned to thinking in terms of his own
exclusive pleasure or profit, or fear of being thought ridiculous,
or alternatively to never thinking at all, cannot overnight,
simply by deciding to, become altruistic, independent,
reflective ; he has not developed the necessary mental and
moral muscles. We react to the present situation, in short,
with our present mental and emotional apparatus, the only
one we have.

There followed another phase in the interpretation of the
probation method. In certain schools of thought and practice
probation was believed to hold possibilities of punishment.
Too great a measure of leniency was thought to be ill-advised.
These people, it was argued, though one hesitated to ruin
them by a prison sentence, yet needed a wholesome reminder
that they could not offend with impunity. So some

magistrates and probation officers deliberately made probation as unpleasant as possible. Probationers were asked to report at the most inconvenient hours, a Saturday afternoon for instance, thus preventing industrial workers from their only chance of outdoor recreation. They were expected to travel long distances to see their officer and to pay their own fares. They were subjected to military discipline at the office, told to stand at attention and take their hands out of their pockets, to come with clean fingernails and collars, and to answer deferentially when spoken to.

This kind of thing is now seen to have little remedial effect on character. The selfish, unstable or unscrupulous person does not become generous, steady or upright because he has been humiliated in this fashion. He merely hates it : hates the authority that imposed it : is more than ever convinced that life is hard and he is unlucky ; and makes up his mind not to get caught again, but to get his own back if he can.

Probation officers have now come to see that the law governing probation permits of another interpretation— treatment. A year or two of close personal contact between the offender and the probation officer may be an opportunity to improve the former's health, to enlarge his legitimate interests and scope, to re-direct his feelings and emotions along healthier channels, so that his outlook on life and attitude of mind are altered, and new mental and moral muscles developed. Instead of having a negative function saving the offender from a worse fate, or teaching him not to do this again, probation has assumed a positive one, intro-ducing him to a better way of life.

A new factor has come into the situation since 1907, which has greatly contributed to this interpretation of the probation provisions. This is psychiatry.

The lay public do not always distinguish the many modern developments connected with psychological research. The two sciences which concern behaviour problems are psychology, the science of human behaviour, and psychiatry, the science of healing the mind. A psychologist is one who has made a study of the way the mind works, and a psychiatrist is one qualified to treat mental diseases, that is to say, a fully qualified medical practitioner with additional qualifications in psychology. Further, psychological treatment is not synonymous with psycho-analytical treatment, as is commonly supposed. Psycho-analysis is one method of treatment only, by which a psycho-analyst helps people to analyse themselves and see their motives as they really are, and so to understand and manage themselves better. This is always a long process, and often a painful one, for the picture so revealed is usually less flattering than had been imagined. Because it takes a long time it is expensive ; and because it is painful not everyone can face it ; because it requires a degree of insight and reasoning ability not everyone is a good subject for it. Psycho-analytical treatment is analogous to surgery. Most doctors hesitate to recommend anything so drastic as a surgical operation unless there seems absolutely no alternative. Even then, some patients are so ill that the risk of surgical treatment is a greater one than the risk of letting things take their course. And some patients are so horrified at the thought that they will not give their consent. So it is with psycho-analysis. There are other and more common methods of bringing relief to sick minds, and this applies as much to delinquent as to non-delinquent patients.

The psychiatrists established themselves in public opinion in Great Britain first during and after the 1914-1918 war, in treating shellshocked soldiers and sailors. Their reputation and sphere were vastly enlarged during the last war, when every reception area in the country clamoured for their immediate assistance in dealing with children who before evacuation had been regarded as normal. Between the two wars Child Guidance Clinics began to be set up, and to

establish a reputation for giving sound advice and help
in the handling of difficult children. Many of the bigger
hospitals also opened psychiatric clinics where similar advice
and help was given to adults labouring under distress of
mind.

The great contribution which psychology has made from
the point of view of probation is that it has led us away from
the purely legal or moral approach to delinquency to the
scientific or curative one. It has taught us that all conduct,
good or bad, has a reason, and that if the conduct is bad, one
must first look for and find the reason before one can hope to
correct it. The scientist, when his experiments take an
unexpected turn, does not pass judgment, " This powder
ought not to have turned green ". He says, " Good heavens,
it has turned green ; now I wonder *why* ? " In seeking an
answer to this why, his knowledge of the matter is greatly
increased. Similarly, the probation officer's attitude should
be not " That man ought not to beat his wife, or that girl
to tell lies ", but rather *why* do they do so ? Unless he can
discover why they do these things, he cannot hope to help
them, for he will be working blind.

Looked at in this way all delinquency takes on a highly
individual aspect. For instance, what might be the reasons
for stealing ? Some steal for the excitement it brings them.
The small boys who compete with each other up and down the
street markets to see who can pinch from most stalls without
getting caught are an example of this. Older boys who steal
motor cars and plan burglaries also sometimes come under
this category. Some steal to impress. The child, for
instance, who feels despised by teachers and fellows alike for
his ineptitude in school may win a dare-devil name for himself
and so considerable esteem at any rate from a circle, by his
thieving exploits out of school. It is the applause he is after,
not the things he steals. Some steal out of a genuine desire
to help somebody. A child might steal coal to help his

mother, for instance. Some steal because they badly need affection, and by stealing pretty little articles and giving them away as presents they hope to win it. Some steal out of funk. A youngster is dismissed from his job, and not daring to return home without his wages, steals the money to make up. Some steal out of sheer irresponsibility. This is called " borrow- ing ". It seems quite clear that in some cases the offender never meant to take, much less to keep, what did not belong to him. Some steal from a deliberate wish to hurt someone. A girl, for instance, may have been jilted by her lover or reproved by her employer, and steals to spite them. Some steal because they cannot help doing so. This is called pathological stealing, or kleptomania, and is a recognizable disease. The symptoms of pathological stealing are that the offender has no use for what he steals, and takes none of the usual precautions against detection.

This list is not, of course, by any means exhaustive, but is sufficient to serve the purpose of the argument here. The point is that, to be effective, treatment must be related to the cause of the trouble, and therefore it will in all cases be highly individual, individually planned, to meet individual needs. Whatever else may form part of the plan of treatment, the child who steals for excitement must be provided with legitimate outlets for his high spirits and wits ; the child who steals to win approbation must be given more approbation in the normal way, and his self-respect built up by those who have care of him ; those who steal because they want to help someone must be shown better ways of helping ; the child who needs affection must be given it, and, if he is unwanted or unloved, possibly found other more affectionate people to live with ; those who steal out of funk must have their self-confidence built up, so that they can face their difficulties courageously. For the malignant or pathological thief it is well to seek the guidance and help of a psychiatrist. The reasons for these reactions are harder to find for the lay, and therefore treatment without expert advice is likely to be ineffective.

In short, to mete out the same treatment to all offenders is as ineffective as to dose all out-patients in a hospital with cough mixture. There must be individual treatment to meet individual needs and conditions.

But a good doctor does more than treat the immediate symptoms of any illness ; he also has an eye on how his patient's general resistance can be built up so that he does not so easily fall a prey to infection again. That is to say, he not only studies factors conducive to illness, he must also have regard to those that build up health. Similarly, good probation treatment must seek not only to alleviate the immediate problems which may have contributed to or arisen from the offence, but also to develop factors which conduce to moral health.

We must therefore consider what attributes go to the making of moral health. The actual circumstances of life, wealth or poverty, good or bad health, success or failure, are not the factors which exclusively determine our happiness or mould our natures. Some people brought up in abject poverty and want, in the midst of friction, frustration, anxiety and ill health, grow into the saints of the earth, strong, true, generous and courageous folk ; while others born into easy affluent circumstances, who have never been crossed, some- times grow up into lazy, selfish, irresponsible, good-for- nothings. It is not only what happens to us, but how we react to what happens, that affects our characters and peace of mind. So that material circumstances, though no doubt they contribute, are not alone decisive in forming character.

There are four factors which it is here suggested are impor- tant constituents of sound moral health : affection, friends, interests, and faith or philosophy of life.

By affection is meant love ; not the hot, passionate emotion of love affairs, but the deep, strong, abiding ties of concern

c

and regard that bind one person to another or to others. Psychologists tell us that it is absolutely essential to the human spirit both to love and to be loved.[1] Our own observation tells us as much. One has only to compare a completely independent person, who is bound to nobody by any bonds of affection, with an ordinary individual who loves those near and dear to him. The one is wrapped up in himself and views everything that happens as it affects himself only ; the other is concerned for the welfare and happiness of those he loves, and takes a wider view. It is when we begin to love another that we learn naturally and spontaneously, not by effort of will, generosity, tolerance, responsibility and courage. When we love another we do not lightly destroy his peace of mind or his belief in us by doing what would horrify or disappoint him, and thus we learn to modify our own inclinations and wishes. A person who loves no one has neither the same incentive to moral qualities, nor the same restraining force. Love is the basis of our moral standard.

Similarly friends or the lack of them have a profound effect upon character. A person who has no friends loses his sense of proportion and judges everything from his own exclusive point of view, thus becoming narrow in his outlook and ego-centric in his interests. If he loves those in his intimate circle, then without friends the love becomes exclusive and possessive and therefore loses some of its potency for good. Good fellowship leads to large-heartedness and large-mindedness within the group. Social approval is a great restraining force on behaviour. Indeed, it sometimes seems too much so, as if we bowed to the dictates of public opinion, rather than exercising our own discrimination. The child at school and the man in his profession alike are sensitive to what is and what is not " done ", and take trouble to conform to it. This is not to say that adults as well as children do not frequently try to assess how far they can go without evoking the

[1] See *The Origins of Love and Hate*, by D. I. Suttie (Kegan Paul), pp. 50 ff.

displeasure of the group and sometimes assess it wrongly. But a person who keeps his own company and shuns the society of his fellows has less opportunity of sensing public opinion and less incentive to conform to it.

Interests have considerable power to shape character. People who have hobbies or purposes of their own to pursue develop powers of imagination and initiative, judgment and self-discipline, persistence and skill in carrying them out. Further, these interests often lead them to seek the advice and therefore the company of others of like interests, so that interests often lead to friendships. Those, on the other hand, who have no interests and have never found anything they think worth pursuing lose the sense of enjoyment and purpose which others have, and tend in consequence to become restless and unsatisfied. Those who know they have abilities but feel unable through circumstances or temperament to use them, tend to become irritable or cynical. Unsatisfied people are apt to become unsatisfactory people.

By faith is meant faith in a living God, by philosophy a sufficient answer for the time being to life's enigmas. Without some belief in an ultimate purpose or scheme of things, people begin to feel just so much flotsam and jetsam, meaningless, purposeless, worthless. People who are able by reason of their faith or philosophy to feel there is something worth living for, have an ideal to live by, and a scale of values whereby to develop judgment. These things give the ability to see things in better perspective and to take a long view. Such people are not so prone to hasty judgment or action or to the hopelessness of despair or bitterness as others, and hence have a staying power or a resilience in adversity which sees them through.

All these things are what the psychologists mean when they tell us that we are motivated by our emotions rather than by our reason. Emotion in psychology means not hysterics but feeling.

"All the motives which govern and drive our lives are emotional. Love and hate, anger and fear, curiosity and joy, are the springs of all that is most noble and most detestable in the history of men and nations" says John Macmurray.[1] It is what we care about and the extent to which we care that the psychologists mean when they say our lives are governed by emotional factors. And it is this, what we care about and the extent to which we care, that makes our characters. We are beginning to realize that our emotions exercise terrific power over our bodies. We turn sick with fear ; or an invalid like Elizabeth Barrett Browning leaves her sick bed when she falls in love ; worry is recognized as a potent cause of illness. It is true also of the mind. We like to think we are rational beings, who govern our lives by reason. It is true we are endowed with the gift of reasoning, but most of us feel first and think afterwards. We think and act according as we feel. A man feels angry, and hits somebody, metaphorically or actually ; then he thinks, and he thinks he finds very good reasons for justifying his action.

If this is true, then if we seek to reform a man's character we must look to his emotions ; engage his interests and inclinations ; awaken, mend and redirect his capacity for feeling. Punishment is an appeal to reason ; it is most effective when the emotions are concerned in it too. A boy is distressed and concerned when someone whom he loves and admires reproves or punishes him. But if he has no regard for the punisher, he simply dislikes the man and the system more than before, and justifies or excuses himself in his own mind for what he did. Love is the basis of our moral standard. He may decide not to venture that way again if he has been punished, but if so it may merely indicate a surrender to "Safety First" or self-defence, rather than a moral preference.

Insofar, then, as probation is considered to have the

[1] *Freedom in the Modern World*, p. 146.

positive function of introducing the offender to a better way of life, the art of the probation officer lies in arousing and re-directing his emotions.

The extent to which the emotional factors here mentioned are at present operative or deficient varies of course very greatly, from one offender to another, just as factors conducive to physical health are operative in varying degrees with different patients. The contention here is that these things profoundly affect character, and therefore must be considered by anyone seeking to reform character. Effective probation must begin with careful enquiry into these matters, and the nature and extent of the enquiries necessary will now be discussed.

III

Enquiries

The necessity for investigation before deciding upon treatment is recognized in the Criminal Justice Act and in the juvenile courts generally, but not so generally in the adult courts. Why less careful investigation should be thought necessary in the case of adults it is difficult to see. It would seem axiomatic that sound treatment in either case depends upon right diagnosis, and diagnosis upon thorough enquiry, yet in numbers of adult courts offenders are charged, found guilty, and bound over on probation all within the space of a few minutes, the magistrates having no more to guide them than a police report. The probation officer's enquiries are distinct from those of the police or education authority. The police have to report upon the offence and the circumstances relating to it, any previous known offence, and, in adult cases, particulars as to the financial circumstances of the prisoner, in case the magistrates see fit to consider imposing a fine or costs. The local authority in juvenile courts may give particulars of the type of home, wages, rent, and a report of the offender's behaviour and progress in school, which together give a picture of his present situation and attainments. The object of the probation officer's enquiries is quite different. He wants to assess the factors which have so far contributed to the offender's outlook and character, and how far harmful ones may be modified and better ones developed. In juvenile courts there appears to be provision for this in pre-trial enquiries.[1]

Legalists object to pre-trial enquiries on the ground that British law holds a person to be innocent until he has been

[1] Ref. Children and Young Persons Act 1933, 35 (1).

26

found guilty, and if the child is thus still held to be innocent, there having been as yet no hearing, he and his parents should not be subjected to investigation. There is something to be said for this point of view, but since in many cases pre-trial enquiries save the child and his family a long period of suspense (for in some rural areas juvenile courts meet very infrequently) and since they certainly contribute to the wise handling of a case, there is also something to be said for them. In juvenile cases where there has been a finding of guilt, and a remand in custody is held to be necessary, there is not much difficulty now. Most areas have access to a Remand Home, at least in the case of boys.

In adult courts, however, there is no legal provision for pre-trial enquiries. A chat in the forum of the court, or in police cells at the back, will not suffice for the kind of interviews that are necessary. The prisoner's mind is a chaos of disturbing emotions in court. He is obsessed with self-pity, " It's unfair. I'm no worse than other blokes " ; with horror, " Shall I lose my job over this, or my pension ? What will the wife say ? (or mum, dad, or my husband ?). What will happen to the kids ? " ; with apprehension, " What can they do to me ? I'm in their power " ; with humiliation, " I've made a proper mess of things ". There are several ways of reacting to this state of mind. Some keep a stiff upper lip, determined to hide their emotions ; they are monosyllabic. Some play for mercy, and sob. Some are dazed, incapable of thought or feeling, oblivious of what they or anyone else says or does. Some few are unfortunate enough to show their emotion in a silly nervous giggle, quite involuntary, but often cruelly mistaken by the court for levity. Others take the dare-devil attitude, " Oh well, I'll get my own back one of these days. They need not think they'll down me ".

People in these states of mind are incapable of giving a balanced account of things. They have not got their situation in perspective. Further, for a thorough investigation other parties have to be consulted, and the home visited. There must therefore be a remand for enquiries. "Remand" means keeping control of the accused during an adjournment.

The practice with regard to remands in adult courts, whether in custody or on bail, is fortuitous. In big cities where there is a prison on the doorstep it is not unusual for most of those found guilty (and some who have not been) to be remanded in custody. The justification for remanding in custody is that in some cases the court may have reason to fear that the prisoner might disappear or tamper with witnesses, or commit further offences. But that this fear is not a real one in the majority of cases is seen by the fact that in country areas, where a remand in custody involves the arrangement of special transport and escort at considerable expense of time and money, remands in custody are very rare. The arguments for remanding prisoners in custody in these cities with easy access to a prison are various, none convincing. In many cases the avowed motive is punitive. " Let them have a taste of the inside ; it will do them good." But the probation system was designed for the very purpose of saving people from this degrading experience. Remand prisoners, we are assured, are kept separate from convicted ones, so there is no fear of contamination. This may be ; but amongst the remanded prisoners there are some first offenders, some old hands ; some young girls[1] from respectable homes, and some brothel keepers. In any case, all prisoners, remanded and convicted, are conveyed to the prison together in the same " Black Maria ", and on the journey a young first offender, for instance a respectable postman, may have to travel with

[1] Under the Criminal Justice Act 1948 arrangements are to be made for young people under the age of 21 to be sent to " remand centres " wherever possible, instead of to prison. This will protect them from older offenders, not necessarily from persistent offenders and very evil influences. A remand in custody will remain a very serious responsibility on those who order it, but there are no remand centres yet (1955).

verminous, mad, drunk, diseased, or depraved fellow pas-
sengers. And on arrival at the prison all will be subjected
to the same humiliating routine of being stripped, searched
and bathed.[1] The bold bad ones thenceforward have
nothing left to fear. They now know the worst that can
happen to them, and it is not as bad as it might be. The
more sensitive and decent ones have suffered a shocking and
lowering experience from which it may take their self-respect
a long while to recover.

Another reason commonly given is that a medical report
can more easily be obtained in prison. But there is no need
to go to prison to get a medical report. In many adult cases
the offender is quite capable and very ready to take himself
off to the doctor or clinic, and ask that a confidential medical
report be sent on his behalf to the court. In the case of more
irresponsible persons the probation officer may feel it wiser
to take them personally. A preliminary telephone call to
the almoner or doctor concerned will prepare the way and
expedite matters in either case. Every locality has its V.D.
clinic, which gives free examinations on request, and if a
medical overhaul is desired, better facilities for this exist at
the general hospital, with its specialists and up-to-date
apparatus, than in a prison. Thus, though extra trouble may
be required, this will devolve on the prisoner and the probation
officer, both of whom in the circumstances would doubtless
far prefer to take it.

A third reason sometimes given for remanding in custody
where a prison is at hand is that some prisoners " have no
fixed abode ". This is not a sound argument either, because
homeless persons charged in the country are not remanded in
custody, and for those charged in cities alternative accommodation is available. The Church Army and the Salvation

---

[1] See *They Always Come Back*, by Cicely McCall, ch. 1, and *Gaol Delivery*,
by Mark Benney (1948), pp. 45 and 46, for a description of the reception
routine in a prison.

Army make special provision for homeless people of all ages
and both sexes, and the Moral Welfare Societies have shelters
for stranded girls in difficulties.   The practice has sprung up,
and might well be much more widely adopted, of remanding
homeless prisoners on their own bail and asking the probation
officer to make temporary arrangements for them at one or
other of these places.   The difficulties commonly argued
against this procedure are not insuperable.   First, who is to
pay ?   The very moderate expense is not an unreasonable
charge on a city court with a poor-box to save some offender
from the degrading experiences already described.   Some of
the agencies concerned will do it for nothing.   If the prisoner
is destitute, and would otherwise be a charge on public funds,
the Assistance Board or Social Welfare Committee may pay.
The prisoner, though homeless, might be in a position to pay
himself.   Secondly, who is responsible for the offender's
re-appearance in court at the adjourned hearing ?   The
offender himself is.   Experience has shown that the arrangement is not abused.   If there is any real doubt about his
due re-appearance there is justification for a remand in
custody in city or country.   If the alternatives and advantages
of the arrangement are explained to the offender, there is no
question where his interests lie.   He is anxious to get out of
this tight corner as soon as possible.   The road to freedom
clearly lies through co-operation and good faith at this
juncture.   To jump his bail now would undoubtedly lose
him this sympathetic attitude.   A third possible objection is
again that it involves the probation officer in much more work.
The arrangements have to be made, and time has to be found
to take the offender to the place, and introduce him there ;
also, possibly, to meet him and bring him to the court at the
end of the remand.   But this is not waste of time from the
probation officer's point of view.   The journey to the shelter
is a priceless opportunity for getting to know the offender and
the way his mind works.   He can maintain contact with him

during the remand much more easily at the shelter than at the prison. And he can obtain from the Superintendent a much more intimate and personal account of his behaviour and mentality than is available from a prison. So that the extra work has a value, and most probation officers would not grumble.

Some magistrates argue that it is not necessary to have a remand at all ; the probation officer can quite well make the necessary investigation after the order is made. This is a queer inversion of what would appear to most people to be the natural sequence of events, as well as of the provisions of the Criminal Justice and other acts. To decide upon the treatment first, and then to set about making a diagnosis sounds like " Alice Through the Looking Glass ". A number of courts do work in this way, and, not surprisingly, it militates against good probation treatment. For one thing, many an offender placed on probation without any enquiry has disappeared out of court and never been heard of again ; it is easy enough to give a false address if no enquiries are made. Where the right address has been given the probation officer sometimes finds that a false story has been told, and the real state of affairs is very different from that described in court. Had the true facts been given, probation might not have been deemed the best treatment, or perhaps special requirements, such as residence or mental treatment, might have been included. Sometimes it transpires that the offender is mentally deficient or deranged, requiring institutional care, rather than the freedom of probation. But the real difficulty about this inverted procedure is that once the prisoner and his family are relieved from the dreadful suspense and fear of being sent away, they become much less communicative. Before the order, when the prisoner's fate is still hanging in the balance, the parties concerned are more prepared to talk freely and frankly, in the desperate hope that the officer may see their point of view and interpret it to the magistrates, or see that they are co-operative, and report it. Once the decision is made, and the offender safe, there is no longer any need to be expansive. If no enquiries have been made the probation officer begins the probation a complete stranger representing the court, instead of the already proved family confidant. Months of precious probation time then have to be spent slowly beating down these reserves, and building up an atmosphere of confidence, before the necessary knowledge, basic to good treatment, can be acquired.

Time and the right atmosphere are required to make these enquiries. The probation officer does well to begin these from the outside sources and to leave the interviews with the family and the offender until last. His greater knowledge will then help him to piece together the threads of the picture into a coherent whole, and the lapse of a few days will give the family as well as the offender time to get used to their situation, and to have reflected upon it.

First of these outside sources of information come the police. They can give much more detail than is required in court as to how, where, when, with whom, and in what circumstances the offence was committed. They may have had this individual or locality under observation for a long time, and will then know the people, street corners, public houses and fun fairs that should be avoided in the future. They know the type of home and neighbourhood the offender comes from ; his reactions to discovery and arrest ; and many other illuminating details, as well as the previous criminal record, if there is one, of the offender and his family.

An even more illuminating source of information is the school, and this applies in the adult as well as in the juvenile courts, certainly for offenders up to 21. In most areas in the juvenile courts the actual school report is given to the court by an officer of the local authority. This relates to the child's attainment, conduct and health in school. Whether or not he goes on and submits in his report also details as to salient home circumstances, the children's officer will certainly have this in his possession, and like the police he will know a great deal about the family which would be helpful for the probation officer to know before he visits the family himself. It is important for the officer to know the financial details of the family's circumstances, both the earnings and the individual contributions to the family exchequer, but these are of secondary importance to the underlying emotional factors, and are indeed often related to the latter. The children's officers as well as the police often make a point of getting full particulars of these financial details from the family. If the probation officer gets these beforehand from one of these officials, he both saves his own time and also spares the family the annoyance of giving the same information to three different officers.

Then, too, a list of the names and ages of all the members of the family is invaluable to the probation officer. The ages of the family, parents included, are significant. Great disparity of age between the parents, or between the parents and the children, brings its own difficulties of divergent outlook and different needs and habit of mind. Big gaps between the children may or may not indicate the spoiled darling or an unwanted extra in the family. A boy following a long string of girls may or may not be the king of the castle or a victim of petticoat government ; and so on. Without the complete list the probation officer is not to know of the existence of an older married brother or sister, who might be able to help a youngster over a difficult patch. Further, an officer so forearmed can get hold of the family's story better and does not have to keep interrupting, " Who is Edna ? ", to get the hang of things. In areas where a custom of friendly exchange exists, all this kind of knowledge is available to the probation officer from the police or local authorities for the asking, and helps to give him a basis for his further enquiries.

But the teacher knows more about the child than the children's officer, because the teacher has direct and daily contact with him, as well as occasionally with the mother too. The teacher's contribution is therefore priceless. He can, of course, enlarge on the actual school report. " Writing, fair ; Reading, good ; Arithmetic, could do better ; Conduct, not always satisfactory " is not illuminating as a gauge of personality.   But he can expand on the child's abilities and interests, his reactions to praise or blame, and wherein he merits either ; his relations with other children, and the role he plays at school (leader, nonentity, sneak, bully, know-all, baby, or whatever it may be) ; the family standards of health and cleanliness ; their capacity for co-operation and for understanding the child. The teacher always, of course, knows if there has been previous trouble at school and what the child's reactions to this were.   He sometimes knows quite a lot of things the child has let drop about the family relationships, as that there is parental friction, that the child is overworked or overpetted at home, that Dad drinks or Mum lies in bed all the morning.

The probation officer and the school teacher have to be in close touch with each other in any case,[1] and where a cordial relationship exists, as it fortunately usually does, it is not difficult for the probation officer to obtain intimate knowledge of the offender from this source.   So valuable are the teacher's impressions that the school should not be overlooked as a source of helpful insight in the adult courts for boys and girls in their later teens.   A written request to a distant headmaster often brings back an illuminating letter in cases where young people have already left home.

From these preliminary enquiries from police, local authorities and head teacher it sometimes transpires that the

---

[1] Rule 52 of the 1949 Probation Rules lays it down that in case of children of school age the probation officer shall make enquiry of the head teacher as to the child's attendance and progress.

family in question is already well known to one or more of the social agencies in the town, such as the Assistance Board, the Family Welfare Society, the Personal Service Society, the National Society for the Prevention of Cruelty to Children, and further enquiries from such a source are indicated. These will reveal the kind of trouble the family has already suffered, their reactions to it, the assistance received, and the impressions made on the workers concerned. It must always be borne in mind that not all these workers are trained and that trained or untrained, no worker is always infallible.

The family should not be visited until all other sources of information have been tapped. What the probation officer wants from the family is their version of what led up to the offence, their view on this, and their account of the delinquent; their ability to understand and help him; above all their emotional relationship to him. It is this that has shaped his character in his early years more than anything else. For instance, a child who is ignored by callous or pre-occupied parents may become self-centred; one who is bullied or beaten· may become cowed or deceitful or defiant. An over-indulgent parent may make a child inconsiderate, an over-protective one, anxious. The attitude of the parents to each other has an effect on the children. Where one parent despises the other the child may despise that one too, and discipline will suffer; or he may champion the despised one and hate the other. The ill-health of one parent may make a strained unnatural atmosphere in the home, with great restrictions on natural noise and games, or even on food and pocket money. Parents who " keep themselves to themselves " and who " never go out " can hardly be expected to have children who make happy friendships easily. The parents' view of the offence itself reveals to a certain extent their own moral standards, and may reveal something of their philosophy of life.

It is important that the probation officer should meet both

parents where a delinquent is living at home ; the wife or husband of a married man or woman ; or other relative with whom the offender may be making a home.   Where there is a father or husband concerned this usually means an evening visit, possibly more than one, because of the changing hours of work and the tendency of some men to be elusive when there is trouble about.   It is quite a false assumption that one has a pretty good idea of the family and home circumstances, if one has not visited it, nor met personally this most important member of it.   " Dad " is an immensely important factor in the child's life and upbringing and in the growth of character of every member of the family.   Even if he is a nonentity, this is significant.   Why is he so ?   What is the effect of a father who is a nonentity on the character of his children ?   Certainly not nil.   But he may just as likely be the greatest asset for good in the whole situation, capable of making wise suggestions as to treatment which his wife with her often narrower outlook might never have thought of. He may, on the other hand, be a stumbling-block to every suggestion put forward by the probation officer, and in such a case it is important to realize this at the earliest possible stage.   It is amazing that in modern social service more stress is not laid upon the imperative necessity of seeing the father when the child's welfare is concerned.

It not infrequently happens when one is visiting that the family are all out, and a helpful neighbour from next door appears upon the scene, all information and eager curiosity. Sometimes the information is innocuous enough.   " Mrs Green ?   Gawn away, dear.   Went last week.   To her mother's."   But sometimes it is much more suggestive. " Out.   More often out than in, I'm reckoning.   And up to no good either.   I wonder they don't do something about it at the Town Hall.   Shocking, I think.   Some people have got some money to spend at the pubs.   .   .   ."   Give her her head, and she will pour out a long story of their goings on.

This is most dangerous. For one thing it is unreliable; neighbours' tittle-tattle is often mischievous, and at any rate it is a one-sided view. But for another, and this is more important, if it becomes known that the probation officer has lent his ear to street gossip, it is unlikely that the family in question, or for that matter anyone else in the street, will ever trust him again. People's confidence and trust are worth more to him in his work than neighbours' stories.

In some cases there still remain one or two other sources of enquiry before one finally sees the delinquent himself. These are the Remand Home Superintendent where there has been a remand in custody, and possibly the doctor or psychologist where a medical or mental report is thought to be necessary.

The most valuable information the Remand Home Superintendent can give is an account of the offender's reactions to it all.[1] In small Remand Homes where the Superintendent is able to see a good deal of the children individually, both on reception, when they are often in distress, and throughout the remands, as they become more accustomed to their situation, this may be valuable. If the child has opened out and confided in the Staff, they may be able to give the probation officer a clue as to the most useful approach to the child. It must be remembered that the Superintendent sees him in abnormal circumstances of shock and emotion, cut off from his normal *milieu*, and that his knowledge of the delinquent is therefore not by itself a sufficiently all-round one on which to base a judgment of character. This applies also to prison reports.

Medical reports may be asked for by the court, the probation officer, the offender or his family, and arrangements can be made for them either in custody or on bail, as indicated

[1] Under the Criminal Justice Act 1948, Remand Homes or Centres are to be available for all young people up to the age of 21 who are remanded in custody, but Remand Centres for those over 17 are not yet available (1955).

D

previously. Sometimes all that is required is an indication as to the presence or absence of symptoms of contagious or mental disease. Where the medical examination consists of a thorough overhaul, such as can be carried out at a general hospital, physical conditions may be discovered which have a real bearing on conduct, such as a severe state of general debility, a bad heart, delayed menstruation, digestive troubles, and so forth. These conditions may well have been indirectly contributory to loss of work or an outburst of temper which, in turn, led to the commission of the offence. Sometimes much graver disorders directly accounting for criminal acts may be discovered, such as glandular trouble, epilepsy, or incipient mental derangement, none of which may have been obvious to the lay eye. Very careful and expert examination is needed to diagnose their early stages.

Psychologists' reports are now obtainable on the court's request in most Remand Homes and in big cities from a clinic or general hospital. They are always valuable, but are essential when the offence is inexplicable, for instance when people, adults or children, steal things for which they have no use, which indeed they may have promptly thrown away, or steal blatantly, without any of the usual precautions against detection, or when a child in an apparently well-run comfortable home is beyond control. There is always a reason, and until the reason is discovered one is not in a position to prescribe appropriate treatment. If, therefore, the reason is not apparent to the court, a specialist's help should be sought. A good psychologist's report will give not only an indication as to the probable causes of the trouble, but practical suggestions as to possible treatment.

And so one finally reaches the interview with the offender himself. The probation officer may not yet have had any contact with him at all. In country areas where one probation officer serves several courts, offenders may be remanded or dealt with in his absence, and he merely notified that this

Enquiries

has been done. By this time presumably a few days have elapsed. The offender has had time to get used to the fact of his unpleasant situation. He has slept on it, and reflected on it, and is better able to see things in perspective and give a coherent account of them. The probation officer is far better equipped, too, to discuss matters with him than he was on the day of the hearing. What the officer wants to learn from the offender himself, and must ask directly about, is How did all this come about ? What led up to it ? What does the family think about it all ? Who minds most ? It is important to know what the offender thinks the family thinks, even though the officer has been at some pains to find this out from them directly. This is not to catch the delinquent out, but to gauge how far the family understand each other. One wants to find out from the offender himself what his interests are, and whether he can pursue them as he wishes ; and if not, why not ; whether he has friends he cares about, and what they think about this offence. And finally what he thinks is the best thing to do to get over the trouble. From some such direction of the conversation as this one hopes to learn his attitude to the offence, his sense of values, what to him is worth while, and what he feels to be his chief difficulties ; his outlook on life and his ability to understand and cope with himself.

Sometimes enquiries have to be made by proxy. A boy leaves his home in the country, and comes to town looking for work, or a woman leaves her home in the town and goes to the seaside for a holiday. If they get into trouble while away from home, the home enquiries have to be made by the officer in the home district, and the personal interview with the offender conducted by the officer on the spot. The officer who finally takes on the probation if an order is made has to manage on secondhand written reports on vital matters. The offender may be sent home again to be on probation, and will then find himself under the supervision of a stranger whom he has never seen. The officer concerned has to take on a personality he has had no opportunity to gauge for himself. It is never so easy to pick up the threads in these proxy cases. This leads us to consider another dilemma which is apt to occur, usually in the adult courts.

This is the offender who has left home and urgently objects to home enquiries being made. He may even refuse to give the address of his parents, preferring to risk a sentence of imprisonment to letting them know that he has disgraced himself. This is natural enough. Why should the family be dragged in, and have to suffer all the grief and shame involved if it could be kept from them, and if they are in no way concerned with the offence ? If home enquiries are not made on the other hand the probation officer rightly feels he is working in the dark. What is he to do ? He must, of course, be guided by the circumstances, and by the wishes of the court. But unless there are strong reasons against it, he probably does best to respect the wishes of the offender in this matter. To go against these in the case of an adult, and contact the family despite his opposition, is to risk losing his goodwill and confidence, and without this he can do nothing. Probation is built up on goodwill, it cannot function on any other basis. In such cases the probation begins with the officer certainly ignorant of much that he wants to know, but at least recognized as a person of understanding in the offender's mind, and this is better than being in possession of a certain amount of information, but ranked as an odious mischief-maker in the eyes of the delinquent ; or alternatively, if there had been no contact at all, as a complete stranger.

Much depends on these preliminary interviews with the offender and his family. Rightly handled they are a sound basis for any probation order which may subsequently be made. They are so important that some further attention will be given to the art of interviewing in the next chapter.

IV

Interviewing

The initial interview with the offender and his family is an all-important one. It is here that the first real contact is made and the basis of subsequent relationships laid. The probation officer's first aim is to understand as far as may be the situation and all its various aspects. His second is to harness the mind and inclination of the offender to the business of what might be called recovery—recovery of his good name, of his self-respect, and of his better qualities. It is of little avail for the officer (if an order is made) to devise excellent means of recovery, if these are not in line with the offender's own volition.[1] Small good comes of the probation officer pulling a recalcitrant or uninterested probationer along a road which is distasteful to him. The art of probation is to stimulate the probationer's own wish for better things and a different way of life, and then to support his efforts to achieve this end. The officer should be behind the probationer, backing him up in his good resolutions, rather than in front, where he runs the risk of outstepping him without realizing it.

The initial interview should have both aims in mind : to find out as much as possible, and to stir the mind and imagination of the offender on his own behalf. The setting of the interview, the client's reception, the framing of the questions, the manner of the interviewer, must all be planned with this dual aim in view.

[1] " It must be from the aspiration of the common people that the salvation of the people comes. Nothing that is good can be imposed upon people by well-wishing superiors. In education, as in everything that concerns the spirit, freedom is the one condition of progress."—Archbishop Temple, Presidential Address to the Educational Science Section of the British Association, September 1916, quoted in the *Life of William Temple* by Iremonger, p. 73.

The setting of the interview comes first. Sometimes there is no choice in the matter ; an offender remanded in custody must be interviewed in a prison cell. But often there is a choice. He could be interviewed at the office, or at his own home. There is much to be said for and against both, according to the circumstances of each individual case. Some probation offices are situated in a low quarter of the town, approached past fun fairs and shady public houses ; crowded with queuing folk, some crying, some sniggering, some being abusive. Some offices are dark, dirty, hideous, noisy and uncomfortable. Some offices are shared by several officers, and the offender is expected to tell his story with other waiting clients in the same room. This is not a setting likely to enhance his self-respect, or to encourage confidences. Other offices, on the other hand, may be situated in quiet side streets, overlooking trees or flower beds, comfortably furnished with restful chairs and friendly pictures, dignified, inviting, reassuring. Such is a good setting. Some offenders' homes are tiny little slum dwellings, permitting no privacy, with cats or babies jumping around and neighbours coming and going. Over-protective or antipathetic parents may be listening in, and attempting to make a child give what they consider to be the right answers. This is not a good setting. Other offenders live in quiet, comfortable homes, where it is possible to talk with much less interruption and more peace than at the only office available. In some cases to ask an offender or his parents to come to the office involves them in a tedious journey at the end of a tiring day, and they arrive worn out. Similarly, if one calls without notice at an offender's home the parents are liable to be flustered. Either of these alternatives makes a bad beginning. To get the best out of these vital interviews it is necessary for everyone to be as composed and collected as possible, prepared and reflective. It is not possible to lay down any golden rule. The probation officer must choose the best setting open to him. The home must be visited, and due notice should be given of this.[1] But if on arrival he finds the atmosphere such that it is not possible to talk freely, he must invite the parties concerned to visit him elsewhere, and make as convenient arrangements for them to do so as possible. He should make sure they know the way, and have clear directions written down for finding the place, for they might be embarrassed to have to ask passers-by the way to the probation officer's room.

The offender's reception is no less important. He comes to the interview nervous and on the defensive. He wonders how much this officer will discover ; what ghastly suggestions may be made ; what he will have to agree to. He heartily wishes the whole beastly business were a nightmare. This is all quite salutary, no doubt, so long as it leads on to a more positive constructive attitude, and this is what the probation officer has got to try to engender. The officer should from the start extend the common courtesies. If the interview is at the office he should rise to greet the client, give him his hand, offer him the most comfortable seat. Cigarettes may help to ease the atmosphere. Women officers sometimes do better if they produce a cup of tea. Children may be offered a sweet. The client is anxiously trying to sum up the officer— " What sort of a bloke is this ? Can I trust him ? " It is courteous to look at a person when speaking to him, and if the officer does this the client has a chance to look, too, and to gain an impression. Too many interviewers conduct their business without this courtesy : while addressing their client they sharpen their pencils, sort out their papers, or move about the room, opening and shutting drawers. This is not conducive to confidential conversation, though if during the interview the client becomes distressed, it may be tactful to divert one's attention in these ways for a moment or two, to give a chance of recovery.

[1] The pros and cons of giving notice before a crucial visit to the home are discussed on pages 209 and 210.

The seat offered is important. It should be on the same level as the officer's ; if it is lower the officer will be talking down to the client ; if it is higher the client may feel he is perched on a stool of repentence while the officer reclines at his ease ; neither feeling is good for self-respect. Too low a chair is to be avoided for adults, who may only too likely have rheumaticky joints. It is not kind to put the client facing the light, for if he has weak eyes he will be very uncomfortable. Nor, of course, should he be put with his face in the dark. Both parties want to be able to look at each other. The best position of the chairs is probably both looking into the fire, or if the interview has to be conducted at a desk, the client should be at the side not immediately facing the officer. The impression one wants the client to get on settling down is, " I shall be all right here. This is not too bad ".

If the interview is at the offender's home the technique is, of course, different. The officer is then in the position of guest, not host, and can no longer command the situation, arranging who sits where. He must behave like a guest, and sit where directed. He should not resent such interruptions as may occur—the milkman calling, the baby crying, the kettle boiling over, but on the contrary welcome them—for the way people react to these things is revealing. One can learn a lot as to the relations of the family with themselves and outsiders, and the way they take life, from such occurrences, even though one cannot go as far with the conversation as is necessary.

The questions must direct the conversation into the desired channels. They must suggest by their form that the officer is consulting and discussing things with the client, rather than dictating to him or interrogating him. They should be so framed as to invite the truth rather than a lie.

All interviewers should equip themselves with what is now called a " framework of enquiry "[1] before they begin. That

[1] The National Institute of Industrial Psychology has suggestions on techniques of interviewing.

is to say, they should come to the interview fully prepared with a clear picture in their mind of what they want to find out. It is a safeguard to do this, otherwise the interviewer can easily get carried away by a sensational aspect of the situation—the terrible parental friction, the baby's serious illness, the shocking state of the house—and leave the interview with his mind seething with possible remedial measures but without the necessary knowledge of other aspects.

FRAMEWORK OF ENQUIRY

Name ⎫
Age ⎬ all previously supplied by the police.
Address ⎮
Offence ⎭

Economic Factors. These should as far as possible be ascertained beforehand.

Emotional Factors

  (i) *Family Relationships*

    A. Offender's position in the family.

    B. Who is most interested and attached to the offender? Is there any degree of insight or understanding, or is it likely that it could be evoked?
To whom is the offender most attached?
Who is most likely to be able to help the offender?

    C. Prevailing atmosphere in family (anxiety, friction, easygoing tolerance, high moral rectitude. . . ?).
What is the focal point of this atmosphere? (Granny, Dad, debts, spoiled little sister, an invalid. . . ?).
What is its effect on the offender?

  (ii) *Interests*

Has the offender any interests or hobbies, or has he ever had?
How are, or were, these viewed by the family? (with pride, contempt, indifference. . . ?).
Have the family interests or hobbies? If not, have they ever had? Why have they lapsed? Could they ever be resurrected?

Are there facilities for recreational interests in the home ?
Is the offender interested in any feature of his work, or has
he been, or could he be ?

(iii) *Friends*

Has the offender any friends ?

Does he make friends easily ?

Does he keep them ? If he loses them, how does this
happen ? Does he throw them up or they him ?

Are they older, younger, of the same or the opposite sex ?
Are the family socially inclined ?

Do they encourage or take an interest in each others'
friendships ?

(iv) *Philosophy*

A. How does the offender (and his family) view this
offence ? Is there any indication that he has
offended against his own moral code ?

Does he appear to have a moral code ?—e.g. what does
he think is really wrong ?

(N.B.—Nearly everyone, offenders and their families,
are ashamed at this juncture ; some are merely
ashamed at the show-up, and this would indicate
that they have not really offended against their own
idea of right and wrong. It does not indicate that
they have no code.)

B. What does the offender (and his family) appear to care
most about in life ? (the struggle for promotion and
success, academic or athletic prowess, exciting
pleasure, money. . . ?). (Few people reveal these
intimate matters to strangers. All the officer can
do under this head is to bear it in mind, watch and
listen.)

Intellectual Factors

Supposed mental ability of the offender. This is usually taken
from the teacher's assessment on the school report. Clear
distinction must be made between attainment at school,
which may be low, and ability, which may be very high.
Unless tested by a qualified educational psychologist, ability
is a matter of conjecture only, even by the teacher.

Reasons for any marked retardation in attainment (physical,
such as short sight, anæmia, etc. ; or emotional, such as
obsessions or anxieties).

If possible, an educational psychologist should be consulted as to the reasons for his failure ; it may be due to persistent truanting, but why does he truant ?

Supposed mental abilities of the family (e.g. child may be the only stupid member of a brilliant family, or the only normally intelligent one in a dull-witted family ; a mentally deficient mother may account for the child being undisciplined).

Physical Factors

A. General impression of health of offender and his family.

B. Medical report. The doctor should be told the reason for asking for an overhaul, and given the health history as recounted by the family.

Social Factors

A. Attitude to neighbours ; the family may be extremely exclusive, and almost afraid or suspicious of neighbours, or they may live in a little fraternity of families, all of whom share everything that happens. These are the two extremes.

B. Neighbourhood, e.g. overcrowded tenement in a slum, or remote cottage on a moor.

Facilities for work, recreation, education, interests and friendships in the vicinity.

Before the interview it is necessary to run through some such basic lay-out of the relevant aspects, piecing together the strands already gleaned from other sources, and noting where the gaps come, and what points need corroboration or further elucidation. The points so arrived at form the framework for this particular interview. This should, of course, be used not as a questionnaire, but as a guide in directing the conversation. The fewer questions the better. There are in the main three different ways of gathering the knowledge required—direct questioning, observation, and sympathetic elicitation.

There must be a few direct questions to start the client talking, and to introduce different aspects of the case. " Tell me all about it from your point of view. How did this come about, and what led up to it ? " is an opening invitation to people to tell their story in their own way. " How does Lily get on with her little brother . . . or her step-father ? " " Has George been a trouble to you for long, or was this a surprise ? " " What does the family feel about it all, Doris ? Who do you think minds most ? " " Did you tell your mother about this when it happened, or your father ? Whom do you generally confide in ? " These kinds of question lead on to family relationships.

But a great deal can be gleaned by observation, by careful listening and watching without any questioning at all. One observes, for instance, something of the family relationships by the way people speak to or about each other, or refrain from doing so ; something of their moral standards by the way they talk about the offence. One can gain an impression without asking as to the general happiness or otherwise of the parties, their outlook on life, and the existence of any nervous tensions. In the home one can observe the family's standards of comfort and cleanliness, and by noting the kind of para-phernalia lying about—books, musical instruments, knitting, bicycle lamps, pets—or the absence of any, what their interests or their hobbies are. One should note, too, where the client begins his tale, where he leaves off, and what, if anything, he leaves out. These things reveal the way his mind works. Some people begin, " Well, it was all my fault, really . . . " ; others with a long, involved rigmarole of times and dates and places. This may indicate (or it may not) that the first has already faced the issue, the second is still evading it. Some leave off where other people begin to be involved, others where they themselves are. Some leave out what is painful or hurtful to them, while others somewhat over-emphasize this. These things give pointers to the temperament and personality of the client. One should mark where people begin to colour up, to shift uneasily or to cry, for these suggest that one is near a sore spot, and therefore a vital one. It may be best to make a mental note of this, rather than to pursue it at the time.

By sympathetic elicitation, that is to say where the interviewer has succeeded in establishing an expansive atmosphere, much can be learnt without interrogation, by skilful direction of the conversation, about his attitude to life, his work and its suitability or difficulties, his relations with his neighbours or workmates, his health, and so on.

The art of these interviews is really the art of listening. Left to themselves, if they are sufficiently at ease, people will tell their story their own way. They may begin with their sensations now, or with what happened last Wednesday night ; they may proceed backwards or forwards, or first one way, then another. An interviewer with a logical mind is again and again tempted to interrupt to get what seems to him a rational sequence. If he interrupts, damage is done. The client is telling what is uppermost in his mind, and it is illuminating to the probation officer to know what he thinks is important. It is easy enough to go back again afterwards and pick up the missing links, rehearsing the story in sequence, so that the client can see both what he has left out, and whether the interviewer is getting it right. By interruption the client is put off his stride, and maybe fussed or piqued, while the interviewer has lost a valuable glimpse into his way of going about things. One is also sometimes tempted to interrupt with criticism or advice. Both are equally fatal to further revelations. Once suggest " Oh, I would not have done that " or " I think you made a mistake there ", and the client's whole attention will be turned, not on giving his own account of things as they seem to him, which is what the interviewer is trying to get, but on trying to defend what he did, or to put it in another light, on covering up other aspects to which he thinks exception might be taken. The interviewer must be absolutely unshockable if he wants his client to speak freely. The conversation is similarly diverted if the interviewer interrupts to give advice. Apart from being inappropriate at this juncture, advice given now will be based on inadequate knowledge of the total situation and the personalities concerned. The time for giving advice comes, if at all, after the preliminary interview, not during its course.

Many of a probation officer's clients are inarticulate people who do not easily express themselves in words, and feel dumber than ever when called upon to do so in such an anxious situation. The probation officer should take these interviews at a much slower tempo, remembering that an inarticulate person is less embarrassed by long pauses than he is himself. He should adapt his own manner of speech as far as possible to that of his client. This most probably means monosyllables and clipped sentences. A flow of words, however encouraging they are meant to be, simply silences an inarticulate person. He knows he cannot compete. A conversation on these lines might run in some such vein as this :

" Mum ? "

" Out." . . . Pause . . .

" Row ? "

Grunt of assent. . . . Longer pause. . . .

" Old man ? "

" Clipped 'er ear'ole." This may be followed after another long pause with a sudden burst of confidence, which would never have come if the client had been rendered speechless by embarrassment at the interview : " See, me mum and dad aren't married ". Translated, this conversation would run something like this :

" What was your mother doing that night ? "

" She had gone out."

" Had there been some little misunderstanding ? "

" Yes."

" Your father was a bit upset, I dare say ? "

" He hit my mother on the side of the head."

This kind of thing can, and must, be done with the greatest

respect and perfectly naturally. One wants to put people at
their ease. It is the worst possible manners to talk down
to people.

It is unwise to be too reassuring in these conversations.
Too easy reassurance about a serious situation simply indicates
to the parties that the interviewer has failed to grasp it. In
such cases it is much more reassuring to become serious and
thoughtful than to say breezily, " Oh well, Mrs Green, don't
worry too much ; I'm sure things will work out all right in
the end ". Such a statement is rarely true, for one thing.
Few probation officers can really be sure that things are
going to work out well. In too many cases the dice are
heavily loaded on the side of continued misery, ill-health,
misunderstanding, limited facilities, or whatever it may be.
It is most unwise to venture any forecast as to the magistrates'
decision. The probation officer never knows whether his
usual magistrates and clerk will be sitting on the day of the
adjourned hearing—they might be taken suddenly ill,—nor
what new factors may unexpectedly be brought to light.
The only assurance that can be given—and if it is genuine
it can be comforting—is that of the officer's personal concern
and sympathy.

One question which must always be asked, of both the
offender and his family, is, " What do *you* think should be
done ? " or " What is the best thing to do about it now ? "
It should be asked towards the end of the interview, when all
the factors leading up to the situation have been examined
and when, perhaps for the first time, the parties see for
themselves the natural sequence of events, and how one thing
has led to another. Sound suggestions are often put forward,
even by quite young children. " I think I'd best not play
up Back Alley any more. I'll go to my gran's. I'll be all
right there ; see, she's got rabbits." One girl, after one of
these serious talks, volunteered that she thought she had better
cut right out her association with a married man who had

been taking her out. Many offenders, asked this question and reflecting upon it deeply, realize that their only chance of making good is to take some really drastic step—to leave the district, perhaps, to change their job, or to offer restitution. The fact that people have themselves come to such a conclusion after serious reflection introduces a hopeful new factor into the otherwise gloomy situation. It is the essence of probation that the offender's own mind should be working on means of recovery, and any ultimate plan of treatment is more likely to succeed if it is based on suggestions thoughtfully made by the offender himself. If the offender himself has no suggestions to offer, the probation officer may perhaps make one, and discuss it with him. In this way the offender's mind is accustomed to some new and perhaps startling idea, as that he should leave home and go into a hostel or a residential job for a time. The probation officer gains light on the wisdom of this tentative plan by watching the reaction of the offender to it. If it seems clearly unlikely to meet with the offender's co-operation it is unlikely to succeed, and the probation officer had better think again. To insist on a course contrary to his feelings or judgment, and to try to drag him along it by means of commands or threats, is to court either rebellion or deception. If the offender is resistant to every suggestion the probation officer can think of, and the officer left in consequence with little idea as to how he could be helped to take a different attitude to things, then it would appear inappropriate to make a probation order, and if asked he should say so.

The question, " What do you think can be done about it ? " must be asked with some reservation and with a due reminder that it is the magistrates who take the final decision as to what should be done, and any plans now discussed can only be tentative ones therefore. Some magistrates are interested to hear what views the offender and the officer hold on the subject of appropriate action, and always make a point of asking ; others apparently are not.   It is a vital point in any report the officer may give to the court.   If the officer is able to report that the offender has thought seriously about the whole situation and now suggests that he would do such and such if given a chance to try and put matters right, it may weigh very considerably with the magistrates in making their decision.

One cannot discuss the question of interviews without paying some attention to the matter of lies.   Truth is many-sided, and therefore a true picture of any situation is always difficult to convey.   One always sees one's own aspect, and therefore gives a subjective view.   Human minds, especially when they are on the defensive and seeking to justify them-selves, become muddled.   Hence garbled accounts are not necessarily deliberate attempts to deceive.   They are more likely indicative of self-deception.   This is true of all inter-views.   But the probation officer is often dealing with shifty unreliable people who have much that they desire to hide, and who have not for a long time had the experience of thinking straight, and with neurotic or unstable people whose thinking apparatus is out of gear for the time being.   A certain amount of lying must therefore be expected, and should never come as a surprise to the probation officer.   It is important to get at the truth, and to help the offender to see, think, and speak truthfully.   The art of doing this should be one of the officer's special studies.

The aim is to prevent rather than to detect lies.   Occasions or temptations to lie should therefore be reduced to the minimum and everything possible done to make it easier to tell the truth than untruth.   Much depends here on the attitude of the interviewer.   If the interviewer adopts a high moral tone, a critical attitude, or a challenging menacing note, he will be encouraging lies.   No one would wish to confess their shadier thoughts and motives to such a person. If, on the other hand, one meets someone who seems to see

E

and understand one's point of view, to have followed sympathetically the story of one's difficulties, who does not appear
to be critical or shocked, though he clearly sees the seriousness
of the situation, it is conducive to making a clean breast of
the whole horrid story and getting the benefit of some sound
advice and help.   This should be the attitude of the officer.
Direct questions around delicate matters should be avoided.
Rather one should lead up to them by identifying oneself
with the client's mind, and foreseeing how he might naturally
have reacted, even sometimes suggesting this, so sparing him
the embarrassment of having to confess it.   " You must
have been afraid by this time that someone would find out.
What did you do with the stuff, burn it or hide it or what ? "
" I hid it in the garden."   One must try to establish sufficient
confidence for the story to be begun truthfully far enough
back, then as one nears the crucial and compromising points
the listener may be presumed to be already deducing what
happened next, so there is no point in suddenly beginning
to lie.   To do so would be to upset the story already told.

One advantage of seeing the offender and his family last,
after information has already been gathered from all other
sources, is that one has a pretty good idea as to the direction
in which truth lies, and can more easily detect deviations.
The officer should always make it clear that he already knows
a good deal about the circumstances, and that he has had a
chat with the schoolmaster, the police, or the N.S.P.C.C.,
whatever the case may be.   Not to disclose this is as good as
setting a trap.   The officer's object should be not to test his
client's ability for telling the truth, but to help him to do so.
But if he does detect a lie, he should neither confute the liar,
nor yet give the impression that he is gullible.   Sometimes
it can be passed over for the moment, as if the interviewer had
not registered that one, and later returned to, the way being
more carefully prepared for truth this time.   It is usually
a mistake to confute the liar in these interviews.   To do so is

tantamount to a declaration of war, and the client is likely either to cease talking any more, or to lie yet more furiously.

If the officer is going to demand or expect truth, or hopes to encourage it, it stands to reason he must himself maintain a high standard. This cuts out bluff. To threaten or promise something when there is no possibility or intention of carrying it out, is a deliberate intention to deceive. It is at times tempting to resort to bluff; it may be the means of achieving our purpose quickly and easily for the moment, but it is a short-lived victory, and in the long run not a cheap one. Bluff is based on an utterly false philosophy. It is a disregard of truth.

It should be remembered that lies are revealing. Why does a person lie? Professor Burt has analysed many different reasons for lying in his *Young Delinquent*,[1] and readers who do not already know this section are recommended to read it. For example, is it a lie of vanity, or of shame, or of loyalty, or of malice, or of confusion, or of fear, or because he can't help it? Each of these represents a different type of personality, and one can hence learn a good deal about a person from the kind of lies he tells.

The desirability of taking notes during the interview is often discussed. It is a great mistake to make running notes all the time the offender and his family are speaking. Everyone minds their step when they think they are being reported verbatim. It detracts the officer's attention from the client's expression and bearing, and tends to slow up proceedings as well as to chill them. Still less is it desirable to bring out and attempt to fill up in their presence any form which the court may prescribe for probation officers' reports. This makes a very formal official business of the interview, and kills the spontaneity one wants to engender. Such forms should be filled up in the office afterwards. The atmosphere of the interview must be easy and informal if it is to be as helpful

[1] See *The Young Delinquent*, by Dr Cyril Burt, pp. 376-98.

as it might be. Nor is it a good plan for the officer to refer
to notes he already has, or to his framework of enquiry. The
natural reaction to that is, " Heavens ! what's he got written
down there about me ? You have to be careful with these
people." Officers should train their memories to avoid these
things, and make a habit of very careful preparation before
embarking on serious interviews. At the end of the interview
it is a different matter to take out a notebook and make a note
of a soldier's number, an address, relevant dates, or things
of that kind, which must be remembered accurately, and upon
which, very often, subsequent action depends.

One sometimes hears it said that treatment begins with the
first interview. Rightly conducted, this should be so. The
offender should leave the interview feeling better than when
he came in. He should feel better for having talked everything over so fully. His own ideas about his situation should
have clarified a lot ; his own mind should be working in the
direction of recovery. His self-respect and self-confidence
should have been geared into the situation. He should feel
that the officer has taken trouble to understand him, is
interested in him and concerned on his behalf, and that he has
obviously put his mind on his affairs. This is gratifying and
comforting. Even though his fate still hangs in the balance
and nothing is yet decided, if it has achieved all this the
interview will not have been in vain. If it is followed by a
probation order, such an interview will make a very good
beginning.

V

Planning Treatment

Let us assume that the prisoner has been found guilty ; that he was remanded for enquiries to be made by the probation officer ; and that these have now been completed on the lines suggested here. The probation officer has next to consider his findings, and to decide upon his plan of action. He must first make up his mind as to where he thinks the trouble lies, and whether or not he might be able to help matters ; if so, how. He must then compose a report to the magistrates, outlining briefly this situation as he sees it. And finally, if a probation order is made, he must explain the whole nature of the business to the probationer and to his parents or guardians, if there are any, so that they may clearly understand what is expected of them. We will consider each of these stages in turn.

1. The Officer's Assessment

If the enquiries have been as full as are here recommended, the officer will find himself with a great mass of detail. This may be bewildering by its very amount. Some aspect may stand out predominantly, or strongly stir him emotionally. He may be revolted, for instance, if cruelty or sexual perversion has been involved, or his sense of pity may have been stirred, as in the case of a child who is in great misery. The officer must endeavour to see all the salient factors in the situation in their true perspective, and to rid his mind of strong personal prejudices or emotions. To do this it is helpful to have a definite scheme or lay-out by which to analyse all the predominating factors, so as to ensure as far as may be that none escapes consideration and all are seen in relation to each other. An outline such as the following may be helpful :

OFFICER'S PROVISIONAL ASSESSMENT AND PLAN OF TREATMENT

I. Principal factors leading up to this offence :
> Economic
> Emotional
> Intellectual
> Physical
> Social

II. Offender's needs (with above classification in mind).

III. Assets :
   - (a) Personal : offender's own good points.
   - (b) Social : factors in the general situation which are helpful.

IV. Obstacles :
   - (a) Personal : offender's own weaknesses.
   - (b) Social : factors in his general situation militating against easy recovery.

V. Proposed plan :
   - (a) How these needs might be met (e.g. change of environment, attention to health, help in easing family tensions, building up his own self-confidence, assisting him in some ambition, enlarging his interests, etc., etc.).
   - (b) How the assets may be used to best advantage (e.g. ways of drawing out and making gentle demands on his good qualities, developing helpful factors, e.g. the interest of an older brother or friendly teacher, backing up and cultivating a perceptive parent, introducing in due course any available interest, etc., etc.).
   - (c) How the obstacles might be met (e.g. by helping him to discover and recognize his own weaknesses for himself, so that he can take these into account and guard against them, or by considering possible changes which might be made, or practical remedial measures, such as medical attention, leaving home for a while, change of employment, etc., etc.).

It will be easier to illustrate this method if a real story is thus analysed.

Alastair A., aged 13, was charged with breaking and entering a store with various other boys. None of the boys had any explanation to offer. It seemed they had nothing better to do, and wondered if they could. Alastair's father was an unskilled labourer, who had himself been in Borstal as a lad, and had known long spells of unemployment since. He was an aggressive, abusive and socially embittered man. The mother was a poor weak creature, suffering from a suppurating sore which badly needed and was not receiving medical attention. The tiny home was dirty, evil-smelling, comfortless, and in shocking disrepair. There was friction between the two parents. There were six children : one older, four younger, than Alastair. He, like the others, appeared to be a normally amenable and gifted child, but with little scope for legitimate outlet in his own home or immediate neighbourhood.

PRINCIPAL FACTORS LEADING UP TO THIS OFFENCE
1. Emotional
   (a) *Family Relationships.* The outstanding factor here was the parental friction, partly no doubt due to, partly causing, the wife's ill-health. There was no evidence to show that there was any fundamental lack of affection. Although the quarrelling was continuous, and maybe sometimes violent, this was probably due to the nervous tension of husband and wife, arising from his temperament and her state of health. Mrs A. was too ill to be able to show any normal parental instincts ; Mr A. in too abusive a mood. Time and an easier domestic atmosphere would be required before their feelings for Alastair and the other children could be safely diagnosed.

    (b) *Interests*. None of the family had any rational interests or hobbies. The disorder and unhappiness of the home was such as to drive everyone out of it. The immediate neighbourhood had little to offer.

    (c) *Friends*. Mr A. had pals at the pub. with whom he let off steam every night. Mrs A. had no spirit for outside friends. The children were sociable enough, but had only the streets in which to meet their friends.

    (d) *Philosophy*. Mr A. was an ardent advocate of social justice. This much was clear from his declamatory speeches against the Government and the Housing Authorities for permitting people to live and work in such conditions as his.

2. *Intellectual Factors*. Mr A. seemed an intelligent man, without education or adequate scope. Alastair seemed from his school report, and the others by all appearances, to be of normal intelligence and suggestibility.

3. *Physical Factors*. Mrs A.'s health was pivotal to the family situation.

4. *Social Factors*. The neighbourhood was a bad one, with tumble-down houses and few amenities, except for low-class public houses and a few commercialized fun fairs here and there. It was a slum area, badly blitzed.

5. *Economic Factors*. Mr A. had been born and bred in great economic insecurity, and even in times of comparative prosperity as this was, six growing children and a sick, incompetent wife present a difficult economic proposition. There was great poverty in this home in spite of Mr A.'s comparatively decent wages at the time.

THE OFFENDER'S NEEDS

   (1) A calmer, steadier, happier home life.
   (2) Legitimate scope for his normal high spirits and
       abilities.

ASSETS IN THE CASE

   Mr A. was intelligent ; so was Alastair. Alastair himself
   did not appear to be a vicious, neurotic or unhappy child
   requiring much personal help. His offence and his
   difficulties arose not from within, in his own personality,
   but from without, in his social setting and the conditions
   of his family life.

OBSTACLES

   Mr A.'s hot temper would need careful handling. Mrs A.'s
   hopeless mood of complete surrender and inability to cope
   was the most serious drawback. The neighbourhood's
   lack of amenities was a drawback, but closer scrutiny of its
   possibilities might reveal more.

PROPOSED PLANS

   (1) It is of foremost importance to secure Mr A.'s goodwill
       and respect. Nothing can be done with the family
       situation if he remains antagonistic. He must be
       met on his own ground and allowed to let off steam,
       then slowly and imperceptibly directed into ways of
       setting about an improvement. For instance, an
       approach to the Housing Authorities in his present
       abusive mood could only do harm. But if in time
       he himself distempered the place, and then
       approached them civilly, they might well be induced
       to repair the roof. To achieve something like this
       would be very good for his injured self-respect. To
       hurry things here is to court disaster. He must
       first come to regard the probation officer as a decent
       enough, sensible, well-disposed kind of person
       before he could be expected to consider any
       suggestions.

   (2) Mrs A.'s health needs urgent attention, and because
it has so completely broken down she is likely to
resist any ameliorative plan which involves her own
effort. Gentle, kindly concern and sympathy are
necessary. A lift to and from hospital in a car
would, of course, go a long way to ease this situation.

   (3) The neighbourhood must be combed for recreational
outlets for the children, and if necessary the local
Youth Committee or Education Authority, churches
or chapels, must be approached on the necessity
of starting some. Mr A. might be directed eventually towards politics, where his declamatory
tendencies might be made use of.

RECOMMENDATION

A two-year probation order.

Some might suggest that the obvious course here was to
remove Alastair to the more salubrious setting of an Approved
School. This would seem to shelve rather than solve the real
problems. Alastair was not in himself a difficult child who
needed special handling or a great deal of personal help. His
difficulties lay in his home, and would continue to lie there
even if he were removed from it temporarily. To remove
him for a while to a totally different setting from that in which
they rose, and to which he would have to return, after possibly
only eighteen months or a couple of years, without any attempt
at improving them, would not appear to be constructive. To
send him to an Approved School would be to give him a stigma
for many years to come and, incidentally, leave the other
brothers and sisters unaided in the same unsatisfactory
circumstances.

Probation treatment which deals with the offender only,
leaving out of account his relationships and his situation at
home, is likely to be ineffective, if indeed not positively
harmful. If, for instance, Alastair were singled out to join

the Scouts, provided with a uniform and the money to go camping, his brothers might not unnaturally be envious, and the result be heightened family tension and jealousy, making life more difficult for him rather than more satisfying. If all the children were found recreational outlets, and the parents left antagonistic towards themselves and society, the prevailing atmosphere at home would remain anti-social, and the tendency of the children to keep out of the house and pursue their own ploys without reference to their parents' feelings, or, indeed, without their parents' knowledge, might be increased. Alastair can only be helped in, with, and through his family.

It is important that the officer should have some kind of purpose or plan of campaign in mind when he suggests probation. The plan may not always be as well defined as in this case. With a dark horse it may simply be " I must get to know this person before I do anything else ". But remedial measures are much more likely to present themselves to the mind if all the possible factors are weighed up in some such method as that suggested here.

It is equally important, however, to modify the plan as time goes on and knowledge increases. Not to modify an original plan of probation does not indicate so much that it was a perfect plan in the first instance, as that the officer has learnt nothing fresh of the personalities that he is dealing with, and is unobservant of their changing situations. Regular periodic overhaul of all probation cases is necessary, when the total situation is re-assessed in the light of subsequent happenings or further enlightenment.

Another danger about making a plan is the temptation to execute it as quickly as possible. This in other spheres is not dangerous, but meritorious. In probation, speed is fatal. It is essential to keep step with the probationer and never to outstrip his confidence or inclination. One of the commonest causes of failure in probation amongst inexperienced officers is their desire to better the situation immediately, and to have something to show for their endeavours. But to travel faster than the client concerned is to confuse him, and so to call out his antagonism in sheer self-defence, whether in open rebellion or in passive resistance. The best results in probation, as we shall see, are achieved by slow, almost imperceptible progress over a long time. The probation officer has done well if within the short span of the actual probation order he has set this progress in motion along acceptable channels.

2. *Report to Court*

The officer's next duty is to compose a report for the magistrates.

The style of the report and the manner of its presentation vary from one court to another. Some courts provide a standard headed form, and where this is done the officer's task is comparatively simple. He has only to fill in the required details from the mass of information now at his disposal. In others the whole composition of the report is left to his discretion, and the onus of deciding what information to give and what not is entirely on him. It is bound to be a short report ; few magistrates would wish to plough through the detailed account which the officer should by now be in a position to present. He must summarize the points which seem to him to be relevant to the question of treatment, as briefly as may be, but be prepared to give further particulars, if cross-questioned by the magistrates, the offender or any solicitor acting in the case. In most juvenile courts a written report is given ; in most adult courts the report (if there is one) is given verbally from the witness box. There is a strong feeling amongst many people that the report in either court should be given verbally, so that the offender and his family can hear what is said, and have a chance to challenge it if they wish. If a written report is made, the law requires that an offender over 17 shall have a copy. In the case of a juvenile the rule is that the substance of certain material points must be communicated to the offender and his parents. The objection to this is that the parties have no assurance that all the relevant points are read out: to them it seems as though their fate hung on a secret document.

The matter is a delicate one, for much that is relevant may also be confidential. If it is read out in a juvenile court, the parents of other children involved in the same charge may hear all their intimate concerns ; and in an adult court the general public and the press are there to lap up anything sensational. It is difficult to give the magistrates the necessary data and the parties full knowledge of what is being said, while at the same time protecting their privacy and confidences. Further, it is bad for a child to hear derogatory statements about his parents or about his own birth (sometimes for the first time) in a court. Here again, some magistrates direct that the child should leave the court while such evidence is being given, but unfortunately this is not always done. It is usually best to tell the parties beforehand what is going to be said, and to give those that are of age to understand a copy of any written report.

In some courts the magistrates look for some suggestion from the officer as to what he considers might be the best treatment, and if none is given, the officer may be regarded as incompetent or unimaginative. In others, any suggestion of this kind coming from the officer is greatly resented. The officer should therefore try to find out beforehand the kind of thing the magistrates look for.

It stands to reason that there will sometimes be an adverse report. It can be adverse in different ways. If the home is an ill-kept one, or the parents of the offender negligent, it will be an adverse report from their point of view. And if the officer is unable to recommend probation if asked, or thinks

probation unsuitable in the circumstances, it is adverse
from the offender's point of view. Both occur not infrequently.

If the officer is asked to express an opinion, and has one,
he is bound to say what he thinks.   If he feels the offender has
no intention of changing his ways, or is insufficiently concerned about the offence to take probation seriously, he is
bound to say so.   The decision rests with the magistrates,
and if they decide nevertheless to make a probation
order the officer is in a difficulty. The effect of the Criminal
Justice Act is that he is obliged to undertake the supervision
of any offender put on probation by the court. The fact that
in the offender's eyes the probation officer "tried to down him"
in court makes an unfortunate beginning.

There is an element of chance in the matter which the court
may often feel should be decided in the offender's favour.
Much depends on the individual gifts and outlook of the officer.
One officer is better at handling people of a sulky disposition,
another those who are hot-tempered ; one is good with the
swaggering kind of young man, another with neurotics.   If
an offender had been charged at an adjacent court, therefore,
the officer there might have reported in a much more optimistic
vein, and been far more likely to help him to recovery.   This
element of chance cannot be avoided.   Probation officers are
human and therefore limited, like everybody else.   In a large
court served by a team of officers the difficulty can sometimes
be overcome by a certain amount of interchange.   In areas
where there is only one officer of each sex, both are bound to
have some offenders under their care whom they are not
really fitted by temperament to help.   Officers have to accept
the fact of their limitations and be as tolerant and generous as
possible in their handling of probationers they find difficult.
It is possible for an officer to be mistaken in his summing up
of an offender's attitude, just as it is possible for the court to
make mistakes.   But the final decision rests with the court.

The art of writing unfavourable reports has to be studied,

and two examples would perhaps best illustrate ways of conveying to the magistrates a true picture of the situation, while at the same time attempting to preserve the dignity of the parties concerned.

The case of Alastair A., just discussed, provides an example of a report which needs delicate handling. The relationship between the officer and Mr A., which as we saw was reckoned to be fundamental to effective treatment, would be jeopardized if Mr A. heard derogatory statements made about him and his home in open court.

After the preliminary details of name, age, address, offence and so on had been given, the probation officer's report might run as follows :

" Alastair does not know why they broke into the warehouse, except that they had nothing to do that evening, and wondered if they could. The home is an unhappy and disordered one, owing partly to Mrs A.'s present very poor state of health. Much could be done to remedy the home situation. Alastair is a responsive child who, given sufficient legitimate outlets, one would expect to do well."

This would indicate to the magistrates that the officer did not think Alastair a vicious child, or the home so bad that he should be removed from its influence, though it makes perfectly clear that home conditions are far from satisfactory. From the A.'s point of view the implied criticism is covered by mention of Mrs A.'s bad health. The report further indicates that the officer feels he could do something constructive in the case. This, for most magistrates who had any confidence in their officer's judgment would probably be sufficient, but if they, or a solicitor on behalf of the A.'s, challenged the probation officer, plenty of precise details could be given.

" What do you mean by saying the home is an unhappy and disordered one ? "

" I heard Mr A. shouting as I came up the alley. He hit one of the children in my presence, who came in to see what was happening. He told me with some heat that he was disgusted with the landlord for not mending the hole in the roof, and with the Government for permitting people to live in such houses. Mrs A. was obviously in great pain, and I thought she had been for some time. The family slops and garbage had not been emptied for some days ; decaying food and soiled garments were lying round the room. . . ." There is no need to regale the court with these lurid details unless they are specifically called for.

Mr A.'s abusiveness is relevant to any probation officer who had to visit the family, but there is no evidence in this case that it was contributory, except in an indirect way, to the offence. There is therefore no need to mention it specifically in the court report, unless more precise details are asked for. If, however, the officer had felt that his father's truculence would militate against Alastair's recovery at home, and that he should therefore be removed from home, it would be necessary to mention it. " Mr A. is a hot-tempered man. Alastair appears cowed, defiant, unsettled (whatever was the case), and I think needs steadier influences for a time." If this were to be given in the report the probation officer would be well advised to tell Mr A. about it beforehand, explaining what he meant and why he was going to recommend that his boy should leave home. " Alastair is in a difficult mood. You have done your best for him, and failed. There is good in the lad, and we want to bring it out. He is of an age to leave home now, many boys of his age go to boarding school. You are worried by him, and get short-tempered, and I think that makes him worse, so if the magistrates ask me what I think I shall suggest that he should leave home for a while." A discussion on these lines with the officer before the report is made to court should help Mr A. to take the unwelcome criticism and suggestion more reasonably than if it was first made in court without any explanation or discussion.

Perhaps it is even more difficult when the officer feels that probation would serve no useful purpose.

Delysia D., a young married woman of 23, was charged with shop-lifting. It was her first appearance in court. Her husband was described as " a wireless mechanic, working on his own ". There was one child, aged three. The officer suspected that the D.'s made their living by professional shop-lifting, and were related to a well-known gang of professional shop-lifters who lived in the district. However, there seemed no evidence for this, and suppositions do not make evidence.

The officer's report in this case was given verbally, and ran somewhat as follows :

" Mrs D. lives in a humble street, but obviously in affluent circumstances." (Evidence, if cross-questioned on this point, (1) her well-tailored clothes and immaculate furs ; (2) the sumptuous furnishings and labour-saving devices in her home ; (3) her husband drove up to the door in his own car at 11 a.m. on the morning of the officer's call, dressed in a well-tailored lounge suit, obviously not working.) " No explanation is offered for the offence except ' sudden temptation '. Mrs D. and her husband seem somewhat aggrieved by the charge. Neither seems to realize its implications or to be much concerned about it." The implication of this report (given to a court which did not like suggestions from its probation officers) is that probation is not recommended, but that a substantial fine could be paid. A probation order was made. Neither husband nor wife were charged with any further offence during the period of this supervision, but neither so far as could be discovered ever did any work, and the probation officer's suspicions were authoritatively confirmed.

F

3. *Explaining the Order*

In some cases, where full preliminary enquiries have been made on the pattern here outlined, the officer will already have had an opportunity to talk to the offender, and his parents if there are any, about the offence and plans of recovery, and their minds will already therefore have been attuned to this line of thought. Even in these cases, however, and much more in those where there has been no opportunity for preliminary talks, the actual terms of the probation order, the conditions of release, and the nature of the undertaking which has been given to the court must be carefully explained again. How this is done varies in each individual case, according to the offender's age, mentality, and present emotional state; the facilities provided at the court for private interviews; and whether or not there has been any contact before the bind-over. A child needs more simple direct language than an adult; an educated, intelligent person needs a different presentation from a simple, illiterate one. A person in a dazed or hysterical state is not able to profit from any discussion on these lines at all, and this explanatory interview must be deferred. A hungry person cannot concentrate on abstract talk of this nature. This should be remembered. People who have been remanded in custody have sometimes risen at a very early hour; have been quite unable to choke down the unappetizing hunks of bread, plates of porridge, or mugs of tepid tea provided by the prison as breakfast; have been rattled around in the Black Maria depositing different prisoners at different courts; or possibly motored anything up to fifty miles; waited interminably in the police cells which are often cruelly cold and draughty; and finally, late in the morning, or even in the afternoon (for remand cases are usually heard after new charges) consented (if over 14) to the probation order, which as we have seen, may or may not have been fully explained in court. These people need a meal and a smoke, time to thaw and recover some ease of mind, before they can be expected to follow intelligently all that the probation officer has to say. Some courts have no facilities for private interviews. It is impossible to explain the terms of a probation order, and discuss plans for a different way of life, standing in a corridor, or sitting on a bench in a crowded office where people are banging in and out, type-writers clicking, telephone bells ringing and onlookers standing around. In such circumstances the whole thing must be deferred until the officer and his new probationer can meet in a quieter atmosphere at the former's office or the latter's home. Where the officer and the offender have already made good contact, the conversation can sometimes be more or less picked up where it then left off. But in many cases the officer may never have met the probationer before, or had any opportunity of sounding his mind and hearing his point of view. A long serious talk is involved, which cannot be scamped or hurried through without detriment to the probation.

Perhaps the most important thing to be explained and underlined is that he has definitely given the court an under-taking. The magistrates have taken the view that he is a fundamentally decent person, who can, and will, make good. They believe that they can trust him, and are prepared to do so. They are bound to consider the offence seriously ; it is their job to protect the public and stop this kind of thing happening, but since he, the offender, has given this under-taking to the court, they are prepared to believe him. The conditions of the probation order must then be enumer-ated. He has agreed to endeavour to be of good behaviour, and to see that this does not happen again; he has agreed to keep in touch with the officer, coming to see him as and where requested, and notifying him of any change of address. If other requirements are involved, these must be explained.

He must think carefully over what is involved. If he has

not already done so in a preliminary interview he must be
helped to see for himself what led up to this offence, and how
his way of life must be modified to ensure that it does not
happen again. The officer must explain what he wants in
the way of contact—a weekly interview at first, probably,
at a time fixed for the convenience of both. The reasons for
this contact, and the nature of the probation officer's relationship, must be explained. The magistrates want the offender
to make good, but realize that it may be no easy matter.
They want him to have help. The probation officer's job
is to advise, assist and befriend him. How can you befriend
or assist someone whom you rarely see? How can you
advise anyone if you are not conversant with his affairs?
The offender must think this over seriously. It is essential
here to emphasize, as outlined in Chapter I, that the officer
is *not* in authority over him ; the offender is to manage his
own life and make his own decisions. The officer has to
report to the magistrates how things are going, and is obliged
to report if he thinks things are going wrong.

As he has entered into an agreement on these terms it must be
regarded as a binding agreement, which he has freely accepted.
It means that if, having given his word, he forgets, or changes
his mind, and breaks his word, the magistrates have the right
to summon him back to court and reconsider his offence and
their decision. They could have sentenced him to punishment
to-day, and if he breaks his word or fails to keep his agreement,
he could be punished for it any time within the specified
duration of the probation order.

If it should happen, as it occasionally has, that the probationer then declares he certainly did not understand all
this: he would never have agreed to probation if he had
realized what was involved, the officer must point out that
whether he understood the implications or not the arrangement is in his own interests; he surely does not intend to
offend again; he must make up his mind, either to accept

the opportunity given sincerely, and make the necessary effort to change his way of life, or to take the consequences; better at least give the business a fair trial. The requirements of the order could be modified in due course if need be, on application of the officer or the probationer.

The interview should throughout emphasize the positive aspects of the situation. Some offenders, if asked what probation means, reply at once, " They watch you ". The answer is, on the contrary, " They trust you ". No one could watch another through all his waking hours to ensure that he did no wrong. Where a parent has been bound over, that can be brought in here. "Your dad believes in you, too. He is so sure that you can and will pull straight that he has undertaken to pay £5 or £10 to the court if you get into trouble again ".

If the officer has already had an opportunity of forming some opinion as to the probationer's qualities, it is helpful at this stage to underline some of his good points ; he is normally by this time feeling very shaken and humiliated. The family who turn out so staunchly to testify for the delinquent in the witness box—" He's always been a good boy at home, sir ", " He's the best husband in the world, sir "—once they are relieved from their own horrible tension of suspense often react at home with torrents of abuse and reproach, and even blows. No one can pull himself together if he is utterly without self-confidence, and it is good for the delinquent to be assured of someone's belief in him at this stage, however limited this may be.

The first interview is not the time to read the offender a lecture on the enormity of his offence. No one cares for this kind of assault. Most people can only take it—and make use of it—if it comes from someone whom they know and regard, and therefore the time for it comes, if at all on probation, much later when friendly relations have been established. One wants the offender to talk freely to his officer about what is passing in his mind, in order that in the telling he may come to see more clearly for himself what is wrong. A severe dressing down or strong personal criticism in the opening phases, while the officer is still a stranger—and not a very welcome one at that—is to court quite the reverse effect. The probationer will conceive a strong dislike for the officer, and determine to have as little to do with him as possible. People who try to inculcate shame in others generally only succeed in arousing antipathy against themselves. We are moved to shame when we meet someone whom we recognize to be infinitely better than ourselves. A necessary prelude to shame is, therefore, the capacity to appreciate good.

But there is more in it even than this. The offence is symptomatic, and one must endeavour to treat not the symptom but the cause of the trouble. The offence is not an isolated, unconnected occurrence, but the result of a habit of mind and the culmination of a sequence of events. There is probably no such thing as sudden temptation. The very word temptation indicates that battle has been done with impulse, otherwise the word impulse would be better used. People are not tempted to do what is completely alien to their way of life or habit of mind, unless they are suffering from mental disease. Those who snatch some desired article from the counter when no one is looking, or commit a sexual offence when opportunity presents itself, have generally played with the idea before, reflected that other people get away with this sort of thing, why shouldn't they? Thus with normal people it is more helpful not to scold them for this particular act, but to help them to see what led up to it. This is not to say that later on in probation the offender should not be led to consider how his actions may affect other people, and his responsibilities towards his fellows. This must be done, but by a different approach at a later stage.

How much can be done at this early stage in discussing the

details of future plans varies naturally with different persons
and their varying circumstances.   But inasmuch as this term
of probation is intended to be reformative, attention must in
the course of it be gradually but persistently directed to those
factors which most affect the formation of character.   While
his material circumstances may greatly affect the offender's
outlook at present, his moral stamina will most surely be built
up, it is suggested here, through his interests, his friends, his
family ties and his faith.   All these factors will therefore now
be discussed in turn.

VI

Material Help

In planning effective treatment for any probationer, the aim is always to help him out of the mentality or circumstances which led to the commission of the offence, to turn his mind to a new conception of life, and its possibilities of both enjoyment and responsibility, and to build up his confidence in himself and his own powers to do better. Sometimes a certain amount of material help seems to be a necessary prelude to better things. Some probationers, for instance, are destitute, or stranded, and immediate arrangements must be made for food, shelter, or clothes. Some are suffering from infectious diseases like scabies or venereal disease, or from some incapacitating disease like tuberculosis or chorea, and need immediate medical attention, and the help of the probation officer in arranging it. Some probationers are in acute distress : for instance married men with dependent families who have been dismissed from their jobs, and cannot put their minds on any other issues until the immediate problem of providing for their families is solved. Some are so worn down and distracted by the chronic struggle of life and its problems, or so accustomed to living in purposeless monotony or horrible piggery that it seems as though some material help is necessary in the early stages to act as a tonic or spur to their failing energies or self-respect. On the other hand, there are others, like Delysia D. described on page 69, who seem to require no material help. Their offences do not appear to have arisen from any kind of material stress, nor to have affected their material position. Treatment must be planned for each separate person individually, according to the probation officer's estimation of their individual needs.

Material need usually arises from some degree of either poverty or ill-health. These things are sometimes interdependent. They are always relative. What is poverty to one, may be riches to another ; what is a prostrating illness to one, is merely a customary weariness to another. The factors leading to poverty and ill-health are various, and so are their effects on character. We will therefore consider each separately.

1. Poverty

If the reasons for material want in any particular family are analysed one finds, as might be expected, different contributory causes. There is sometimes ill-luck. Factors beyond a man's control have power to throw him out of work these days—a new process in the industry, the labour laws in Japan, the economic recovery of Germany. Hard work and loyal service do not defend a man against economic depression such as we experienced for instance in 1931. Whole works close down. Whole areas are hit. Failing health is a potent cause of poverty, as poverty itself is a menace to health. Many fall a victim to this vicious circle. A delicate man in poor health continually loses days of work through sickness, and thereby wages. His one anxiety is to get back to work, so he never gets a chance to recover properly and build up his reserves of energy between each bout of sickness. He runs his family in consequence on continual short money. This means less food, and so less energy, a lowered resistance to infection, and more strain and anxiety. All this in turn militates against his health. In this same kind of way the wrong kind of job may be a contributory cause of poverty—a person with bronchial tendencies, for instance, should never be working as a postman, continually exposed to all kinds of weathers ; nor should anyone threatened with tuberculosis be doing heavy muscular work, whether

indoors or outdoors. Poverty may be aggravated by ineptitude and bad management. Some people are born house-
wives ; many are not. This applies to all walks of life.
One woman can make 30s. go twice as far as another. Few
teachers of domestic economy could teach or suggest anything
to the capable wives of the very poor. In fact we expect
untrained people to do what trained ones could not possibly
do. It is of little avail to attempt to instruct the very poor in
domesticities. One worker showed a woman how to make
a nourishing supper dish for her large family out of odds and
ends. " Now, Mrs Smith, just pop it into the oven half an
hour before they come home, to brown it over," she said as
she left. " I didn't like to tell her, miss," said Mrs Smith
afterwards, " that my oven don't work. Never has, miss.
It's cracked. The landlord won't do nothing about it."
Low income means not only shortage of food, but of cooking
utensils and storing space. The very poor often have only
one kettle and one saucepan for all purposes, no mixing bowls,
no gas, no electricity, and nowhere to keep coal.

Some ineptitude is caused by poor mental capacity, which
can never be rectified, some by emotional causes. People,
for instance, who feel hopeless and despairing may begin to
let things go and to take the easiest way. The whole situation
is bleak and cheerless ; what is to be gained by worrying
oneself, or struggling with the inevitable ? These people
do not need instruction, nor even the settlement of some
outstanding debt ; they need to be fired with new enjoyment
of life, to give them renewed zest and purpose in living.

One of the most insidious effects of extreme poverty in this
country is its prevention of rational occupation. One sees
this continually with the slum child. In his tiny overcrowded
little home there is no room for even a chair apiece all round
the family (meals have to be taken standing around or in
rotation), let alone for a child's paraphernalia of toys and
hobbies. Alfie, aged 5, spent a happy afternoon in the

country picking up conkers. All the way home he chattered busily about what he was going to do with these prized possessions. And what did he do with them ? " Me muvver froo vem on to the fire. She said she'd no room for such rubbish." The tragedy of this story lies in its truth. She literally did have no room. Bertie, aged 10, spent his Bank Holiday tramping through the crowded streets to a common, some five or six miles distant, in search of grass and trees and a pond to fish in. Sensible child, perhaps you think ; why do not more boys do the same ? Not at all. He was rewarded on his return home with a terrible hiding and weeks of nagging from his overwrought mother. He had worn his boots right through, and how could she ever get them mended ? So the slum child grows up idling round the streets. There is no chance here of developing powers of concentration, as the more privileged children do, poring over their paint boxes and puzzles. Even street games are constantly interrupted by passing lorries or policemen.

Within the very poor home long-continued undernourishment and overcrowding tend to produce irritability and nervous tension. These in a tiny home where one cannot easily withdraw without giving offence, lead to rows, blows, and sometimes fights. Habits of impulsive unrestrained behaviour may develop, or sometimes a somewhat exaggerated egotism, " You have to look after yourself in this world, nobody else will ".

Extreme poverty narrows the circle of acquaintance. People are ashamed to meet their friends, fearing embarrassing though kindly meant enquiries or visits ; or the indignity of not being able to return hospitality. So " We keep ourselves to ourselves " is the easiest way out, but a disastrous one.

People living a hand to mouth existence are apt to lose the capacity for thinking ahead. The immediate present is in itself such a problem that the future, or long-term planning, is ruled out. A child who is being taught to save up his

money has the dismay of seeing his money box broken open
when the landlord begins getting nasty about the arrears of
rent, or when father is suddenly taken ill.   No child who has
once had this happen to him, or seen it happen to another,
will ever be so silly as to run the same risk again.   He will
cash in on every sixpence or halfpenny as soon as it comes his
way, and secure its value for certain.   Thus is developed the
" eat, drink, and be merry " philosophy of life, which the
more privileged classes reckon as irresponsibility.   We have
yet to see what the effects of our new schemes for social
insurance will be.   Whatever they are, we have reared many
generations under the old regime of extreme economic
insecurity, and the character and outlook so moulded is now
part of our national social heritage, with which we must
reckon, for it will not be quickly or easily eradicated.

This brief survey may be sufficient to show that money
alone will not undo the effects of prolonged poverty and
economic insecurity.   This book attempts to show the wide
range of factors—friends, interests, affection—which are
necessary for any real counterbalancing in the formation or
change of character.   None the less, money can be useful in
the process, and the probation officer must be conversant
with all the possible agencies which might help in a material
way.   There are many.   The main sources of possible
material or financial assistance open to the officer and his
probationers might be classified roughly under four heads :
funds available to and administered by the court or the
probation officer exclusively ; funds subscribed to voluntary
societies and administered by them on behalf of the charitably
minded public ;   public money administered by statutory
authorities ;   and the self-help of the parties themselves,
through some re-arrangement or modification of their private
lives.

The funds available to courts and probation officers are
variable. The Metropolitan Magistrates' Court Poor Boxes are

reputed to be very well to do. In times gone by wealthy benefactors left them large sums, which bring in a steady income, and this in turn was sometimes re-invested. (The Metropolitan Juvenile Court Poor Box, on the other hand, being of later date, has nothing like the same amount of money, though, on the whole, probably greater need.) In other big cities there is sometimes a Poor Box, in enterprising places where the magistrates have themselves been at pains to collect one and contribute to it. In many areas there is none. The Police Court Mission sometimes has funds available to help individual persons recommended by probation officers. A Befriending Fund is available for any area that makes application for it through the Probation Department of the Home Office, the Exchequer contributing on a 50–50 basis with the local authority. This Befriending Fund is limited to the use of probationers. Some probation officers have privately collected funds of their own to administer, given to them by personal friends or by the churches or chapels to which they belong. A good deal of money sometimes comes through the press when a pitiable story is written up in a sensational way. Sometimes as much as £50 will reach the probation officer in odd sums through the post for " Lily, the Lonely Girl " or " the Boy who had No Home ". These sums can be embarrassing, for the story told in court, which was written up so appealingly by the reporters, is sometimes found to be totally false upon investigation. Where the donors append their names and addresses it is possible to write and tell them the facts of the case, and to ask if they would prefer their kind gift to be diverted to some other person whose need is greater. Some officers do well out of advertising their needs in the local press. Prams, bedding, barrows, tools, typewriters, and such like, have all been obtained as gifts through suitably worded appeals in the local paper.

Hence it will be seen that, one way and another, probation officers often have money available for use at their discretion, or, in the case of Poor Box or Befriending Funds, upon their application and the magistrates' approval. They certainly need it. The odd cups of tea, cigarettes, meals, which they are continually providing, although trivial in themselves, are of great value in the establishment of a happy relationship or a brighter outlook, but in the course of a year mount up to not a few pounds. Bigger sums are often needed, fares, for instance, of parents who cannot afford to visit their children in Approved Schools, or of persons going home to relatives; fees for special types of training; loans to purchase stock or start a little business; odd medical or psychological fees, and so on. To meet these the officer may have recourse to some of the voluntary or statutory funds already referred to.

In most towns of any size there are large funds subscribed by the public to different trusts or societies, and administered by such bodies as the Family Welfare Society, the Personal Service Society, the Soldiers', Sailors' and Airmen's Families Association, to mention only a few. Probation officers should be acquainted with them all. A handbook of classified funds and agencies, *The Charities Digest*, is published annually by the Family Welfare Association, and the officer can add to this as he discovers other possible local sources of help. There is no lack of money for charitable purposes in this country. The art is to know the most likely funds, and to put the case in the most convincing way. It is always worth while to *ask*. Officers who make a practice of asking for what they want, get much more than those who don't. It is always easier to get money for a long-term scheme than for immediate relief, and hence it is often easier to get big sums than small. The agencies, of course, have to have full particulars of the whole situation, and usually make their own investigation and assessment.

All officers have to be acquainted with the powers and duties of the various statutory social services, and should never tap private sources if there are public funds available.

There are the local Education, Health and Housing Authorities, each with a wide range of duties and powers, with every one of which the probation officer is bound to have constant dealings. The Assistance Board or Social Welfare Committee has wide powers for relieving material need. The Ministries of Labour, Education and Health, through their local officers, have a different range again. Knowledge of the spheres of all these authorities is essential to all probation officers.

One sometimes hears said, somewhat petulantly, " Don't we do enough for these people ? Surely there is now public relief for every kind of contingency or distress ? " The trouble is that it is all so departmentalized, with little elasticity or chance of interplay between the various authorities, so that some unfortunate people whose dilemma is multiple fail to get the necessary co-ordinated assistance. The story of Mr and Mrs J. illustrates this well. Mr J. was a lorry driver, suffering from severe gastric trouble. For many years he had been constantly off work sick, and his wages, checked with his employers over the last eleven weeks, showed that he had been earning an average of less than £3 a week. He had six children, three of school age, three babies at home. The family lived in a small back-to-back cottage, one room up and one down, sharing a water closet in the yard with three other families in similar cottages. During all his long history of ill-health extending over years, the public assistance Authority had brought his money up to 50s. a week when his earnings fell below this. Clearly the man's health was pivotal to the family's poverty. Lorry-driving is the worst job that he could have tried to do ; with its long hours of sitting in a cramped position, and irregular sandwich meals, it was bound to aggravate his complaint. No one had thought of a change of job for him. A visit to the man's doctor, followed by another to the Employment Exchange, armed with a medical certificate, might have secured him a much more suitable job, chosen to suit his physical strength.

If this had been in some large works, of which there were many in the neighbourhood, with little extra fuss or expense he could have got from the works canteen the light regular diet his condition demanded. His teeth were in a bad state, contributing to his complaint. His insurance society were prepared to help him with the cost of extractions and new dentures, but no one was prepared to help him with the loss of wages involved in attending hospital for this purpose—there were no evening dental clinics in the town apparently. The family were on the priority list for a better house, and were actually offered one with four rooms on the new housing estate outside the town, but they could not afford either the moving expenses or the cost of black-out (which was then necessary) for all the extra windows, so they had to let their chance go. The three babies were not getting their orange juice or cod liver oil ; the clinic from which these were obtainable free for children under the age of five years, through the local Health Authority, was a mile and a half distant ; Mrs J., herself in very low health on account of prolonged undernourishment and her constant confinements, had no pram and no money for bus fares, and gave up all idea of trying to get them there to claim these foods. The three schoolchildren were not getting milk or dinners at school. The reason for this, given by the Education Authority, was that the family were above the income level for free meals, and the children had complained that they did not like the milk. Mrs J. had recently had her sixth confinement, at home, and served two short sentences of imprisonment for shop lifting. While she was in prison no arrangements had been made for the care of the children, their father being either ill at home in bed or out with his lorry. The parents had none the less recently been fined £2 by the local court because the two eldest children had not attended school regularly It will thus be seen that without some collaboration between our various statutory social services, not only will some families fall between them all and remain in desperate straits, but their position may be made worse by the unco-ordinated action of the different departments concerned. The probation officer often has to serve in the role of liaison officer between them all.

Finally in this review of possible ways of relieving poverty, there is self-help. Sometimes the family is so worn down with worry and the continual strain of trying to better themselves without the adequate means or knowledge, that some outside help is necessary. A change of work, as we have seen, may be the most constructive way in which to help a man to help himself. Sometimes the wife is prepared to take on extra evening or part-time work for a while, if she knows of it, can get to and from it easily, and still be available at home at the important times. People are more likely to take on such extra effort if there is a goal in view, such as, for instance, the purchase of a bicycle which would thereafter save several shillings a week in fares, as well as provide the means of week-end pleasure and exercise ; or of a typewriter or sewing machine which would enable extra part-time work to be done at home in the evenings. But the main road to self-help is the emotional one.

Mrs Q. was quite worn down with her utterly dreary and squalid existence, but she had become accustomed to this, and did not notice it until the war came and her children were evacuated. She was then invited by their hostess in the country to come and spend the week-end there and see how they were getting on. She did this and found an adorable little home, cosy, comfortable, clean, pretty, beyond her dreams. It upset her, and she went home and cried on the bed in disgust at her own miserable, dirty, dishevelled rooms. Then she pulled herself together and marched off to the hairdresser for a shampoo and set—a thing she had never thought of doing probably since her children began to arrive many years ago. This so restored her pride and

G

dignity that she set to work at once, first to spring clean, and then to distemper her little house. Money did not produce this transformation. The spark that fired her into action was an emotional one, first the beautiful hospitality she had received in the country, and then the stimulating and reviving effect of the shampoo on her failing spirits and self-esteem. And so it often is. If one can introduce some new factor which makes life worth living again the barometer goes up, and natural resourcefulness and resilience with it.

2. *Health*

The factors which contribute to health or ill-health are just as varied and multiple as those which contribute to poverty. In some cases the ill-health may be attributable to congenital physical weakness, such for example as a weak heart, delicate lungs, inherited syphilis. More often a person's physical resistance to infections has been worn down by social or economic conditions, perhaps still more often by emotional factors. Some people's health is affected, for instance, by living in noisy, overcrowded, smoke-ridden cities ; by working in unhealthy conditions—underground, or in certain chemical processes ; or by neglecting the basic rules of personal health. These might be termed social causes of ill-health. People's health is affected if they are unable to get sufficient food. This is an economic cause. It may be that there is a world-wide shortage of food, or a faulty distribution, as in 1946, when whole continents faced famine. It may be that though food is plentiful, this particular person has never been able to earn enough money to buy sufficient for A.1 health, as was the case with vast numbers of our lower-paid workers in this country before the war.[1]   It is significant that

[1] See *Food, Health and Income*, by John Boyd Orr (Macmillan, 1936), and compare tables on pp. 21 and 34.   See also *Poverty and Progress*, by B. Seebohm Rowntree (Longmans, Green & Co.), particularly Chapter VII.

people tend to buy food when they can afford to ; a rise in income is always first reflected on the table. But in this country at the present time the greatest toll of ill-health comes probably from emotional causes. Worry gets people down ; it saps their energy and powers of resistance ; it interferes with their digestive processes, and stops them sleeping.

Health has a bearing on mentality and behaviour. Our moralists may deny that this should be so, but few would deny that it *is* so.[1] People who are suffering ill-health are tired, and tend to give up easily. They get irritable or listless. Their judgment is affected ; they lose their sense of proportion and become intolerant or sometimes selfish in their assessments of people and situations. In consequence quarrels and misunderstandings may arise ; and impulsive people in the desperation of the moment may throw up their jobs, leave their homes, or assault someone, thereby adding greatly to their difficulties. It is important for the probation officer to investigate health history when problems arise. One girl was the despair of her officer. She would *not* work, and openly proclaimed that she could not endure working and did not want to work. It was quite by chance that she let drop one day in the course of casual conversation that she had spent the first eight years of her life flat on her back in a spinal carriage. The orphanage where she had been brought up had not thought it worth while to mention this, in spite of more than one earnest plea for information about her background. Hence the poor girl in failing to keep all the many unsuitable jobs that had been found for her—all of the kitchen-hand, wardmaid type, involving heavy scrubbing and polishing—had been passed as a lazy, idle incorrigible. A child's failure at school may often be traced to lack of

[1] Burt, *Young Delinquent*, p. 280 : Any physical discomfort will sharpen general nervous irritability, a sore gland, a bad tooth, a stomach-ache make for restless fretful petulance and impatience. Cool reflection and calm reactions are difficult.

sufficient sleep, or to chronic constipation—easily remediable states, but quite enough to account for restless inattention and tiresome behaviour in class.

The possibility of there being some physical cause for unsatisfactory behaviour should always be remembered, but there are certain circumstances in which attention to health is pivotal to effective treatment, and basic to recovery.

For instance, over and over again in the juvenile courts when enquiries are made at home one finds, as in the case of Alastair A. already quoted on page 59, that the mother is in a bad state of health. Deterioration of home discipline, a low standard of comfort and cleanliness with consequent family friction and nervous tension, and a child's failing sense of security, may àll be directly attributable to the mother's wretched health. Many mothers in the lower-paid wage groups suffer from chronic malnutrition or debility, or from neglected abdominal trouble following the birth of the last child. The quickest, surest way to a recovery of the young offender may be to build up the mother's health and strength, and thereby a happier, more satisfying home life, and more consistent home discipline.

Attention to health is also of importance in the case of drunks and prostitutes. It is frequently found, if investigation is careful enough and goes far enough back, that it was some physical weakness that originally led to the beginning of these excesses. A man or woman suffering from some lowering or weakening physical ailment, failing in business or in personal relationships, depressed, unsure of himself, fed up, may seek relief and stimulation or escape in drink. Once people take to constant drinking in excess their physique is lowered more and more. Their digestions go to pieces ; they cannot take normal food. Further, they often contract severe chills from exposure to damp and cold while in a helpless state of intoxication. Similarly with prostitutes, the world-wide enquiry

conducted by the League of Nations[1] between the two wars
has established that more often than not some innate physical
weakness caused them to fail in respectable life and so to drift
down the social scale. It stands to reason, then, that if one
wants to help these offenders one must take into consideration
both their normal physical strength, as far as this can be
ascertained, as well as any subsequent damage to it. They
must first have their health built up as far as may be, and then
be found more congenial work, more suited to their physical
strength and quite different from that in which they have
already failed. These people need to be literally " nursed "
back to a better state of physical health and strength before
they can be expected to take on normal responsibility for
themselves and their fellows again. They need humouring,
careful feeding, and warm affectionate personal care. This is
what society cannot bring itself to give. Inebriate and Rescue
Homes are sometimes dour, grim places, with the accent on
somewhat rigorous discipline. Society is terrified lest
" over-pampering " should make people parasites. The
answer is, these people are parasites already; and they will be
just as much parasites if they are eventually relegated to prisons
and workhouses as they are now, pursuing their excesses.

There is an interesting account of successful treatment of
prostitutes along these lines of extra attention to food, comfort
and physical well-being in Russia after the revolution, in the
book *The Great Offensive*, by Maurice Hindus.[2] Individual
officers who have worked on this principle in this country
have been very successful.

Most people react well to concern about their health.
They take it as kindly personal interest and often thankfully
welcome any suggestion that might elicit sympathy or explain

[1] *The Prevention of Prostitution*. League of Nations, Advisory Committee
on Social Questions.
[2] Pages 139-40. But it must be remembered that Russia's problem of
prostitution was at that time abnormal. The recent revolution had
suddenly reduced all girls of noble and bourgeois rank to penury.

in part their failures and difficulties. They are for the most part therefore prepared to fall in with suggestions related to medical examinations or treatment. The exceptions are the timid people whose imaginations at once conjure up dreadful visions of the horrible possibilities which a visit to hospital might entail—bed-pans, students, anæsthetics, unsuccessful operations—or those who are so overwrought that they have begun to regard themselves as indispensable, and the neurotic folk who all unconsciously are clinging to their maladies as a cloak to their inability to manage themselves better. The two former need a supporting friend to go with them to the medical examination and see them through the business. The latter need psychological treatment, if it is to be had, and if they can take it, to help them to understand themselves better, or to incite them to new interests which will take them out of themselves.

It is not difficult to plan medical treatment—less than ever since the National Insurance Act, 1946; but the road to its practical achievement is fraught with endless petty difficulties and frustrations, which must be accepted as part of the game, and reckoned on beforehand. For instance, an appointment may be made for a probationer to see a specialist, or to attend a clinic. This is often quite genuinely forgotten. One day is so like another to dreary people that there is nothing to distinguish Tuesday from Wednesday, and the great majority of probationers do not have engagement diaries or calendars. Another appointment has to be made, with suitable apologies and explanations. When this day comes there may very likely be a quite unpredictable change in the working shift, making it impossible for the patient to attend. More letters of apology and corresponding delays ensue, and letters are exchanged between the probationer and the officer, the officer and the hospital, and back again, before a third date is arranged. On the appointed day the patient has to hurry home from work, wash and change his clothes, and rush off, often without having time for a meal, to queue for a tram. If he has not been to this doctor or hospital before, he will almost undoubtedly lose his way, and thus arrive late, only to be told that the doctor has just left, and he must attend again in a fortnight's time.   Or a mother has to arrange for relations or friends to mind her children.   She gets up incredibly early to wash and dress them and take them to these friends, and arrives at the hospital puffed and exhausted before 9 a.m. to take her place in the out-patients' queue. Usually it is some four or five hours before she has finished, and when finally examined she may merely be told to attend again for an X-ray examination or to see another specialist in a different department on some future date.   She gets home late in the afternoon, famished and worn out, to find the fire out, no shopping done, and all the family coming home for their cooked high tea as usual.   No wonder their spirits quail at the inordinate trouble of seeing this specialist, and at the prospect of going through all this fuss week after week if treatment is ordered.   Surely the mild backache or headache to which they have become accustomed is preferable to all this terrible rushing about and exhaustion.   If goodwill prevails, however, to oblige the probation officer, this further appointment is remembered, but when the day comes, as likely as not, one of the children will be taken ill, and the mother must stay at home to nurse her, or the wage earner will have to go to the chemist's for a bottle of medicine.   The next week the same stupendous effort may be made to reach the place in time, but because the preceding appointment was not kept they were not informed that this week the department would be closed, or the particular doctor in question away on his holidays, so the effort is made in vain.   This picture is no exaggeration.   People living in rural areas or in huge cities often have long journeys entailing changes of bus or tram, each with its queue and uncertain stopping places, to reach the appointed hospital or clinic, and to persons jaded or ill, or unaccustomed to travelling outside their own little world, great expenditure of fatigue and anxiety is occasioned. It sounds so simple on paper to persuade poor Mrs A. or Mr J: to go and see a doctor, but in actual fact it often takes weeks to accomplish.[1] Furthermore, if it is achieved, it is often difficult to get patients to carry out their doctors' instructions. This difficulty is not confined to delinquents. Highly respectable people in all walks of life forget to take their medicine, lose heart about the treatment, or faith in their doctors, and give it all up. And even if it is faithfully taken, the poor little bottle of medicine has so much to compete against—inadequate diet, monotonous or worrying work, anxiety or friction at home, a joyless life—so that the results of all the effort are sometimes not spectacular. Another difficulty is that people suffering from long-standing or progressive ill-health need far more to build them up than mere treatment, even effective treatment, of the immediate symptom—clearing up the current whitlow, extracting an angry tooth, provision of a surgical belt.

And so the question of convalescence has to be considered. It is not difficult to arrange convalescent facilities, though this usually entails more ingenuity and bother on the part of the officer. Most big hospitals normally have their own convalescent homes for those of their patients who need it most urgently. Many philanthropic bodies will arrange it if appealed to. The Salvation Army, for instance, have facilities for holidays for overdone mothers, and the Invalid Children's Aid Society for children. Often the patient himself has relatives or friends in the country to whom he could go if the expenses were covered, and here recourse can be had to one of the funds mentioned in the last section.

[1] To obtain a medical report on remand is quite a different matter. Then, while his fate still hangs in the balance, and the awful horror of a possible prison sentence looms above everything else, the offender will usually go to any lengths to do as he is advised by the officer. Further, doctors and clinics will usually give priority to remand cases.

Government grants are now available under various heads towards the maintenance of probationers required by the terms of their order to live away from home. (See Appendix II, Home Office Circular 216/1949). Arrangements for the suitable care of children during their mother's absence on convalescence are not an insuperable difficulty. Frequently relatives, friends or neighbours are ready to step in and help temporarily here. The Children's Committee will sometimes take charge of the children in these circumstances temporarily.

The real obstacles to convalescent treatment are the emotional ones. The people who most need it are often the most loath to go. The effort needed to pull oneself together, make the necessary personal adjustments, think ahead, face the unknown and the unfamiliar, are often altogether too much for sick persons, and they simply cannot contemplate it. In the case of married women there may have been unhappy marital relationships for some time past, partly no doubt exacerbated by low health, partly contributing to it. These women, though they may not always confess it, sometimes doubt their husband's good faith (sometimes with good reason). What about his late nights? Could he be trusted to pay the rent? With these gloomy fears crossing their minds they will not hear of leaving home. If convalescence or a change of air is achieved in these cases the results may be remarkable, and have quite a transforming effect. But though on this account it is tempting to press it, to try to force it on parties who resist never works, and nearly always ends in failure and vexation, which may do more harm than good.

A country holiday or a change of scene is sometimes recommended for children who have been sexually assaulted, to help them to " forget " the unpleasant experience. But in actual fact emotional factors often operate here, too, in an adverse direction. What these children need is a much greater sense of comfortable security for a time to get over the

shock. To send a timid, frightened child in these circumstances away to strangers, into the unknown, out of reach of
her mother and her home, and all that is familiar, may be to
add a second emotional shock or horrifying experience to the
first. Better treatment may be to add greatly to the pleasantness, comfort and security of life at home. All such children
need a talk with an expert child psychologist about the
incident.

As an alternative to convalescent treatment, where this is
resisted, or in addition to it, much can be done by food. Food
is an under-exploited factor in the treatment of those in
physical or mental low water. Good food brings an immediate
rise in the emotional barometer. A cup of tea, even, can
bring about a mollified attitude in the space of a very few
minutes, while a good dinner produces a warm, comfortable
glow of well-being ; life takes on a different complexion
altogether and the prospect, so intolerable before, becomes
comparatively manageable again. This is one of the reasons
why the probation officer needs money. Meals, particularly
good ones, are expensive, but they can be highly effective as
an incident in probation. Much more could be made of
food in many of our institutions for delinquents. There
would be less running away and more running back again in
some if there were a more generous standard of feeding.
Lowered vitality as well as high nervous tensions respond to
good food, and need it. It would be interesting to get
qualified dietitians to explore this field. Thus where ill-
health or malnutrition is diagnosed or suspected it is well to
try to raise the standard of feeding. For instance, Bournvita
or Ovaltine may be advised at bedtime. Or if appetites outdo
the housewife's imagination or energy some of the hungrier
members of the family might be encouraged to make greater
use of works' canteens, thus relieving the resources at home.
Obvious as this suggestion sounds, if the family custom has
been for the workers to take their own sandwiches or to come

home for their mid-day dinner it takes a lot of ingenuity to break the habit. Similarly, if the family or the individual is accustomed to living mainly on bread and margarine and tea, it is no easy matter to institute fruit, fish and vegetables in addition. Hence in cases where a new job is being sought, attention might well be directed to jobs which carry food with them. Plentiful food of good quality is often provided for the workers in hotels, restaurants and some hospitals.

For many persons suffering ill-health, whether delinquents or not, psychological rather than medical treatment, or in addition to it, is necessary. It is at present much easier to obtain a psychological diagnosis of the trouble than treatment for it. There are too few psychological clinics, and they are for the most part badly understaffed and overworked. Nevertheless the more help is sought from this quarter, the more will be forthcoming. The value of seeking psychological help is that the officer, and sometimes the patient, gets more light on the reasons for the trouble, and also suggestions as to possible treatment. The treatment most often recommended by psychologists is something which can only be provided or carried out by the lay—a change of environment, for instance ; a different kind of job ; attention to some physical defect ; and in the case of children, over and over again, " adult affection ". Where something more than this is required, as in the case of neurotic invalidism, undue worry, compulsive theft or sexual trouble, skilled psychological treatment is needed. As things are at present the most that clinics can usually offer in this way is a weekly or monthly visit to, or interview with, the psychiatrist, the gist of which may be a measure of explanation, reassurance or suggestion to the patient. In the case of children much can be done by means of play therapy in skilled hands.[1] Insofar as drunkenness is a form of escapism (this seems often to be the case), intelligent

[1] See e.g. *Child Guidance*, by Burbery and others (Macmillan & Co.), Chapter X.

drunks may benefit from psychological treatment, in being thereby helped to see for themselves that they are running away, and what it is they are running from. As already indicated (page 18), psycho-analytical treatment is only rarely either suitable, available, or recommended.

"Just so much common sense" say many people of psychological treatment, as if thereby to decry it. It is, of course, true that psychological treatment if successful must be founded on sense, but it is not nearly so common as these speakers seem to suggest. Good psychological treatment is not only based on gifts of temperament and insight which are not at all common, but on a degree of intensive study and specialized experience which is quite beyond the beat of the ordinary person. Naturally, as in all professions, there are both good and bad practising it, and the same psychiatrist has varying success with different patients.

Both health and poverty, often closely related to emotional outlook, can be affected by a change of job. People often find themselves by force of circumstances, by ignorance, or during wartime by direction from the Ministry of Labour, in jobs for which they are temperamentally unfitted. An office-boy yearns for an outdoor life ; a girl is miserably worried by an over-exacting or over-attentive foreman ; someone finds himself committed to close meticulous work requiring a degree of concentration and a precision of eye or touch with which nature has not endowed him. Examples could be multiplied. Such people continually feel irked and fretted and may begin to lose their health. Because they are unsuited to the job they tend to do it badly, and suffer the consequent criticism or sense of failure and inadequacy. A change of job, obvious as this would appear to be in the interests of health and vitality, is not as simple as it sounds. There may be strong family prejudice to overcome. In the case of skilled or professional workers, or of those with dependent families or relatives, considerable risk is involved in a change. People who feel they have been a failure at one job often feel diffident about their powers of making a success of another.

A change of environment may make a great deal of difference to health. This is patently so in the case of anæmic youngsters who change from a city job to one in the country or at the seaside ; or of workers who change to jobs nearer home, thus cutting out hours of weary travelling and bus-queuing every week. In these circumstances health may improve enormously, and even cease to be an adverse factor. To move a family to a new environment is more difficult and less likely to succeed, however sunny and spacious the new home, or squalid and uncomfortable the old. The immediate effect is bound to be much harassment ; money has to be found for the move ; belongings have to be assembled—a depressing business, they look more than ever bedraggled out of their familiar setting ; a better house almost invariably involves a higher rent, frequently higher fares to and from work, more rooms to keep clean ; and the family may find themselves in a strange area, with no nice friendly neighbours running in and out, no old familiar tradesmen ready to oblige with a little credit, no comfortable landmarks, church, club, Assistance Board or Insurance man. This fundamental uprooting takes a lot of getting over. During the period of adjustment the family's nerves, spirits, and health may all suffer. It is important to foresee all this ; and if the family is keen to move, and an opportunity to do so presents itself, they should be prepared beforehand for the difficulties that lie ahead, and helped as far as possible to meet them as they arise. It is most unwise to put pressure on a family to move if they are resistant to the idea.

Finally, the little things must not be forgotten. Some probationers have *never* had new clothes, bought specifically for them. The very poor buy their clothes second-hand at market stalls or jumble sales. All element of choice in the matter is ruled out. A dowdy, dejected woman who comes by some new clothes and suddenly finds herself attractively dressed feels different all over. To a child a new overcoat or set of underclothing heralds a new era in his life. A visit to the hairdresser in the same way, as we have seen, can have a transforming effect on self-respect and spirits as well as appearance. Many a probation officer can testify from experience to the value of these seemingly frivolous attentions in bringing about restored self-confidence, a different outlook and a determination to make a " fresh start ". As in all other remedial efforts there are, however, dangers which must be borne in mind. It is unwise, for instance, to dress up one member of a family alone. The others are likely to feel jealous. The smart one may be ashamed to be seen out with her shabby family. Family tensions may thus be increased. If one wants to give a girl new clothes to keep up her appearance at a new job, or to give her more zest for life, it is well to give her mother or sisters something at the same time. This sends the probationer's stock up, and instead of being angry and jealous the family are interested and pleased. The possibility of jealousy between mother and daughter must never be overlooked. It is one of the fundamental principles of sound probation treatment that the probationer must be helped in relation to his total situation. One must avoid the one-eyed piecemeal kind of treatment which clears up one difficulty by making another. The probationer's whole setting must be taken into consideration, and treated as a whole.

3. Pitfalls

There is something attractive about giving. All of us like to feel we have helped somebody, made a difference or been of some value to them. It is gratifying to us. This is how charity affects the giver. The effect upon the recipient is not so happy. People's dignity may suffer from being the recipients of charity. It is hateful to feel that we are the object of pity, or that we are dependent upon someone cleverer, richer, or more fortunate than ourselves to extricate us from our difficulties. It makes one feel inadequate and pathetic, and puts one under an uncomfortable obligation to another. This is sometimes overlooked by social workers. It is a very serious oversight in the case of a probation officer. The probation officer's main job is to build up his people's self-respect, to help them to stand upon their own feet, and to feel competent to do so, and he should be wary of using a tool which may damage rather than enhance this attitude of mind. For this reason some strong-minded probation officers will have nothing to do with money, and spurn poor-boxes. If help is needed they refer their people to agencies who cater for those needs, and take no active part in the business themselves. There is something to be said for this attitude.

Any trained social worker can think at once of innumerable ways in which the lot of the A. or the J. family could be improved by recourse to the existing voluntary and statutory services—medical treatment ; convalescent treatment ; birth control advice ; a new house ; new furniture ; a new job ; new interests for parents and children alike. Their whole lives could be re-made from top to toe in every department. All that is required is that the families in question should put themselves unreservedly into the hands of a competent social worker, meekly fall in with every suggestion and follow out every instruction. Go there ; attend here ; sign this paper ; do this ; fill up this form ; answer these questions. This kind of help involves such an invasion of people's independence, and of their most intimate personal concerns that in actual fact few will permit it. People would rather live their own lives their own way, in a degree of poverty or discomfort to which they have become accustomed, than in a brand new clean house the social worker's way. There are three common reactions to this kind of well-intentioned but unacceptable management of their affairs by other people—passive resistance, complete surrender, or an assertion of independence.

One sometimes hears an exasperated social worker complaining, " After I'd made all the arrangements for convalescence she never even went to the station ! " This is passive resistance. The plans miscarry ; Mr A. does not attend there ; the necessary form is lost ; the appointment is not kept ; the social worker is frustrated ; and the client gets a bad mark for being unco-operative or irresponsible, or even with a young impatient worker as " Hopeless ! ". But the worker might have saved herself the trouble of making all the arrangements. If she had been more perceptive of the personality she was trying to help she would have seen long since that the client in question neither wanted nor intended to do what was suggested.

Complete surrender on the part of the client is the most lamentable reaction of all. Mrs F., a young woman in her thirties, was expecting her fifth child, her husband being in prison, and she entirely dependent on Public Assistance. A worker visited her near the expected date of her confinement and asked her what plans she had made. Was she going into hospital, or going to have a nurse at home ? " Oh well, dear, see, they arrange all that, don't they ? I don't have nothing to do with it. They do things their own way, see. Wait till the time comes, then they send you where they want you to go. They don't never tell you nothing." Who was going to look after the other children while she was in bed ? Would she arrange for her mother to have them in the country, or for some neighbour to take them, or what ? " Oh well, dear, see, they look after all that, don't they ? It's not for me to say nothing. They fix it up their own way." Had she any little garments ready for the new baby ? " Oh no, dear, see, they give you all them things, don't they ? . . ." Everything this woman said, shocking as it sounds, was literally true. None of these important decisions and preparations were any business of hers. If she had gone to the Relieving Officer and said, " I am expecting a new baby on October 19th. Could you book me a bed in St Andrew's Hospital, please ? I've been there before, and I know the Sister. And could you arrange for my children to be sent to my mother in Norfolk about October 12th ? She could meet them at King's Lynn. And if you will kindly give me some money for flannel and wool I can be getting a few baby clothes together . . . "—what would he have said ? That is not the way these things are done. It is literally true that beggars can't be choosers, so unfortunate people sometimes lose their power of decision and execution. A surrender to the dictates of organized charity is the most disastrous reaction of all.

A third possibility is an assertion of independence by the client. The worker discovers that all the lovely new furniture or clothes, which she took so much trouble to get for the family, have been sold ; or the family have just decamped from their new home and disappeared, leaving no address ; or where she looked for a warm and friendly welcome she meets angry hostility and complaints. Probation officers should watch out for this reaction, and when they meet it learn from it. It indicates that they have overdone their philanthropy, and must go about their business much more slowly and observantly. It indicates, too, that the parties concerned still have spirit and are determined to preserve their independence of initiative and judgment and, looked at in this way it may be, though very dismaying at the time, a not unhealthy reaction.

It is not always that the schemes one envisages for helping people are in themselves bad ones. Much more often the fault lies in moving too quickly, and forcing the pace. People do not want to be hurried and hypnotized along into unfamiliar ways. They want to go their own way about things, and have

H

the satisfaction of achieving their own purposes. Most people's minds work very slowly, particularly if they are in a rut and unaccustomed to thinking at all about future potentialities. It takes time for a new idea to germinate. It takes time for people to learn by experience the best way of going about their purposes. But if our purpose is to help people to profit from experience, to develop strength of character, imagination and initiative, the slower method is much the surer, just as it is in the nursery. The probation officer's role is to stimulate the probationer's conception of possibilities, be behind him in his efforts, back him up with interest and concern and friendship, help him here and there as unobtrusively and as acceptably as possible, *not* to do everything for him. Excellent plans miscarry if the pace is forced.

Cecilia C., aged 16, was an intelligent girl who had several times run away from home, and was finally charged with travelling on the railway without paying her fare. Enquiries showed that she had won a scholarship to a secondary school, but her parents had not seen their way to allowing her to take this up. The psychiatrist in the Remand Home confirmed that she was highly intelligent. He thought she was quite capable of doing well at a University if only she could settle down again. She had been leading a very wild life, lorry-jumping up and down the country, sleeping in ditches, and feeding at coffee stalls. A great deal of time, thought and trouble was taken by her probation officer. The girl was capable of better things, and a better way of life must be made as attractive as possible. Her self-respect must be built up. A job was found for her in a large store ; smart new clothes were given her, in keeping with this work ; a place was secured in a hostel for working girls of this kind of standing (not a hostel for delinquent girls) ; not very far away was a progressive evening institute with a varied programme of educational and recreational classes, which it

was hoped would attract her attention before long. The
officer took Cecilia along to the hostel and personally introduced her. They had a cup of tea together, and then the
officer left. So did Cecilia. She decamped that evening
and never returned. The officer herself was the first to see
where the mistake lay. It was all too quick. This wild
young hoyden could not change overnight into a respectable
little business girl. Spread out slowly over a couple of years,
taken step by step, at Cecilia's own pace, the same programme
might have been very successful.

One must therefore be careful to respect the dignity of
those we are trying to help, watch and learn from their
reactions, and go about the business slowly, making sure that
any line suggested commends itself to the client in question
before it is pursued.

Finally, it is perhaps worth emphasizing again that the
provision of material necessities is very rarely enough. " Man
does not live by bread alone." Our happiness and peace of
mind, our moral standards and our relations with our fellow
creatures are dependent on other factors than board, lodging
and health, important as these are. It is what we care
about, and the extent to which we care—the state of our
emotions—that most powerfully affects our characters and
behaviour. We must therefore pass on to a consideration of
these emotional factors.

VII

Interests

Many people comment these days on the limited range of our interests and the vogue of " spectator sports ". We sit in the cinema and watch other people having adventures, or in our armchairs at home listening to other people making music, and we go to sporting events and watch other people performing. At the same time the trend of industry sets up a great need for something more creative if we are to preserve our natural endowments, for the great majority of people now work in subordinate positions where judgment and initiative are not demanded.[1] Work itself is becoming more and more specialized and departmentalized. A nation of specialists is dangerously near to becoming a nation of narrow-minded people, unaccustomed to thinking of things or situations as a whole or to watching the interplay of different factors.

So much is true of our society in general to-day. When we come to consider the leisure interests of delinquents we find various degrees of satisfaction. Some are interested in criminal professions, and all the strength of character and fine qualities from which society could have benefited, had these been directed into a legitimate channel, become a menace instead of an asset. Some steal the wherewithal to pursue their interests, like the small boys who steal wood to make trucks or scooters. Some seem fully and legitimately satisfied with the lives they lead, and their offences to have nothing to do with their interests or lack of them ; some sex offenders come into this category. But on the other hand there are

[1] See *Democracy and Industry*, by Reaveley and Winnington (Chatto & Windus).

numbers of delinquents who appear to be absolutely purposeless in life ; to lead empty, meaningless, drifting existences,
without one glimpse of an idea as to the manifold possibilities
of enjoyment and value which life holds. It is shocking, for
instance, to meet a party of adolescent girls at some of our
probation homes and hostels who cannot read (for pleasure),
or write, or sew, or cook, or swim, or walk (except to the
nearest bus stop), or bicycle ; whose span of concentration is
twenty minutes at most ; whose skill in handicrafts is no more
than that of a child of five, and therefore no satisfaction to
them ; and who take no pleasure at all in team games or
sports, indoor or out. Their minds are a seething chaos of
fantasy and sex ; they spend their time by preference doing
up their hair or lips, quarrelling with one another, and fretting
to " go out ", i.e. to walk up and down the streets picking up
boy friends. These girls are not mentally deficient, as some
might suppose from this description : far from it ; while
most are of average intelligence, some are well above it.
They are suffering from a most insidious rot, which attacks
empty minds and purposeless lives. It springs from lack of
mental stimulus and scope, from social and emotional inani-
tion. It is this type of youngster which presents the probation
officer with his greatest challenge, for youth should be the age
above all others of idealism and enthusiasm and drive.
Others, while they have not reached this extremity, are yet
dreary, purposeless, frustrated. The tendency of people who
have no interests in life is to become abnormally interested in
themselves. To an egoist molehills become mountains, and
reality fast fades into fantasy.

The probation officer's task here, then, is a double one.
He must both stir up latent faculties, and find them legitimate
scope and satisfying outlet. The approach varies with age
and circumstances. We will consider the question of interests
first in relation to children at school, then with wage earners
at work, and finally with both in leisure.

1. School

Many delinquent children are doing badly at school. Some are educationally retarded, that is to say, below the normal standard for their age. Some are truants. It is ineffective as well as unkind to deal with them simply by exhortation, threats or punishments. A properly qualified educational psychologist should be consulted to discover the causes of their failure before remedial measures are planned. It is quite common for a child who always does badly at his lessons to be dubbed " mentally deficient ", and thereafter to be more or less passed over as hopeless. Intelligence tests administered by a qualified psychologist are necessary to assess scientifically a child's intellectual ability.   He may have first-rate ability, but for some reason or other not be using it. Most neurotic children are behind with their lessons, but they are often above the average in innate intelligence, doing badly because they are emotionally disturbed. Their minds are obsessed with inner fears and fantasies which they cannot control and which distract their attention. They need skilled help to dispel these obsessions, such as can be had at a Child Guidance Clinic.   If, on the other hand, the test shows the child to be really mentally deficient or below average intelligence, a special class, or school, or even residential institution suited to his mental range is indicated.   There may be a physical cause for the child's inattention or failure— such as defective eyesight or hearing, malnutrition, constipa-tion, or lack of sleep—and then his mother must be consulted and steps taken to remedy the condition.   Occasionally some specific hold-up is the cause of the trouble, such as an inability to read or a failure to master some one mathematical rule or process—the child may have been having measles when the rules for long division were explained, and never since have discovered them.   Some Child Guidance Clinics provide skilled coaching for children in this dilemma.   Once he can grasp the lacking technique, the child often picks up quickly at school, and if he thus wins his teacher's approbation and more prestige in class, with gathering confidence and enjoyment he may become quite a reformed character. Some probation officers give their children individual tutorial help of this kind. There are dangers here. Such help should only be undertaken in consultation with the teacher, for if different methods are introduced by untrained hands, the child may become more hopelessly muddled than ever. Officers interested in this field—and it can be a highly constructive one—would do well to read some of the modern literature on the subject. They should, for instance, know something about the educational value of play and different play materials,[1] the project method, the Look and Say method of teaching reading, and Marion Richardson's method of teaching writing. They should read David Wills's chapters on this subject in his book *The Barns Experiment*,[2] and try their hand at picture dictionaries.

There are in the main two types of truanting : a child may run away from fear, or in search of excitement. Both are really forms of escapism. The great majority of truants are in the first category. They absent themselves from school or home because they are unhappy or unsure of themselves there ; are afraid of punishment or ridicule, or bullying or feeling out of it. More rarely a boy plays truant because he is downright bored. The school is generally at fault in these cases in not providing sufficient stimulus, and failing to use his abilities to the full. It is important to diagnose the cause correctly, for the treatment is, of course, quite different for the two different types. With the former it will lie in gentle reassurance and affectionate comradeship, aiming at building up the child's confidence in himself ; with the latter it will

[1] See *The Growing Child and his Emotional Needs*, by Dr Emmanuel Miller and others (Kegan Paul), Chapter I.
[2] *The Barns Experiment*, by W. David Wills (George Allen & Unwin), particularly Chapter XI.

involve making increased demands upon the truant's intelligence and powers, and in providing him with greater scope. Sometimes, in either case, a change of school or teacher is helpful, but this is rarely sufficient in itself to stabilize the child.

It is a good plan to begin probation with a discussion of the child's school report. He may know that the magistrates saw this, but he should now be told its contents in detail. It is helpful to consider it with him, without reproach, but with interest and as much encouragement as can be squeezed out of it. " Writing fair ; well, that's not too bad. It shows you can write, anyway, and you will probably improve. Reading good ; that's grand. That's most important of all. You need never be dull if you can read. . . . What kind of books do you like best ? . . . You could borrow some of mine if you like. . . . Arithmetic, could do better ; I think that's good, too. It would be much worse, wouldn't it, if he'd said ' He *can't* do better ' ? You've got wits, evidently, you see. You are not a stupid. I wonder why you find it so tiresome. (It is the probation officer's business to try to discover this.) Conduct not always satisfactory. Evidently, then, it is sometimes satisfactory. That's good. What sort of thing do you think is most important about conduct ? What is the best kind of person like ? Clever, or kind, or brave, or straight, or what do you think ? " This is an important thing to discuss with children, and if they do not feel able to talk about it in the first interview it should not be pressed, but returned to later. It is important always to emphasize the positive side, to discuss the value of good qualities rather than the harm of bad, and the fact that he *can* do what is required rather than that he does not. The fact that he can do it is a thought to underline again and again, all through probation. Praise is a better spur than blame, and encouragement is better than censure. One wants to build up the child's damaged self-confidence and self-respect.

The amount of reasoning which a child can take depends on his emotional state. A normally well-balanced youngster responds well to a rational approach, but delinquents are often emotionally disturbed, and unable to apply their minds to reason, being too much obsessed with their inner, sub-conscious fears and fantasies.

It is part of an officer's prescribed duty[1] to make enquiry of the head teacher from time to time as to the child's progress in school (though the child himself must not be visited there), and this provides a valuable occasion for serious discussion with the youngster both before and after. "I am going to see your headmaster next week, Raymond ; what do you think he will tell me about you ? Will he have anything nice (or bad) to say ? " The child's own view of his progress, successes or difficulties at school should then be talked over frankly with him. After the visit the officer should report to the child what the headmaster actually did say, and wherein his account of conduct or achievement or any particular incident differed from the child's. Genuine pleasure and delight should be shown over all the encouraging aspects. " I *was* pleased, Raymond ; the first thing I saw when I went into the school was your picture hanging on the wall. Why didn't you tell me it had been chosen ? Have you told them at home ? They'd be proud of you, you know." Interest rather than criticism should be shown over the bad reports. " He told me there'd been a bit of trouble about a cricket ball . . . or a bottle of milk. . . ." This must be discussed. It is important for the child to discriminate in his own mind between serious faults and trivial ones. Jumping on the desks, messing about with the chalk, talking in class, are not in the same category as bullying younger children, cheating, lying, stealing, or temper tantrums. " Conduct not always satisfactory " is not sufficiently illuminating. The former kind of offences against school discipline are very

[1] Rule 52 of the Probation Rules, 1949.

trying to the teachers, and it may be this kind of thing that lies behind such a report. A probation officer was once sent for to "speak" to a youngster in a Probation Home about her misconduct. The offences were thus enumerated to the officer in front of the girl : she had tried to commit suicide by drinking Lysol ; she would leave her stockings lying on the bedroom floor ; and she had laughed in prayers. This kind of confusion of trivial with serious is damaging to a child's moral sense, and the probation officer must seek to help the child to moral assessment. Many children nowadays are utterly neglected at home as far as any character training goes, and have never been taught to consider other people, which is the basis of good manners, nor the reasons for having and observing rules. All children want to be a success, but a great many simply do not know, because it has never been explained to them, that inconsiderate, irresponsible behaviour is wrong because it makes life more difficult or unpleasant for other people, and that is unkind.

The officer's attitude to really serious failings, unkindness or dishonesty, should be absolutely sincere. If it is true it may be quite helpful to take the line, " Well, I must say I was surprised to hear that about you. I didn't think you were that sort. In fact, I don't think you are that sort. I think this was a mistake, and not like you at all . . . " and then to get on to the question of whether the child could show whoever is concerned in some way that he is sorry, and wishes it had not happened. This kind of line may be helpful if it is true, because few things are so shaming or so stimulating as to fail in a friend's estimation and yet to retain the friend's confidence. But often in probation it would not be true to say it was a surprise. The officer has been aware of, or suspected this habit, and to express pained surprise would be insincere. Children quickly detect and always despise insincerity. The reason for these serious faults must be discovered. There always is a reason. One suspects, for instance, that children who are cruel have been cruelly used themselves, either mentally or physically. But it is not good enough to rely on guesswork. Reference to a Child Guidance Clinic can be helpful in cases of serious moral weaknesses. The attitude of the officer should not be critical, but concerned. What a delinquent child needs more than anything else is affection. It is affection, genuine affection, coupled with larger scope and wider friendships, that is ultimately going to help him to more acceptable conduct. If the officer or the Child Guidance Clinic can help him to understand himself better they will have helped him a great deal.

School is vital to children in this country. It is school which introduces them to the larger world and to relationships with their fellow creatures on a wider scale, as well as teaching them the basic techniques of reading, writing, and manipulative skill. It should, of course, teach them something more vital even than these. It should teach them how to form judgments, to weigh evidence and assess values, to think ahead, and to see more than their own point of view. It should give them growing self-confidence, respect for other people's feelings and opinions, enjoyment of their company, and the capacity to co-operate with them. It should open their eyes a bit to the immense possibilities of life, and to its responsibilities. How far the schools of this country do prepare children for adult life in these ways is a different question. The point here is that it is the probation officer's business to help his juvenile probationers to get the most they can out of the schools they go to. This involves intelligent understanding on his part of the child's situation and temperament.

2. Work

Some probationers seem never to have regarded work as an activity which might be enjoyed in itself. The fairly ordinary question, " What kind of work would you really like to do best if you could choose ? " is often met with an incredulous stare, which seems to say, " How can you be so silly ? Who would *like* to do any work ? " Work is just an evil necessity, an unavoidable grind, a means of getting money. The reason for this attitude is not far to seek. In a highly industrialized country like ours the unskilled monotonous jobs far outnumber the interesting ones. There is not enough skilled work to go round. Further, the question is a foolish one to ask, considering that the probationer's knowledge of all the available possibilities is usually so limited and the actual practical choice so often restricted by circumstance. The deciding factor is in most cases the immediate earnings—other considerations weigh very little if there is any choice of wages. This applies to all walks of life. Money is our main criterion of value in this materialistic age. But the choice is also limited to a certain extent by the industrial facilities of the immediate neighbourhood and the natural endowments of the probationer.

Perhaps the probationer can give a surer guide by saying what he does *not* like in the way of work. Why did he leave his last job or jobs ? Some people unaccustomed to thinking in terms of why, cannot answer this question either ; they simply say " Fed up " or " Browned off ". Others, however, can be much more explicit. " It was so noisy ; it got on my nerves." " I hate standing in the same position all day without moving." " The lifting made my back ache.". " I don't like working indoors." " I was so lonely there, there was no one to talk to." All these are sensible enough reasons for seeking a change, and give the officer a clue as to the kind of work to avoid or choose, if possible, in the future. Some jobs are definitely more companionable than others ; light assembly work in electrical engineering, for instance, may be done by groups working together ; so is callender work in laundries and some work in wholesale tailoring firms. A youngster dismissed for " always talking " should be directed to a sociable job such as one of these, where chatting does not interfere with the work. Some jobs are definitely solitary, as in much machine work, the power press or the lathe, and those who are not sociably inclined and cannot stand the gossip and twitter of workmates round them do much better in some of these. There are jobs that involve moving about, such as waiting, and motionless jobs such as that of a cashier. There are open-air jobs and indoor jobs. Some work calls for a considerable degree of dexterity or precision of eye, and a worker not gifted in these directions is bound to do it badly and find it irksome and fatiguing.

Some probationers have already failed in one kind of work, and are much more likely to make a success of their probation and to right themselves if they can start fresh in quite different employment. The commonest example of this is domestic service. One meets little servant girls or wardmaids who have had dozens of places and either walked out or been dismissed from them all. It is abundantly clear that they are in no way cut out for this kind of work, and have absolutely no interest in it. It would therefore seem fatuous to keep on finding them other posts of the same kind. Many social workers think girls are " safer " in residential employment, under the employer's eye, where late night hours are likely to be detected and frowned upon. But the fact that it would be safer if it worked does not make a plan workable. The " safest " way is to find a totally new kind of life, not associated in the girl's mind with failure, which she herself thinks is attractive, and where she expects to be happy. Factory work, with its more regular hours and cheery companionship, is more likely to suit many of these youngsters, and if they live in Approved Lodgings they can still have evening supervision, of a more congenial and sometimes even maternal kind.

There are certain types of offence which require specific consideration when it comes to finding work. Prostitutes, for instance, are usually congenitally and temperamentally unfitted for heavy manual work. Hence, the laundry work so often provided in training homes for this kind of girl is quite unsuitable, as well as unacceptable. Waitressing is similarly unsuitable, by reason of the heavy lifting so frequently involved. Jobs as usherettes, receptionists, flower shop assistants or mannequins, which require good appearance and attractive manners but not a great deal of physical exertion, are much more likely to appeal to them. Some of the more intelligent ones would probably do well if trained as hairdressers or manicurists. One hears it said that to train such girls for these beauty trades is simply to train them to command a higher price in prostitution. This is not a valid argument. Any help given to any person may be abused. That is not a reason for giving no help. Why try to educate delinquent boys ? You are simply training them to become more intelligent thieves. This is a parallel argument. A prostitute's life is not normally a happy one ; it has no future, and it is exhausting and devitalizing. Many girls may approach the business in their search for " a good time ", but if their normal life and work brought them more legitimate satisfactions there would be less incentive to seek such desperate means. Respectability should be made as attractive as possible to these girls. Some have no intention of giving up what they consider to be a profitable and legitimate profession ;[1] they are giving value for money. Obviously these are not suitable cases for probation. Others are weary of the whole business, but despairing. " It's no use you wasting your time over me, miss ; you don't understand ; you think I'm good, but I'm not, I'm bad "—this, actually voiced in so many words by one girl, represents the attitude of many. It is not that they are determined to keep on with the business, rather that they are absolutely devoid of hope or purpose ; completely devitalized and emptied ;

[1] Prostitution by women is not illegal in this country. Soliciting to the annoyance of passers-by is.

and though they are often sick enough of their way of life, they have no longer sufficient energy of mind or belief in themselves to contemplate anything different. Probation has been of considerable help to some of these girls, but is of necessity a long, slow business of building up.

Similarly, drunks should not normally work in jobs where they are left alone for long hours together, as is often the case in domestic service ; nor yet in fatiguing, worrying or exacting posts. Light work in a companionable setting, such as some unskilled factory work, or as a cloakroom attendant, where different people come and go all the time to give diversity to the day's duty, is called for in their case. Mrs R., an elderly woman with innumerable convictions for being drunk, whose sore-tried family had several times cast her off, and several times forgiven her again, found real happiness for many months at the buttonhole bench in a big tailoring factory. She was scandalized at the goings on of the young girls there, diverted by the gossip of the older women, and willingly harnessed herself to the life and traditions of the place. She went for many months without a lapse, and spoke with pride of having held the job down for so long. When at last she lost it after recurrent days of absence due to drinking, she was heartbroken, but the experience of belonging to a big firm, and having been respectable for so long, and the stimulation and interest of the life there, did a great deal to build up her self-respect which had been utterly lacking before, and to set her a new standard of her own to live up to.

With both prostitutes and drunks it is good where possible to plan evening work. This leaves them free to lie late in bed in the mornings, to which they have probably become accustomed, and at the same time keeps them busily engaged at night, when soliciting is at its height and the public houses are all open.

The probation officer must obviously have a wide range of knowledge of all the possibilities which the employment market holds. This involves several things. First, he needs to cultivate close and friendly contact with the officials at the Employment Exchange, so that he can discuss the needs and temperament of any one of his probationers individually with them and enlist their personal interest and effort in finding the most suitable job possible. Employment Exchange officials are generally most sympathetic and helpful when consulted in this way. The probation officer can greatly enlarge his knowledge of the different kinds of work there are, and what each demands and has to offer if he is adept at getting people to talk—and of course all probation officers should have this gift. It is not only a matter of getting his own probationers to talk naturally and discursively about their day's doings. Much relevant information and enlightenment can be gathered on this matter in trains and buses, queues and pubs, by anyone who keeps his eyes and ears open and has the gift of drawing people out. A certain amount can be learnt of the way other people live and what kinds of work there are to be done, from current fiction. The officer should have wide contacts. He should work on terms of reciprocity with his colleagues in town and country. It is very valuable for him to have links with bodies like the Rotary or Soroptimists Clubs, or Toc H, where he can meet people of wide interests and in all walks of life, employers particularly, and have opportunities of talking to them informally and personally.

Many young unskilled workers flit gaily in and out of work with never a thought for references, and their offences seem to make little difference to their prospects of employment. Professional and skilled workers, on the other hand, are expected to produce testimonials, and hence the story of their offences may follow them around, closing one door after another. While the former are generally quite capable of finding themselves " a " job, they are not always successful in finding one best suited to their needs and abilities. The latter really need assistance, and are usually glad to accept it. Where a job calls for a high degree of reliability, as in teaching, banking, or nursing, a person who has shown himself seriously lacking in a sense of responsibility may quite rightly be deemed unsuitable for this profession and, however grievous to him and his family, the probation officer could not rightly seek to re-instate him in such a calling, nor could employers if they knew of the lapse, properly take him on again in the old capacity. These will need all the more help in finding alternative employment that will call out their best and use their gifts. But a finding of guilt in a court of law does not always necessarily indicate this degree of unsuitability. Where an officer has reason to believe that an offender could be trusted to make good in a responsible position, much can be done by a direct approach to likely individual employers. This can only be done on the definite understanding that the officer is free to tell the whole story, and the offender should know this, and give his consent before any approach is made. Where this is done it is often successful, and probationers have made good in positions of trust found for them in this way. It must be remembered, too, that sometimes as a result of successful probation treatment, unreliable people develop a strength of character and a new sense of responsibility in the course of years which fits them for more skilled work than was conceivable at the time of their offence. It is the belief that people can be helped to mend their ways and recover their better qualities which inspires the whole probation system.

In this aspect of probation, as in every other, officers must be prepared for much frustration and disappointment. For instance, officers who have good facilities in their districts may have recourse to vocational guidance specialists for advice in the matter of finding suitable employment. There is first the usual kind of bother in arranging for an appointment and getting the probationer to attend for interview.[1] Appointments

[1] Described on pp. 90 and 91.

I

are often missed through one mischance or misunderstanding or another. Then money has to be found for the fees. The officer may then go all out to follow the recommendation made. He rings up firms and agencies; seeks apprenticeship grants; goes to see employers or other persons who may have influence, in the hope of getting introductions. Someone at last agrees to see the boy in question, but by this time the officer may discover that he has already fixed himself up in some quite unsuitable work with none of the advantages they were looking for, but which offered acceptable wages without delay. If the lad goes to the interview, not surprisingly he does not always impress, so the lengthy business begins all over again. Occasionally the desired opening is actually offered, on reasonable terms, but even then the officer's troubles are by no means always over. He may find the lad hesitant and dubious. "I'll think about it, sir; I'm not sure I couldn't do better elsewhere," he says. He may have lost his nerve (Isn't this flying rather too high? Can he sustain this role? Wouldn't it be better to go as Uncle Jim's errand boy?); or it may be natural repugnance at having his life managed for him.

Every probation officer has to be prepared to take setbacks at every juncture, including final frustration of his efforts, without losing patience or faith in his job. It is a mistake to go faster than the probationer can travel, and if such a boy begins to hesitate it may be an indication that he is right, and could not sustain the role. True, he may have said he always wanted to be an architect above all else, and here at last is the chance of a position in an architect's office, the first rung of the ladder leading to his ambition. But boys, like other people, do not always know what they really want, and sometimes change their minds. This is human nature. It does not help anyone to make up their own mind to have it made up for him. The important thing is not that the boy should accept this proffered opening with all its possibilities, but that he should learn personal responsibility. To dominate another is always dangerous, and it is not synonymous with helping him to manage his own affairs. Officers have to be continually on their guard against their own pride of work, their own ambition, and their own wish to see results. It would be grand to see this ne'er-do-well lad a qualified architect in a few years' time ! And it would make the officer look extremely silly to have to explain, after all the employer's kind interest and trouble, that the lad did not want the job after all. Though it may be easy enough to jump the boy into acquiescence by an outburst of impatient indignation or by vehement persuasion, this would not ensure that he made a success of it when he got there. This is what is meant by saying that officers must be prepared to modify their plans and go slowly. It is a good rule to hand responsibility back to the probationer. " Yes, that's right. Think it over carefully. You don't want to make a mistake. Be sure to let Mr —— know what you decide." Very often if this line is taken, the boy will come back smiling. " Well, I've thought it all over, and decided I couldn't do better, so I'm starting to-morrow." This is not cheek, it is the legitimate assertion of an independent personality, and to have come to the decision himself in this way is better for his self-respect than to be dragooned or hypnotized into doing so by another. But if his nerve fails, and he gives up the golden opportunity which took so much trouble to get, his self-respect must not be allowed to suffer, for if he has made a mistake he will need self-respect to get over it. And he may not have made a mistake. Vocational guidance specialists as well as probation officers can make mistakes sometimes. They are bound to.

But this is not all. Very often plans are frustrated by forces quite beyond the control of the probationer or the officer. It is strange how often misfortune seems to dog the unfortunate. The lad begins the new job, and before he has had a chance to prove himself or learn the ropes, meets with an accident and is relegated to hospital for several weeks. His place has to be filled. Or Mr J.[1] starts off in his ideal new job, and after only a week or two the firm concerned have to close down that branch, or his eyesight proves insufficiently good for the special line in which he had embarked. These kinds of setback are continual in all probation work. They are just part of the game.

This does not mean that the efforts made were not worth while. The constant contact between officer and probationer which all this involves, and the fact that the officer is keenly sharing each disappointment or elation, may be of more value to the probationer than actual success in finding suitable work, for this is real friendship, and it is experience of real friendship which most of these people need more than anything else. Hence it is only when these services are rendered in a spirit of friendship that they are of real value, whether they are rewarded with the result desired or not. If such services were not rendered, and no special efforts made to forward thoughtfully-conceived plans for recovery, there would be less evidence or experience of friendship. The fact that they are bound to be beset by all manner of difficulties, setbacks, and probably by ultimate frustration is no reason for not making them.

Officers should also bear in mind that an early change of job is almost inevitable, however much trouble was taken to secure it and however suitable it may seem to be. Delinquents are apt to labour under a heavy feeling of guilt. They feel that they have failed, and are failures, and hence will always fail. They feel employers, colleagues, friends and family will always suspect them, look down on them or pity them. They are apt to be quite devoid of self-confidence in this respect. Hence it is that so often they feel constrained to tell those with whom they are living or working of their past.

[1] Page 83.

It is as though they were under a compulsion to do so. The building up of a new sense of self-respect to take the place of this besetting sense of failure is of paramount importance to recovery, and this is difficult when the delinquent knows that his employer knows all about his previous offence. Therefore, after a few months of steady work in the newly-found job it is not to be deprecated if the probationer begins looking around to make a change. If this is done in the correct manner, with due notice and explanation, sympathetic employers will realize both its necessity and its desirability from the probationer's point of view, and will not think that their efforts to help him have been in vain. Their role really is to act as a stepping stone. When the probationer has thus " bettered himself " once or twice by his own efforts, he is more likely to begin to lose his sense of failure, and the derogatory feeling of being beholden to others, and so to recover his self-respect. Some people are apt to be disappointed and critical of probationers if they do not settle down at once in the job first found for them, so it is well to bear in mind that changes may be helpful.

If work can eventually be found which the probationer really enjoys, if he begins to look forward to it, to take pleasure in the companionship of the work bench, or in the interest of the machine under his care, or a pride in any skilled process he learns, or in the diverse encounters which his work brings him, then he has been injected with a potent tonic for good. Pleasure in his work will give him a satisfaction in life which makes for greater stability. As his interest grows, so will his sense of personal responsibility. It is difficult to feel responsibility for anything in which one is not in the least interested, but when anyone begins talking about what " we " do at work, as against what " they " do, then it shows that he is beginning to identify himself with the business, and this is the beginning of responsibility.

3. Leisure

Probation officers can help their juvenile probationers to a more satisfying use of their leisure in a number of ways. Many probation officers have libraries of their own children's books housed at the office, for perusal on the spot or to be borrowed and taken home. This is a useful stepping stone towards the ultimate object of introducing the child to the public library. Books can play no mean part, if an indirect one, in a child's recovery. If he reads them the probation officer will discuss them, and this may be his first experience of rational discourse with an adult, of being listened to on his own ground. If he takes the books home, some other member of the family may read them—" I can't change my book this week, Dad hasn't finished it " reveals a very satisfactory state of affairs. Dad and he now have a common interest, which may have been lacking before. A child craves adult companionship on terms of equality, and so many delinquents lack this. Further, if the child brings home readable literature which is enjoyed by other members of the family, then his stock goes up at home, and this is good for him, too.

A few fortunate probation officers are able to have a play room and to make good use of it. Some officers now have an office to themselves with a waiting room attached, and occasionally these are on the ground floor with a yard behind. The whole setting is admirably placed for play. The curative value of play in children's behaviour problems is still much overlooked, and those unacquainted with its role both in mental training and in emotional healing should read some of the literature on the subject before passing judgment.[1] It is through play that a child discovers his gifts and develops them, and acquires rather than learns the art of persistency in

[1] *The Growing Child and his Problems*, by Dr E. Miller and others, has a useful chapter on Play by Gwen E. Chesters.

meeting and overcoming difficulties. The emotionally-disturbed child, battling with thoughts and fancies he is trying to repress, finds relief in the opportunities which play provides for expression. He can bang on the drum, hit nails hard with a hammer, slosh the paint about, cut off the plasticine baby's head, and thus get rid harmlessly of pent-up feeling which only does damage if bottled up. A child who has ample opportunities of experimentation in play is more likely to find his bent and so to spend his adult leisure hours wisely than one who is inexperienced in play. Children brought up by unimaginative parents or in overcrowded homes often have limited scope for play. Both corporate and personal projects are needed in play. It is the latter which are most commonly missing.

A juvenile court probation officer who has in her[1] waiting room books, crayons, plasticine, cut-outs and so forth and a friend, colleague or student to supervise, can arrange for all her schoolchildren to come and see her on a Saturday morning. There is no difficulty about getting them to come if they enjoy it. Further, there is room for friends or brothers and sisters to accompany the probationer, and this is a valuable opportunity for the officer to get to know the probationer's associates and to help them to help him. The officer thus has a chance to see the children off their guard, their own spontaneous natural selves, some murmuring busily to themselves while they pursue their purposes, some becoming expansive in play. This is a valuable entry into a child's mind which a more formal interview denies. With a yard, more enterprising outlets can be provided—wall-painting, sand and water games, gardening on a small scale, and so on. There must be supervision, but with it a free hand to the children to follow their bent—always provided they do not interfere with others, or make a nuisance of themselves. It is easy

[1] Women officers usually supervise the younger boys as well as girls and women.

enough for the officer to watch the play and withdraw children one by one as she wants them for their little private talk, which is one of the valuable parts of probation and must not be overlooked in this group treatment. It would be wrong for probation officers to take matters further than this and to attempt to interpret the child's play to him, as is done in play-therapy at Child Guidance Clinics, without training in the art. Harm can be done by the inexpert and amateur overstepping his province.

Some officers encourage their children to make Christmas and birthday presents for the family, or models or pictures for decorating the office. Many children have never experienced the pleasure that can be had from doing something for somebody else, and this, therefore, is often quite a fruitful field. Further, the child gets recognition and commendation for his efforts, which acts as a spur to further efforts, because recognition and commendation are acceptable.

Most children nowadays pick up one way or another quite a lot of pocket money. Some extract a money commission whenever they run errands for their elders ; some earn several shillings a week on newspaper or milk rounds or for " minding " other people's children. If a child gets enthused therefore at the probation office with model-making, stamp collecting, present-giving, this pocket money can serve a constructive purpose.

Some of the more sociably-minded children can be recommended straight away to join clubs, where there are suitably enterprising ones in the neighbourhood, and then the range of leisure pursuits is often extended to outdoor sports, team games and camping.

All these activities open the mind of the child to further possibilities, and accustom him to creative and purposeful leisure, and to the fact that there are legitimate ways of going about things and enjoying life.

Once a child has left school, play becomes derogatory to his dignity.   All wage earners, even fifteen-year-olds, should visit the officer at a different time from schoolchildren. Treatment of adults and adolescents in this sphere is along much the same lines, except that a slower tempo should be taken with older people, and less expected in the way of results.   The older probationers often take longer than the younger ones to reach the stage where they can listen to anyone else.   The relief of having someone interested enough in them and their affairs to listen is so great that they are inclined to pour out their current troubles and grievances to the exclusion of other topics, and it is not the slightest use trying to get on to other things until they have had at least one innings, more likely two.   This is the direct opposite of children, who are generally quite inarticulate until they know one well, and if there is to be any conversation at all it is up to the probation officer to start it.

Treatment of adults and adolescents in this matter of enlargement of scope begins, as it does with the children, in the office, and quite a lot can be done there to change the current of the probationer's thoughts.   There will sometimes be signs of the children's paraphernalia lying about, and though no wage earner, particularly a young one, wishes to be associated with children or their ploys, he may yet be intrigued with any models, paintings, magazines, to be seen there, and that is a step towards engaging his interest.   Flowers help. One monosyllabic elderly woman suddenly sprang to life upon seeing a bowl of buttercups in the office.   She rhapsodized about these throughout the interview, recalling her childhood days, and becoming positively vivacious.   There should always be plenty of colour in the office or interviewing room. It should be a gay, buoyant kind of place.   Colour for those that can see it has a tonic effect.   Pictures can contribute, especially if they are changed from time to time.   For one thing, they show the officer's own interest and turn of mind, and probationers are legitimately interested in this.   One woman officer always had a photograph of a baby on her desk : it appealed to her married women probationers. Another always had dog pictures ; this at once revealed the animal lovers like herself. Places one has visited give opportunities for talking about travel, other countries, holidays, and stirring people's imaginations that way. Water-colour paintings interest those who " used " to paint well at school. Snapshots of people camping, climbing, boating, will generally turn somebody's thoughts in those directions before long. The conversation is all important, with adolescents particularly. One wants to direct the conversation into new spheres, always and every time trying to stir their minds, inject a new idea, awaken interests and aspirations, widen their mental horizon. One wants to send them away with new thoughts—vocations, holidays, travel, films, politics, ethics, dress, current events, bringing up children, sometimes one's own week-end activities, glimpses of all the manifold opportunities and possibilities which life can give.

Wherever possible one should plan to give them new experiences. This is perhaps easiest done when the probation officer has a car, and can combine giving pleasure to a passenger with normal duties. A drive round the district visiting, with tea somewhere *en route*, is a red letter day for many working women, and gives a wonderful opportunity of getting on to easy natural terms. A longer expedition to the country with younger folk for a picnic, to gather blackberries or bluebells, or perhaps more important than either, to see something beautiful for a change, can help a lot in changing the current of their thoughts for the time being. Some officers are very enterprising in this line ; they will take one youngster skating, another to a horse show, this one to a church play, and that to a political meeting. Actual experience is better than hours of talk. It must not be supposed that one pleasurable or novel experience of this kind is going to reform the ways of a delinquent forthwith, or make him into an ardent enthusiast. Rather it will give him something different to think about and to talk about for a day or two. If he enjoyed it, it may whet his taste for that kind of thing, or for more enterprising use of his leisure. A lad is more likely to begin saving up to buy himself a bicycle or keeping pets in his backyard if he has met, and enjoyed being with, other people who do these things normally and enjoy them.

Music can play a part in the reformation of character, and more than one probation officer has had remarkable results in this line. Professor Burt[1] and others since have drawn attention to the curative value of music in the treatment of the unstable, but it has not yet been generally recognized. Music has powers of healing both to those who can make it and to those who can hear it. It is really ordered and disciplined emotion, for music without rhythm ceases to be music. Officers with musical gifts themselves are perhaps quickest to spot these gifts in others, and moreover usually have a circle of musical friends who are prepared to be interested and to give practical help. One girl, thanks to the unremitting toil of her probation officer over the course of years, won an open scholarship at the Royal College of Music and was able to complete her training there. A boy got expert advice and help through his officer about symphonies which he had been writing. But these are, of course, exceptions. A much larger number of delinquents without going so far have found, and can find, relief and pleasure in much lesser attainment, such as a few piano or singing lessons. These things give a new prestige as well as an outlet for pent-up emotion. Gramophone evenings are a way of combining a little personal hospitality with the beginnings of musical interest. Nearly all towns and sometimes quite tiny villages boast a gramophone club. Percussion bands should not be forgotten. Men and boys, if they can acquire an instrument by their own efforts or by gift, can sometimes join a small

[1] See *The Young Delinquent*, by Cyril Burt, p. 523.

band and get enjoyment as well as a few useful evening engagements playing at local public houses or neighbours' dances. All these possibilities, be it noted, bring the probationer into touch with other people on the basis of a common interest, and the fellowship may be as healing as the music.

Dancing and eurhythmics have a value. Expressive dancing is specially needed by factory workers whose work sometimes involves no change of posture throughout the day. Many young people are already beautiful ballroom dancers, but would no doubt be entranced with the much greater opportunities of movement and self-expression which other forms of dancing give if they knew of them, or tried. Eurhythmics are a real means of self-expression as well as for imaginative powers. More than that, they are dependent upon relaxation of the muscles and breathing apparatus, and highly-strung, taut, nervy folk have benefited very much from this kind of thing. Officers do well to cultivate friendships with eurhythmic enthusiasts with a view to introducing occasional probationers, who can often well afford the fees of these classes if they once get fired with the idea.

Swimming is another form of physical exercise which can tonic up tired muscles as well as give opportunities for happy companionship.

People are much more hesitant about taking up drawing, painting or modelling after they have left school than they are about music, or even about admitting a fancy for these pursuits, which are supposed to be childish, for some reason. But even in the most unpromising places there is often an art class, and such classes have this to be said for them : only enthusiasts go, and they are therefore usually a collection of individualists, even weird judged by the more conventional standards to which the probationer has become accustomed. It may thus rather appeal to him. Here he need no longer strive to appear to be what he knows he is not, exactly the same as his family and neighbours. In exercising independence in dressing, behaving and talking he now has the support of these fellow students, who do not think him at all out of the ordinary. A less independent-minded probationer on the other hand might feel slightly superior to these " odd fish " at the art class, and that would be good for him, too, in a different kind of way.

Politics have proved an admirable outlet for the argumentatively inclined. There is an intellectual kind of youngster, sometimes with some education, sometimes with none, full of headstrong theories based on air, or the aggressive declaiming kind of man. Direct their attention gently into discussion groups, debates and public meetings, and an outlet may be found for their assertiveness, recognition and appreciation for their gifts, and often contact with more educated minds.

The list of possible activities can be indefinitely prolonged. Knowing the great variety of outlets that will be needed, probation officers should go about their business with eyes and ears alert to note any possibilities for future use. For instance, the Town Hall or Public Library may provide lists of recognized recreational or educational associations. Humbler groups advertise themselves in shop or private windows up and down the back streets. Bird-seed shops may have a notice about a meeting of pigeon fanciers or bee-keepers or a rabbit show. Private houses or small meeting halls display little notices about meetings of enthusiasts of one kind or another. The percussion bands advertise their services and their existence in wireless shops or the local press. It should be remembered that a probationer with his damaged self-confidence is more likely to join small, odd, informal groups than well-established, large, conventional ones.

There is no one " delinquent type ", and therefore there can be no one prescription for probation treatment. Some delinquents are well-to-do, some poor ; some educated, some

illiterate ; some intellectual, some dull-witted ; some successful in their circle, some unsuccessful ; some dare-devil in
spirit, some broken. People from all classes and widely
varied backgrounds break the law and disregard the feelings
and welfare of others. Each probationer is an individual,
with individual gifts and needs, and must be treated as an
individual before he can be helped to right himself and take
a more responsible attitude to his fellow creatures.

These activities of school and work and leisure make a
useful initial point of contact between the probation officer
and the probationer. Much importance, however, must not
be attached to them by themselves. They are not fundamental to happiness and stability as affection and satisfying
social relationships are. On the contrary, to a very large
extent they are dependent on the latter ; it is not until the
most fundamental needs have been met that people have
energy and leisure of mind to give to lesser things. Hence
it is quite useless to say to an inhibited youngster, " You
ought to take up some interest ", or expect that if they are
introduced to one, their troubles will be solved. They cannot
get interested in anything until they have emotional stability
or satisfaction. A young probationer may embark on a bit
of embroidery, if she is very compliant, to please her officer
or because she has not the spirit to resist, but this does not
mean that she is really interested in it, and unless she is
interested in it it will help her very little. When a person is
really interested in something, they not only " do " it, they
think about it, talk about it, plan around it. It becomes a
creative purpose, not a mere device for passing time away.
And so, though interests may come early in chronological
order of attention, they are secondary to that far more
fundamental human necessity, happy human relationships,
which we must now go on to consider.

VIII

Friends

Apart from small boys and gangsters, most delinquents in my experience are unsociable. Some are so by force of circumstance only. Older men and women and some young boys may be full of natural social instincts and aptitude, but never have heard of social amenities, or become so immersed with their families that they have never thought of seeking friends outside. But many others, most adolescent delinquents, and nearly all delinquent girls, are inherently unsociable. They are wrapped up in themselves, living lonely inhibited lives, not at all at ease in society. They sometimes say so in so many words, " I don't trouble about friends, miss ", or " I keep meself to meself ". " Sociable I am and always 'as been," one woman is reported to have declared, " but mix with others I don't and never shan't."

The probationer's need of friends is recognized in the Probation Rules. "The probation officer shall encourage every person who is under his supervision . . . to use the appropriate statutory and voluntary agencies which might contribute to his welfare, and to take advantage of the social, recreational and educational facilities which are suited to his age, ability and temperament"—so runs Rule 54 (1).

Our best Youth Clubs are probably one of the biggest social assets of this country at the present time. The Women's Institutes and similar associations are in the same category. Here is to be found social intercourse of the freest, happiest kind ; relaxation and refreshment of mind, corporate purposes and personal responsibility. Not unnaturally these associations would seem to the general public to be the solution of the probation officer's difficulties, and to provide the very form of re-education which young delinquents so badly need. But the framers of the rule already quoted were evidently realists, and recognized the difficulties and subtleties involved, as is shown by their use of the word "encourage". People do not and cannot make friends to order, in the genuine sense of friendship, which is the only operative sense in this context. The vital thing to remember about unsociable people is that they do not like society. It is useless, therefore, urging them to join clubs, however excellent these are in themselves. If they go because they dare not cross the probation officer, or as a condition of their probation order, they will almost certainly hate it, and therefore fail to profit from it. These people are unsociable because they have no self-confidence ; they feel inadequate and uneasy with other people. To push people like this into a hearty, happy group of friends, all taking each other for granted, ragging each other, and knowing about each other, is to underline more than ever that they do not fit in. They see more clearly than before that they are not like that ; they are misfits ; and for very fear of being drawn deeper in and so disclosing their inadequacy, they decline any kindly advances which well-meaning members or leaders may make. So even if they do go, to oblige the probation officer, the effort will fail of its purpose. Usually they don't go.

Yet these people need friends. They will never be really normal until they can take their place reasonably easily with their fellow creatures, and they will miss one of the greatest enrichments of life if they never experience friendship. The probation officer must therefore work to this end, but it is a long, slow business, and cannot be hurried. The unsociable do not turn sociable overnight, simply because it would be good for them to do so. It is disastrous to begin probation by putting pressure on such an offender to join an association against his inclination.

The basis of happy human relationships is self-confidence. All delinquents are lacking in this quality, some more, some less. Their pride has had a nasty knock ; they have made a mess of things, brought grief and shame to their families and queered their own pitch. This applies even to the devil-may-care lads who are deliberately embarking on a life of crime. They got caught, and were not quite so clever as they meant to be, or as their co-delinquents who did not get caught. Some seek to hide this inner loss of confidence by a façade of over-confidence. Officers must not be deceived by this. Ex-prisoners and Borstal people are pitiably unsure of themselves. They deliberately shun company, and are obsessed with the fear that their shady past will be discovered. " I won't go out, thank you, miss," said a newly-discharged Borstal girl to her employer on her first half-day ; " I'll be safer indoors." Before attempts are made to find these people friends, or to introduce them to a social life, essential as these are to any recovery, their self-confidence must be built up. The close, regular, personal relationship of probation officer and probationer lends itself admirably to this end.

It must not be forgotten that in this highly industrialized age and country, many people have never been treated as individuals, and therefore hardly realize themselves as such. People who have grown up in a large family, particularly in circumstances of overcrowding or economic stress, may never have had individual attention from their parents. Many parents in comfortable circumstances, and with small families, fail to give their children personal attention. At school the child may well be overlooked, whether the class numbers 60 or 20, if he is not striking in any way. At work he may be just an unskilled " hand ", one among hundreds. If he dropped out, people would hardly notice ; no one would mind much. In large tenement buildings, blocks of flats, or streets of houses, it is quite possible for a person to be taken ill, and even to die, without this being noticed by the neighbours. In a village, on the contrary, everyone is a recognized personality, and no one can do anything without it being noticed. Probation, in being absolutely individual treatment, is therefore an admirable instrument for helping these people. Week after week, month after month, the probationer will have all to himself, even if for only a few minutes at a time, the undivided attention of the probation officer, an absolutely new experience. From the very first interview, as we saw, the officer's aim is to build up the delinquent's self-respect. The manner of his reception, the framing of the questions, the direction of the conversation, the atmosphere of the room, everything, is planned with this purpose in view. The officer concerns himself with the probationer's health, material welfare, appearance, prospects and fortunes, all intimate matters, which maybe no one has ever troubled about before. With girls their hair styles, colour schemes and clothes can be discussed. " You ought to try your hair brushed up, so, off your face ; it would suit your style of face." " You need a touch of red somewhere." " What a lovely new coat ! Where did you get it ? " It is gratifying to find that one's appearance is an object of interest to someone else ; it enhances a woman's feeling of self-importance, and to these neglected people it can be stimulating. The officer is concerned about his probationer's doings ; remembers what had happened last time they met, and is anxious to take up the story and hear about recent developments. The officer listens—and lonely people have rarely had an audience before. If anyone listens to you it surely means they are interested in you. All these things count. The range of conversation widens ; news, films, books, public people, broadcasts, are discussed on terms of equality. The officer, it seems, regards the probationer as a normal, sensible kind of person, with opinions worth listening to. The officer consults him as to what he thinks should be done. However crazy the probationer's plans may be, they should be discussed respectfully, as a rational proposition, until the pros and cons emerge in a clearer light, and the probationer sees for himself that his suggestion is hardly likely to work. The probationer should never be made to feel silly or feeble. He should leave each interview feeling set up, more assured. Thus he will begin to enjoy meeting the officer—in short, he will begin to enjoy conversation and company. He begins to feel that he can hold his own as well as anyone else in social intercourse. This is the first step. It takes months.

The next step is to introduce new people. The probationer will not always have the officer, and unless his circle widens during the course of probation all this building up will have been to no purpose. Some officers have been successful here in getting a small circle of their own friends interested, and in introducing them at a judicious juncture. " You ought to meet my friend Mr So-and-So ; he's got a marvellous stamp collection (aviary or tool shop, whatever it may be). I'll take you round there one night." Or perhaps this new friend just drops in at the office at a pre-arranged hour and, finding the probationer there, invites him round to his place himself. Some of these friends are immensely valuable to the probationer, opening a door on to new experiences, standards, and widening horizons, of which he never dreamt before. This may be a further stage, but it is not, of course, often a satisfactory final one. It is but rarely that there is a very great or lasting community of interests between the officer's friends and the probationer.

Sometimes the officer can suggest following up some activity which seems to attract the probationer—the painting class, percussion band, rabbit club, allotment guild, which were discussed in the last chapter. The development of social confidence often comes most naturally through a development of some interest, as we have seen. The interest, whether it be music, politics, pets, or anything else, begins to take a person's mind off himself a bit, and this is a shift of focus which is necessary before anyone can feel at ease in society. Knowledge or experience of the activity in question gives him a certain amount of self-confidence to begin with ; and it is easier to feel a person in a small group than in a big one.

It can be valuable at this stage to ask the probationer if he would care to come and help at some project in which the officer is himself interested—to join the carol party which is singing for the Red Cross ; to take part in a concert to be given at the local hospital ; to help, or make something for, the sale at the church ; to steward at a meeting ; or possibly to visit some sick person.

One officer used to arrange Bank Holiday parties at her house for her lonelier probationers. She invited Miranda, aged 17, to one of these, but it did not appear to be at all a success. Miranda sulked the whole afternoon. The next time a party was being arranged the officer said, " I don't know whether to invite you or not, Miranda ; you didn't seem to enjoy the last one much." " I certainly did not," said Miranda, who was always outspoken ; " it was a horrible party." " What was the matter with it ? " said the officer. " I thought you were inviting me," said Miranda, " but there were all those other mouldy people there who had nothing to do with me, and whom I don't care to know." This interested the officer. " I had not thought of it that way," she said ; " I thought they were mostly rather unhappy people, and that if you came and breezed around with the cakes and chatted to them all it would brighten them up." " Oh, in *that* case I'll certainly come again," said Miranda, and she did. She played her part with distinction and grace, greatly adding to the pleasure of the others, and so not unnaturally enjoyed it herself. Thenceforward every guest who was invited to subsequent parties was asked to come in order to help in some way, one to help with the tea, one to arrange the flowers, one to sing perhaps, and so on. This

kind of thing is helpful in a double way. First it enhances
personal dignity to have one's help sought ; to feel needed
and of use is stimulating and a pleasant change from being
the recipient. But secondly, if the project—the carol party,
the sale or the meeting—is a success, the little band of helpers
will feel pleased with themselves, and tempted to embark on
another venture of the same kind, and the unsociable probationer will find himself being caught up in a group of normal,
ordinary people who have no thought of probation in their
minds for the most part. Thus wider social intercourse
begins to be achieved, and in due course friendships may
begin to be formed.

None of these things would work early in probation. They
are only likely to be successful if the way has been prepared
beforehand by systematically building up the probationer's
own inner sense of self-respect and assurance.

Many probationers would gladly render personal service
to the officer. It is unwise to allow this. The officer who
gets his car cleaned, or the garden dug, or the table supplied,
all for nothing, by grateful probationers, is going clean against
the British sense of decorum, and embarrassing misconceptions
are bound to arise. It gets known that Mr So-and-So's
probationers have to work for him if they want to get on.
This situation has actually arisen in one or two cases, all quite
unconsciously from the officer's point of view. But apart
from the unwisdom on that score, personal service to the
officer does not serve the second and most important function,
of widening the probationer's circle. The officer's aim is not
only to relieve the probationer's mind of a sense of obligation,
he wants to get him able to enjoy company, and to mix easily
and happily even if with only a few friends.

Clothes sometimes have an indirect bearing on the making
of wider social contacts, particularly perhaps in the case of
women. A woman probationer is unlikely to accept an
invitation to meet others if she is ashamed of her clothes or

appearance. Invitations have actually been refused on this account. It is equally damaging to the probationer's pride to have clothes given or discussed all in the same breath as an invitation. It is as good as saying, " You are not fit to be seen, you poor thing, in your own clothes ; you can't go like that ", and this, besides being hurtful to anyone's self-esteem, is bound to make the person so addressed self-conscious, a bad attitude of mind with which to set out to make new friends. If the probationer is concerned about her clothes the officer should be aware of this, and do something to help her about them early in the probation, in the stage of building up her self-respect. It may not be necessary or wise to give clothes. If the probationer is clothes-conscious it will probably be sufficient to put her in the way of earning more money, or to comment approvingly when she does look nice, so getting embarked on a discussion of clothes and tastes. If the probationer is not clothes-conscious, and does not appear to notice or mind looking down at heel, well and good. It would seem a pity to draw her attention to the fact, and so cause her embarrassment. A lot of very successful people have no idea how to dress, and are quite oblivious of the fact that other people think they look frights.

The question of whether and in what circumstances officers should lend money arises in this connection. Some officers have none to lend. Some believe that it is in all circum-stances wrong either to borrow or to lend. Some wonder whether it may not land the probationer in a worse pickle. For instance, by borrowing from his officer he may be spared the pains of learning the difficult art of living within his income. Or it has sometimes happened that the probationer finding himself unable to pay back the money as promised, is ashamed to meet the probation officer, and so fails to come and see him regularly, thus breaking one of the terms of his probation order. He may even be tempted to steal, in order to repay his officer. Money in any case has power to ruin friendships. " Never borrow from a friend " has not become a wise saw without reason. These possibilities must be borne in mind. On the other hand, other officers say that to lend money in some circumstances is to enhance the probationer's confidence in the officer, and hence it may be a valuable factor. The probationer in asking for money may be seeking to test his officer's feeling for him, and to discover that he does believe in him, to the tune of some pounds perhaps, is sometimes a turning point. Further, the self-respect which comes from having paid back all that was borrowed may be helpful. Some officers who make a practice of lending money freely say they have lost very little by it financially and that they believe it is of real value. Each officer must do what he feels right in each set of circumstances. Some harm is undoubtedly done sometimes by too trusting or generous a response, while much good has equally undoubtedly resulted from a far-sighted trust and generosity. An example of a constructive loan of money is given in Chapter 12.

Although for the reasons outlined above our Youth Clubs and Community Centres are unlikely to help the majority of probationers much—at any rate in the early days of their recovery—they may be valuable to a few. They are valuable to those of the younger boys and older married folk, who have quite normal social instincts and who are not over-sensitive. If the activities offered by the association attract the youngsters, they may take to it very well and be much helped and stabilized by the group. The individual's code of conduct, ambitions and interests are raised unconsciously to those of the group. He finds stimulus in the group's acceptance of him and in the fact of " belonging " to it. An adult may have been prevented by domestic cares from becoming exclusively wrapped up in himself. While there may be some initial diffidence to overcome, such folk often respond very well to the friendly intercourse they find in these men's and women's fellowships. (It is an interesting paradox that

the cure for exclusive self-interest seems to lie partly in
becoming an object of interest and concern to someone else.)

The gang presents a quite different problem of friendship.
Both amateur and professional gangsters, if one may so
differentiate them, belong to a circle of friends which they
enjoy, and within which they are prepared to share, conform,
obey and to modify their own wishes or feelings where these
conflict with those of the group. There is honour among
thieves, and some things which they would not stoop to.
Here the social instincts of loyalty, responsibility and comradeship are well developed within the group, but used to society's
detriment rather than advantage, and with the effect of
lowering rather than raising the moral standards of the
individual. Inspired by the daring demanded, afraid of
losing the gang's good opinion, the individual does things
he would never have dreamt of doing or had the nerve to do
on his own. Hence the would-be reformer often seeks to
break up a gang, and to remove the individual from its
influence. The leaders may be sent to Borstal or Approved
Schools ; lesser lights to probation hostels ; underlings to
relatives in the country or to residential jobs, or they may
be forbidden to associate with each other by the terms of a
probation order. This in itself is not enough, of course. The
leader still retains his gifts of leadership, which society needs
and, if these are not made use of, and re-directed into socially
acceptable channels, there is danger he may continue to lead
rebels against law and order. The underlings have shown
their capacity to follow. Society also needs people who can
carry out instructions and work loyally to a pre-arranged plan
—who can co-operate in other words—but an undiscriminat-
ing follower is as dangerous socially as an unscrupulous
leader. It is not enough to separate the followers. They
must be helped to develop powers of judgment and the
strength of character to use these. Some people aim to keep
the gang going as a gang, and to treat it as a gang. There is

an interesting account of American experiments along these lines in a book called *The Gang*, by F. M. Thrasher, but some of our own officers here in England have been successful with this method on a smaller scale. It is more likely to be successful with small boys than with older lads or men, but each must in any case have individual help in building up greater powers of independent judgment.

Since the probation officer is often introduced to the offender by the magistrates as a " friend ", and since by the wording of the Act it is one of his principal duties to " befriend " him, this would seem to be a fitting place to discuss the relationship between officer and probationer.

However introduced to the offender and whatever the appearances, the probation officer is at first likely to be the object of suspicion, if not of hatred. This is difficult for many inexperienced and well-meaning workers to take in. Where an opportunity has been given for full preliminary enquiries to be made, on the pattern suggested earlier in this book, both the offender and his family may have reason to regard the officer from the start as a reasonable, helpful kind of person and even to be glad of his promise of continued help and interest. This is another reason for preluding all probation orders with full preliminary enquiries. But it must be remembered that most offenders realize that their fate hangs to a large degree upon the impression they make on the officer, and hence most will receive him courteously if not cordially, but he should not be misled by this semblance of grateful and co-operative goodwill, or take it to indicate that the relationship is already that of a trusted friend. The probation officer, however friendly he means to be, is a stranger ; associated with the police and the magistrates ; known to be consorting with these authorities daily ; having his headquarters at the magistrates' court ; epitomizing in his person all the hateful experiences of arrest, suspense, public shame and family misery. Further, the whole idea of being

" supervised " or of needing help is repugnant to any adult or would-be adult person. The position is derogatory to anyone's dignity. So the probation officer starts the relationship heavily handicapped, with much to live down, and it is a great mistake to assume that he is accepted from the start as the friend he wishes to be. Since this is so, the officer must beware of sentimentality in his view of his role and guard against describing himself as a friend, rather letting his actions and his attitude speak for themselves over the course of time. Friendship is an experience, and time, not words, is needed to prove it.

Yet the more maladjusted and deeply delinquent people need a true friend more than anything else if they are to recover themselves and develop their better natures. A probationer of this type needs something much more than mere happy and sociable companionship, essential as we have seen this to be for true balance of mind. He needs a friend who, seeing him as he really is and recognizing his many failings, yet both believes in him and likes him ; who has time for him, and listens to him ; to whom he knows he can speak freely without fear of snubbing or domination ; to whom it is, in fact, a relief to speak his mind ; to whom he knows he can turn in any extremity whether this is due to his own folly or misdoing or not. He needs someone of whose affection and good opinion he is sufficiently assured to be able to consider criticism or advice. Sometimes such a person can be found within the offender's own family circle. Sometimes one of the staff at a hostel may help him in this way, sometimes a foster-mother or landlady. These possibilities are discussed at greater length in the next chapters. But it sometimes happens that the officer himself fills this role. It is a tall order, and deeply taxing, as most readers will imagine. It is a relationship which grows not so much out of a desire to help other people, or to do one's duty conscientiously, as out of a genuine, spontaneous interest in this particular individual, and a tolerant affection for most people.

It has been found that the badly maladjusted delinquent has usually been starved of normal affection, or thwarted in it, or already badly let down by someone. He is therefore liable to be sceptical and cynical about friendship, and resistant to it. This is recognized as partly a defence measure. He wishes, unconsciously, instinctively, to protect himself against being hurt again. And so probation officers must be prepared for the paradox that the more a probationer needs trust and affection and craves it, the more will he resist and fight it when he first meets it.[1] This makes the business a gruelling test for anyone who sets out to help him. The probationer, hardly trusting his senses or able to believe that here is a person disposed to like him and be interested in him, feels constrained to test the friend and try by all means in his power to prove to his embittered and twisted self that the relationship is not a true one and cannot last. He therefore becomes outrageously and deliberately provocative ; misses his appointments ; throws up his jobs ; is abusive and rude ; lies and deceives ; lands himself upon the wretched officer's doorstep in piteous plights ; squanders borrowed money ; makes impossible demands upon the officer's goodwill, and takes every conceivable kind of liberty. If the officer responds with the very natural reaction, " Now I've done with you " or is the sort who " stands no nonsense ", he has proved the probationer's point. " It was only words. He doesn't really care about me. He only likes me if I kowtow to him. He's thrown me over. I knew he would. Nobody really cares about me. Nobody ever has. I'm no good. I never shall be." And so the last state of that poor irrational offender is worse than the first. The probation officer's efforts may even have done more harm than good.

Officers who find themselves called upon to help their probationers on these deeper and more fundamental levels

[1] See John Bowlby, for instance, *Forty-Four Juvenile Thieves, their Characters and Home Life*, p. 52.

must be prepared for this provocative phase, and go through with it. It means not that the probationer is beyond redemption, rather that redemption is not to be had cheap. It means that the offender has already been stirred, and badly, badly needs the friendship he is spurning. Much of the provocation can be taken with gentle good humour and mild remonstrance. Some can be ignored altogether. Some demands a straight talk in no uncertain terms, but where this is deemed necessary it should always, and at once, be followed by some friendly gesture. No interview with a person in this precarious state of mind should end on a note of disparagement or anger. The good dressing down should always be followed by a resumption of normal rational relations. The offender should feel as he leaves that all is as it ever was between them. If the officer's patience and persistence can hold out over the course of months, the provocation becomes less with the offender's growing sense of security, coupled too with his widening interests in other fields. As his work and leisure interests demand more of his attention and provide greater satisfaction, the interest of testing the strength of his officer's feelings for him becomes less exclusive.

There may follow a second and equally embarrassing phase however, particularly in the case of girls. The probationer may become infatuated with the officer, and seek no other satisfaction than to bask in her favour.[1] This is an immature state. With maladjusted persons such as we are discussing here it may be an inevitable stage in the process of recovery,

[1] One of the difficulties of running a hostel for delinquent girls is that if they develop a strong attachment for one of the staff they tend to desire to be the one and only one, and thus to become madly jealous of one another. If the Matron asks Ella to run upstairs and fetch her handbag, Jessie will retire to the bedroom in a passion of frustrated tears and be unbearable for the rest of the day. The incident to her disordered mind showed that the Matron did not trust or love her, or that she wished to insult or hurt her. Probation is easier in that the " friend " deals with the youngsters individually, and does not have to cope with their reactions to each other.

but it is a dangerous one in two ways. It is dangerous if allowed to continue for too long, because it means that the probationer is entirely dependent for her stability of mind on the officer's favour and approval. If the officer's patience gives out, and she brings the relationship to an abrupt end, or if she changes her work or leaves the district, the sweet pea is deprived of its stick, as it were, and must therefore be expected to flop, since no other social ties have been formed. It is dangerous from the officer's point of view because such affection and devotion are, without doubt, often deeply satisfying to a woman, especially to an unmarried woman with a strong maternal instinct. It is possible for an officer so to appreciate the girl's admiration and dependence that she unconsciously encourages it, to the detriment of the girl's character.

Another danger in this kind of relationship is that it is easy for the enthusiastic officer, particularly one with a strong maternal instinct which has no other satisfactory outlet, to get things out of proportion, with consequent damage both to herself and to her work. Caring intensely as to what happens to this young girl, grieving when things go badly, worrying lest she should make another mess of things, wondering what else could be done, she becomes obsessed with her work, loses sleep and forgets about meals, lets her own friends or outside social contacts go, never relaxes, idles, or takes her mind off her problems for a minute, and so ends up a nervous wreck, incapable of seeing things in perspective, and much less likely to be able to help her probationers as a result. A probation officer needs a sense of proportion as well as strong human affections. For this reason all officers should cultivate outside friendships with people who are not in the least interested in problems of personality or social equity. They should make it their business to take regular and adequate time off, and to use this for refreshment of mind and spirit. All that is reckoned here as necessary to the development of sound and healthy character—family affections, friends, interests, faith, are equally necessary to its preservation. They are necessary as much to probation officers as to their probationers.

A further point to consider in these cases where the officer befriends his probationer in this very real sense is the time factor. A genuine feeling for a probationer does not evaporate automatically at the end of one year or two, the normal duration of a probation order. Neither does a social misfit, of the kind here under discussion, inhibited, solitary, egotistical, develop normal stability and harmony of mind in so short a space of time. Officers must therefore be prepared to be behind such folk, and at their service, for much longer. This is not to contradict what has already been said about the danger of allowing girls to become too dependent. It takes a long time to get girls who have developed a dependent attachment to widen out and grow up to emotional maturity, and the process cannot be hurried.

Clarissa is an example of this kind of relationship in probation. She was 19 when she was placed on probation for stealing £2. She was the illegitimate child of her mother, who had deserted her altogether at the age of 9. She had never seen her father. She was an embittered, quarrelsome, disagreeable and utterly unreliable girl. She had already had one illegitimate child herself before she committed this offence, and this child had been adopted at birth. She suffered more or less chronic ill-health of a mild but disabling bronchial character, which perpetually seemed to militate against steady employment. She was continually out of work, and was moreover never keen on working. Work was in any case difficult to get at this time, and the unskilled work which was all that Clarissa could do was very badly paid. Thus it came about that the probation officer continually helped Clarissa financially. This did not prevent Clarissa from deceiving her on more than one occasion.

Throughout the two-year probation order the officer's home was open to Clarissa, and she dropped in and out of it at will, quite frequently spending her evenings there. She was often vilely rude, and nearly always ungracious. When she had been particularly outrageous she wrote a quite sweet little letter of apology the next day. She was most disarmingly conscious of her shortcomings. So the probation proceeded, with little sign of improvement or of growing stability. Towards the end of the two years Clarissa arrived late one night in great distress. She was given a shake-down bed, and next day confessed in a storm of tears that she was again pregnant. She refused to give any information at all about the child's father, but when it was born she loved it passionately, so much so that the officer thought it might be Clarissa's salvation. Although by this time the term of probation had expired, the officer found mother and child a very suitable lodging, and endeavoured to help them financially to keep them together. This proved impossible, and at last in great grief both decided that it was in the child's best interests to be adopted, and this was arranged. By this time Clarissa was approaching her twenty-first birthday. She still had no trade, and now less than ever any interest in life. The officer gave her driving lessons which enabled her to obtain more interesting work. This was a great success. But there followed the old ups and downs, the uncertain health and temper, with their concomitant loss of jobs. The officer continued to be behind her in everything, visited her when she was sick, housed her and helped her to find other employment when she was out of work, championed her and fought many battles for her. Finally, when Clarissa deserted from His Majesty's Forces the officer went with her to the police station when she gave herself up. Gradually things seemed to improve. Clarissa lived down her desertion and was promoted. She finished her term of service happily and satisfactorily. At the time of writing it is ten years since

Clarissa was charged and bound over on probation. She is now much steadier and more settled. She has friends of her own making, has developed standards of her own and tries to live up to them. She keeps in touch with her officer,[1] but is no longer dependent on her. Clarissa is still heavily handicapped by her temperament, health and heritage, but she has found herself and is no longer a social liability.

It is in the nature of things not often that any one officer can help many of his probationers in this kind of relationship of long-term affection. They do not all need it ; they do not all want it ; and it would be impossible to act as parent substitute to many youngsters in this way. Yet this inner assurance of parental love, or its near equivalent, is undoubtedly what a great many of the worst and most difficult offenders need.

If the officer can help the probationer to a wider range of interests, to greater self-assurance, and to the experience of friendship in some of the ways we have already discussed, the latter will be better able to adapt himself to such relatives as he has, or such friends as he meets. The goal of stability of character must be approached from many different angles simultaneously, in a concerted drive, as it were. All the aspects we have mentioned are helpful, but the fundamental necessity is emotional satisfaction, the experience of both knowing oneself loved for what one is, and of deeply caring for another or others. This leads us to consider family relationships and their next best substitutes.

[1] Not the author.

IX

Family Affection

Many offenders appear to be fully satisfied on the score of affection.   One thinks of the married women shop lifters or gas meter thieves for instance, and fathers in the same category, who seem to be wrapped up in their families and whose thefts are often the result of deliberate intention to ease the family circumstances ; or others, juveniles particularly, who having stolen are overcome with horror and remorse when they realize the devastating effect of their bad behaviour on the family.   But there are many others who one feels have never experienced the emotion of love towards anybody. Some of the children brought up in institutions, for instance, or by a constantly changing succession of not very interested adults, have had little chance of normal emotional development.   Illegitimate children often have good reason to know or sense that they are unwanted and belong nowhere.   Many dutiful parents have no conception that for the development of stable character children need affection, happy adult companionship and attention as well as food and clothing. There are misfits and misunderstoods in many loving and understanding families.   Over and over again we read in modern psychiatric science that disorders of behaviour are more often than not brought about by unhappy human relationships.[1]

[1] (1) See *The Psychological Effects of the War*, by R. D. Gillespie (Chapman & Hall), p. 229 : ". . . Psychoneurotic conditions . . . are primarily the outcome of faulty interpersonal and social relationships. . . ."

(2) In *New Light on Delinquency*, Drs Healy and Bronner estimate that in 91 per cent. of the delinquents examined by them delinquency was due more than anything else to unhappy human relationships.

(3) In *Psychology in General Practice* we read that the pathology of psychogenic illness is the pathology of relationships with other people (p. 30), and that psychoneuroses in particular are essentially disorders of the personal relationships of the patient (para 4, p. 45).

Elementary ethics, with which most of us are more familiar, teaches us the same, but from the positive rather than the negative angle. Of all factors that have power to make or mar human character, love is the greatest. It is love of family, of country, of a cause or a purpose that prompts men to their greatest generosity, courage, endurance. It is love of a person that stimulates them to greater endeavour and better performance. It is this capacity for long-term self-forgetful affection that differentiates us from the animals.

Family life is nature's provision for the natural development of the emotions. It is in the family that the young child normally first experiences love, first as the recipient of their admiration and delight in him, and then in the delight of his own first overtures and expressions of love and devotion to them. He begins joyously planning little presents and surprises for those who love him. It is in the family that he first learns that love is a two-way emotion, involving give as well as take, and often pain as well as joy. He learns to modify his own wishes in deference to those of others ; he is disturbed and unhappy when he sees those he loves upset, or ill, or in trouble. New and exciting friends may come and go, flitting across the scene and drawing his allegiance after them, and this is valuable. It is right and proper that his circle of friends, and of specially loved ones too, should expand, but this will only happen normally if he has first experienced the meaning of love in his intimate circle.

It is probably true that the most precious things in life are also the most costly, and it is just because family ties are so dear and so close that they provide the richest ground for dissension and exasperation. Family friction is universal, and can be devastating. To quarrel with an outsider, or suffer unpleasantness from an acquaintance, is a passing vexation which does not worry us for long. The closer the emotional tie, the more deeply do such situations pain. When a member of one's own family is unreasonable or unkind, or

we think they are, it is intolerable. Further, just as family
life may be the cradle of the finest emotions, so we now know
that it can also be of one of the most insidious and dangerous—
jealousy. This is not so widely or readily admitted, but it
seems incontrovertible that jealousy is a potent factor, though
maybe a hidden one. We recognize it in the little ex-baby
when a new brother or sister arrives, but a new baby can no
less disturb the emotional balance of the parents. Jealousy
appears to be a trait of which everyone is intuitively ashamed,
children and grown-ups alike, and in the effort to disguise or
suppress it, or be blind to it, a new tension creeps in, commonly
known as a guilt complex. One is too deeply ashamed of
inner feelings of anger or dislike towards the family to be able
easily to admit or face them, so they tend to rankle uncom-
fortably within.

Most normally adaptable people accommodate themselves
to this pattern of family life with a degree of tolerance and
goodwill, and learn to take it in their stride. But many
offenders are not normally adaptable people, and in any case
the family humiliation and exposure caused by the offence
and court proceedings are likely to have an exacerbating
effect. So that in every case the probation officer must begin
by discovering what the family relations are, or have been,
as was intimated in the chapters on enquiries and interviewing.
The kind of help which a probation officer can give a delinquent under this head is in the main of two varieties. With
all young delinquents it is essential to try to ensure that
there is someone in their intimate circle who loves them ;
and with young and old alike one must aim to help them to
manage their emotional relationships better. This means
helping them to understand themselves and those nearest
them better, and to learn a greater measure of adaptability
and tolerance.

For purposes of discussion here we shall consider different
categories in turn. There are first those children and young

people with homes of their own, but in which this fundamental need of affection appears to be inadequately met. Then there are the children and young people with no homes or near relatives of their own, and who are therefore in grave danger of growing up with this side of their emotions undeveloped. Lastly there are adults, and the adult experiences of courtship, marriage and parenthood, to be considered in relation to the treatment of delinquency.

1. *Children at Home*

It is family affection and pride that first awakens a child's capacity for love, but love threatened easily turns to jealousy, love thwarted to hatred, and love unreciprocated to desperation.[1] It is here that those family tensions grow up which so often lie behind delinquent behaviour, and which Dr Burbery and her colleagues have discussed in detail and very clearly in their book *Child Guidance*. It is enough that a child *feels* his position in the family to be challenged or unsatisfactory for his behaviour to be adversely affected. He may be just as much loved as the new baby, just as able as his brothers, the object of his new stepfather's real concern and regard, but if he feels inadequate or left out, or that his presence is resented, the consequences are likely to be just as unfortunate as if he really were.[2] Some children withdraw, becoming more and more remote, introspective and retiring, accepting the unloved role they believe life has cast for them. Others fight it. They insist upon being recognized as a force of some kind, and if they cannot shine and attract attention by legitimate means, they will do so by illegitimate. Much bad behaviour has been traced to this fundamental need for recognition and assurance of being of some importance, and

---

[1] See Suttie, *Origins of Love and Hate*, pp. 60 and 61.
[2] " Whether these feelings are justified or not is not the point ; their existence is the point." See *Psychology in General Practice*, p. 117.

before distracted parents and teachers resort to Child Guidance
Clinics they would be well advised to consider ways in which
they can give their child more of both. Very few adults
really understand themselves and their motives : it is not,
therefore, surprising that children do not.   Children such as
are here under discussion, who are emotionally disturbed, do
not understand why they behave so badly ; they do not *want*
to behave badly—they want to be a success, and they cannot
mend their ways without sympathetic and affectionate help.
One way of helping such children is to discuss family relations
with them, impersonally, but on their own pattern, without
emotion or censure. " It's a bit tough on boys, I always
think, when a pretty little sister appears on the scenes.   They
seem to get all the petting and all the second helps and treats,
and one is never allowed to hit them when they tease. But
before very long, you know, the girls begin envying the boys.
Girls always think boys have the best of it.   Boys are allowed
out to play alone, and don't have to stay in and help with the
household jobs so much. . . ." The child can be helped
to realize that these inner feelings of his, of which he is only
semi-conscious, but yet somehow ashamed, are not at all
unusual or terribly wicked. If someone else acknowledges
his unspoken difficulties, seems to regard him none the less
as normal and reasonable, he may be helped to get things
into better proportion and so to manage better. But children
who are seriously emotionally disturbed should be given
skilled help at a recognized clinic by qualified experts.

In many juvenile cases it is not that family relationships
have set up a nervous tension, but that they are so torpid that
they hardly seem to operate at all.

There are parents who seem to have no normal maternal
and paternal feelings for their children, and who have therefore never aroused or awakened reciprocal emotions of love
and affection in them. Babies are fed and washed from time
to time, but never cuddled, kissed or played with.   They are

left severely to themselves and in no way made to feel companions or even acceptable. This type of bringing up is now not uncommon with the intelligentsia, who seem determined not to have their way of life altered in any way by the arrival of a child. Some parents treat their children in this way because their own emotions were never properly developed in early childhood, others because they are afraid of showing their emotions, and some because they never wanted the unfortunate children and are thoroughly bored with them. Children who grow up in this atmosphere from earliest infancy have only themselves to think about and plan for. Their outgoing emotions are never aroused or encouraged. The result is either an urgent, insistent effort to attract attention and affection—a tiresome child, in other words, whom nobody takes to—or an introspective child, living in a dream world of its own, totally uncomprehending of the feelings of others. Both types tend to make a selfish grown-up, unless other influences get working before it is too late. The probation officer's job here is to find some affection somewhere for the child. It is doubtful whether much good can be done by discussing with the parents the desirability of giving the child more attention and affection, though no doubt it is difficult not to do so. If the normal emotions have not instinctively arisen, it is unlikely that they will arise by an effort of will, at the dictate of reason, and unless the show of affection is spontaneous and genuine it is worse than useless. One has seen a mother so instructed dutifully take her child on her knee at intervals and go through the motions of cuddling, but the effect is lamentable, and must merely emphasize to the child more clearly than before that mummy does not really love her. With older children such an attempt on the part of the parents could only mortally embarrass and disgust all parties concerned. Perhaps a better way is to try to arouse the parents' interest and pride in the child by dwelling on his abilities and gifts. This touches them sometimes ; they feel they have evidently produced a child who may be a credit to them after all, so his stock goes up, and indirectly and imperceptibly he benefits accordingly. Sometimes the child himself may suddenly awaken his parents to his own lovability. Stephen, aged 6, away at a residential school for evacuees, began writing regular letters home every week. All the children did, it was part of their normal school routine. His letters were unusually sweet and imaginative. His mother had until then never taken the slightest notice of him, and he had never received letters or parcels from home, but now at last he had an ecstatic letter from her. " Dear Stevie, I think you are a very clever boy. You write better than Alfie and Reggie (neighbours). I am very proud of you. I pin your letters on the wall, dear, so that everyone can see them. Write me some more, dear. Gran thinks you're wonderful. I am sending you a few sweets and comics. Your loving Mother." Stevie made every passing adult read this letter to him for the next two days, until it had positively worn out with being so constantly pulled in and out of his pocket and pawed over. Letters in the same vein continued thereafter at reasonable intervals, and Stevie was transformed from a glum and rather disagreeable little boy into a sunny one. This turn of events was in no way engineered ; it just turned out so. There is a danger in deliberately encouraging such a child to make advances, for if the parents were still unresponsive the child would suffer cruel disappointment.

The school teacher is likely to be wiser and more understanding than such parents, particularly if she is aware of the child's neglect at home. The teacher can look out for opportunities of giving special encouragement and appreciation. It may also be possible through friendships formed at school for the child to meet parents of other children who may elicit by their own warmth the warmer side of his nature. Perhaps the best solution of all is to unearth if possible some relative with normal human emotions, a granny or an auntie. Letters, birthday cards and occasional outings or visits with a really loving relative may give the child deep satisfaction and help him very much. Removal from home altogether to this warmer atmosphere might occur to some as desirable in such a case, but this would be a drastic step, and drastic steps do not always have beneficial results. To sever home ties, however feeble they may be, is to emphasize the fact that they are unsatisfactory. Whereas the child has probably accepted the coolness of his parents' attitude to him as normal, because they are the only parents he has ever had, removal from them suddenly suggests that they, or he, are deficient in some way. If he goes to a happier place, resentment and bitterness against his parents may set in ; or a fierce defensive attitude for them based on fantasy—an untrue picture of what his parents were or are. Moreover, there is always an element of chance in this boarding out of children. Granny may be taken ill, or auntie's circumstances change, and then the child literally belongs nowhere. It would seem better to keep him at home, where he belongs, trying to warm up the parents' interest and at the same time to find him as many outside compensations and as much outside appreciation and affection as possible.

Some people believe in providing unloved children with pets. Certain it is that many children do shower deep affection on animals and gain real comfort from them, perhaps particularly when they find human relations unsatisfying. It may therefore be a thing to try, but love of animals does not take the place of love of one's fellow creatures, and carried to extremes it becomes a perversion, recognized as such when it comes to the lapdog worship of elderly women. If pets are introduced, it should never be with a view to replacing human friends. Efforts should always be maintained to lead on into satisfying human relationships.

It sometimes happens that children who have apparently

had much love and care expended upon them by devoted
parents show grave moral failings. They may cheat, or lie,
or steal, be sexually precocious, cruel, or completely unresponsive and insensitive. It comes as a great shock to such
parents to be told, if they consult a Child Guidance Clinic
or a psychiatrist, that this bad behaviour may be a result of
their own faulty handling, or possibly a reflection of their own
unhappy marital relationships. These situations are very
distressing, but one cannot disregard the advice of a trained
specialist in children's behaviour problems simply because
it is unpalatable. We must none the less, however, admit
that there are some situations which remain a mystery. We
have not yet probed all that lies behind human personality
and character.

2. *Adolescents and the Family*

With adolescents the family situation is totally different.
They are in any case approaching adult powers of reasoning
and discernment, and many are approaching economic
independence, too. There arises a natural urge for self-
expression, to be independent at all costs, to hold and act
upon their own opinions. In well-to-do families, where the
adolescents are despatched to boarding schools and universi-
ties, they are able to build up tastes and friendships of their
own, and to lead their own lives, distinct from the family,
without any comment or fuss. In a few fortunate families
ample scope is given within the home for diverse tastes and
interests and independent thought and action. But without
normal outlets of this kind adolescence is apt to be a stormy,
intolerant phase, either outwardly or inwardly. There is in
some families a real tyranny of tradition—the son must be a
lawyer like his father and grandfather ; everyone automatically goes to bed at ten, or to the same church on Sundays.
Family traditions of this kind, even when apparently trivial in

themselves, may often prevent the youngsters from developing interests and activities of their own which cross the family pattern. In some families, where the parents are partly dependent upon the wages of their children, there is economic tyranny, and the young people cannot leave home or follow their own bent without leaving their parents in financial straits. Some young people exercise this natural urge for independence by being different at all costs, and so giving endless cause for offence. If the parents are Labour, the youngster will declare himself a Conservative ; if they like jazz, he will cultivate Bach ; if they like oil paintings and mahogany, he will hanker after bare walls and steel furniture, openly and heartily despising the taste of his parents. Other young people not so passionately assertive as this may yet silently long for a different way of things, and feel overcome with shame at the supposed disloyalty or ingratitude of doing so. R. C. Sherriff has portrayed this situation most poignantly in his novel *A Fortnight in September*. Such a state of things is absolutely normal. Young people who have not had outlets for expressing their individuality, and who experience no wish to cut across family traditions and strike out on their own, who do not resent in some way the close adherence to family pattern sometimes expected, are not fully mature. They may be seized with these natural growing pains later in life, a much more uncomfortable time to have them ; or else they will remain tethered to their mother's apron strings and not fully mature to the end of their days. But adolescence is a dangerous phase, especially in the case of probationers where the shame and exposure of the offence aggravates existing tensions. It is dangerous because impulsive action in the heat of anger or desperation may lead to the severing of home ties, and this in turn may lead to a false impression of independence, or to an intolerant habit of mind. Fullness of life cannot be achieved through isolation, nor yet through intolerance.

The probation officer can do a great deal to ease this kind of situation, first by making it quite clear to the probationer that he recognizes the hampering conditions at home, regards it as perfectly possible to deal with in an adult reasonable way, and is on the probationer's side in the matter ; and secondly by discussing matters with the parents and endeavouring to secure greater freedom for the youngster. Adolescents, provided they are not severely disturbed emotionally, can take a good deal of reasoning and straight talk. It should be made abundantly clear to them that this is quite a usual situation, it constantly happens ; and that they will only make matters worse by taking an intolerant or inconsiderate line. They must learn to accommodate in the little things. This can do them no harm. They must remember the courtesies of life. To forget this is to be childish. If they expect their parents to make some sacrifice of their habit or preference, then they must do the same. This may pave the way for much more important concessions on the part of the parents—more pocket money perhaps, and freedom to spend it unsupervised ; later hours at night ; permission to go off on a holiday alone, or to change to some more congenial job.

The question of leaving home often arises. Where an adolescent is over-coddled or over-dominated at home, to leave his parents and have to face the world alone may be the only means of helping him to grow up. If family dissension is very severe, this often provides a tempting way out. Indeed, to leave home sometimes seems the only thing to do in the interests of preserving and strengthening home ties. But though much less questionable and difficult than in the case of children, this course has its drawbacks. For one thing, though in well-to-do circles it is quite usual for the adolescents to leave home (and this can be used as an argument), in working-class homes it is unusual. In some working-class families, for a girl to leave her father's home, except on marriage, is a smirch on the family honour, and involves an almost irreparable rift. For another, an alternative to the parental roof equally acceptable to parents and youngster is not easy to find. Hostels for the lower-paid wage groups are almost non-existent, and in any case are usually only found in huge cities. The financial difficulty is overcome in a probation hostel, but there are several snags here—the companionship is bad ; it is only available for a limited sojourn ; and it has a stigma.[1] Lodgings are a possible alternative, and much more use could well be made of the provisions for Approved Lodgings. Residential jobs are a possibility, but often mean going down in the social scale, as for instance if an engineering or dressmaking apprentice were to take up residential work in a hotel or a hospital. Relatives might offer a solution, and they should always be borne in mind. Grandparents are proverbially more tolerant than parents, and there is no stigma about going to live with relatives. It is probably always easier for both parties if the youngster leaves the home town altogether. It is very difficult to explain why a youngster should go into a hostel, or lodgings in particular, in his own home town. It seems simply to advertise the fact that things have gone wrong at home. It is much easier for the parents to be able to say, if questions are asked, " Oh, didn't you know ? He's gone to take up a new job in Westhampton ".

   If departure from home is contemplated, every effort should be made to accomplish it with goodwill on both sides, and with the family blessing and approval. It may be better to keep things going uneasily at home until this is forthcoming than to risk an estrangement by doing without it. A youngster who has the relief of being able to let off steam without restraint to an adult ally like the probation officer, or of having his officer's encouragement and backing to take a line of his own, may be able to manage along quite reasonably

[1] For a further discussion of these institutions, see Chapter X.

in an unhappy or constricting home atmosphere for a while, particularly if the officer is successful in helping him to wider outside friendships and interests.   If it comes to leaving home, much can be done by the officer in unobtrusive coaching of both sides thereafter.   The probationer should be reminded to remember family birthdays, to answer letters, to take a gracious little present when he goes back to visit his family, and his parents can be similarly encouraged.

All this arises fairly commonly without there being any definitely untoward circumstances of family life.   But in the probation officer's circle untoward circumstances are all too common, such as the illegitimate child who is really not wanted at home ; a step-parent who is unkind ; parents who are neurotic in some way.   Henry H., for instance, a lad of 16, was the illegitimate child of his mother.   He was four years old when she married her present husband, by whom she had since had four more children.   There was open hostility between Henry and his mother's husband.   He was a blustering, bullying man, who did not scruple constantly to remind Henry of his birth, and threaten to " have him put away " if he did not behave himself.   Henry's school report described him as " of average intelligence, but resentful of authority, sulky and indifferent in temperament ".   He had already been on probation once, and was reported by his probation officer to be " impatient of advice, determined to go his own way, self-willed and obstinate ".   Removal from home seems clearly indicated in such a case.   The situation must have been intolerable for the boy.   Since he was now old enough to leave home, the plan of treatment for him would surely be to say, in effect, " Life for you has so far been very unhappy.   You are old enough now to go your own way ; no doubt you could make a better job of things if you managed your own affairs. . ."   He should be allowed to make his own plans, with every encouragement and all the backing that his probation officer could give him, and all that could be offered in the way of wider fields of opening opportunities and friendships. But good probation treatment will not end here. More is required for Henry's best development than mere change to a happier setting and the satisfaction of being allowed to make and implement his own decisions. If that were all, one can imagine him becoming successful perhaps in his career but possibly hard and selfish in outlook. This is a danger to self-made men who have overcome great difficulties. The probation officer should discuss the home situation with him from time to time, at first entirely from his point of view, to assure him of full understanding and sympathy. " Things must have been wretchedly unhappy at home. To be in a family and yet not belong to it must be hateful. You were right to leave home, because you were not really wanted there." This is straight talk, but it is the truth ; to have someone else recognize the truth about one's situation is a relief. Later, when the lad is established in a happier setting and is further removed from the painful situation, it can be referred to again, this time from the parents' point of view. " The old man did the best he could for you, you know. He did give you a home, which many men would not have done. He may not have made much of a success of it, but he meant to do right by you. And your mother, too, must have had a tough time of it until she met the old man. Someone let her down good and proper. And she didn't want to give you up, either. Lots of women so placed nowadays are all for bundling the babies into homes or anywhere to get them out of the way. You must never think too hardly of them." All this is as true as the first conversation. It will be easier for him to see it if his own feelings have first been frankly admitted. He is more likely to be able to think kindly of them and to develop in time a generous, tolerant attitude to life and his fellow creatures if he can look at his own situation in this way, than if the whole matter is dismissed without further reference. Great care needs to be exercised in broaching these delicate subjects, because, while some people react to such a situation aggressively, as Henry did, others are much more sensitive, and recoil from facing painful realities. Some, for instance, so much resent their unhappy situation that they cannot bear to have it commented upon, or the slightest breath of criticism levelled against even patently unkind parents. With these the approach probably goes best the other way round. One should begin by putting the parents' point of view, in a sympathetic, explanatory kind of way, and finish up with, "All the same, I am afraid it can't have been very happy for you."

There is often some hesitation about discussing these difficult and painful family relationships with young people, but where they exist the youngster concerned badly needs help in surmounting them. It is these that have power almost more than anything else to mar his outlook. A boy, for instance, who continually hears his mother vilifying or snubbing his father will only be unaffected by this if he is peculiarly and undesirably insensitive. Insensitivity may be a protective covering grown to protect sensitivity, or it may indicate emotional retardation. In either case, therefore, it is a dangerous state. If the youngster is not insensitive, such a state of things will certainly affect his outlook very materially, though variously with different individuals. He may come to regard his father as a milksop to put up with it, and therefore develop an ultra-virile attitude himself as a reaction, becoming a bulldozer in disposition, or contemptuous towards his fellows like his mother. Or he may so recoil from unkindness or unpleasantness that he cannot stand up to the normal rough and tumble of adult life, and so become as escapist. An unloved child may try to harden and deceive himself ; to avoid the pain of admitting to himself that he is unwanted, or of being starved of the affection that human nature craves, he may pretend he does not mind, that he is tough and perfectly happy without family ties. If he is successful in this endeavour he will become a hard, unfeeling person. He is much more likely to be only partially successful and therefore to live in a constant state of inner conflict ; the fact is he *does* need affection, he *does* want to be loved and to feel himself assured of a place in someone's esteem, because he is human. Thus it is imperative for the stability of character and peace of mind of these young people that they should be helped to recognize their family situation as it really is, to see it from a wider viewpoint than their own in relation to society's standards and perspective, and to find compensation where it is inadequate.

This is also the opportunity for directing the thought of the probationer towards the question of responsibility. " At any rate you have learned one thing from this unhappy chapter of your life. Never let your own children suffer as you have done. Learn from your own experience what children need in the way of parental affection and encouragement. Your parents may have been ignorant of these matters, but you are not." Responsibility for the happiness and welfare of others is often overlooked these days. Normal young people are concerned about courtship, marriage and parenthood, and in the case of those who have never had their attention drawn to their responsibilities in these matters, it behoves the probation officer to do so. Adolescents are generally interested in discussing modern methods of bringing up children based on their observance of other people as well as their own early experiences. They are prepared to discuss the ethical considerations of what traits or qualities make the best kind of person, and how these can be developed in young children ; the question of nursery schools or home life ; of boarding schools ; of continued education ; of the right kind of education to bring out the best in children, and so forth.

Much more could often be done in some cases through brothers and sisters. These adolescents who may be going through heavy weather with their parents often have no grudge against little brothers and sisters. If they could spare some attention from battling with their own affairs to give time and affection to a younger child, they would usually be rewarded with joyous appreciation and devotion—the very thing the adolescent most needs at this juncture. To be a hero in somebody's eyes is always valuable. And as love commonly elicits love, the admiration of a little brother or sister is a powerful, though often overlooked, asset for good. Similarly it is often worth while to contact older brothers or sisters, who have already left home, maybe having suffered the same trials there themselves previously. Not uncommonly such older ones can be of real assistance, sometimes in actually offering a home or a holiday, sometimes with moral backing and lesser but valuable tokens of interest and concern.

3. *Young People with No Homes*

So far we have considered only young people who have families and are actually living at home, but a great many offenders have none, and are alone in the world. Children in this condition generally find their way into institutions or are taken charge of by a public authority, so that from the point of view of probation treatment the problem does not often arise under the age of 16, and most often occurs in the adult courts.

It is no uncommon thing for young people in their twenties or later teens to say, when charged, that they have no parents and no homes, but it is by no means always true. They are ashamed, and do not want news of their trouble to reach the ears of the family. Conversations run in this vein : " I have no home." " Where was your home when you did have one ? " " I don't want to say anything about it. What I do is no business of theirs." " Well, it's understandable enough, you would not want your family to know of this trouble.

M

You must have left home some years ago now ? " " That's right. Two years ago. And I keep meself to meself now, see." " Have you ever written to them ? They must be worrying about you." " No, and I don't want to " . . . This is enough to establish that there *is* a home, and that the offender feels very keenly his estrangement from it. Those that do not care and have no feeling or regard for their families have no hesitation in giving the address and any particulars asked. So the position is definitely hopeful, but all the more for that reason delicate. In course of time, if one returns to the subject of the family, it transpires that the offender is the family black sheep. Many of these probationers have no hesitation in accepting all the blame, and freely acknowledging that all that has happened has been their own fault. Experience has shown over and over again that with a little gentle suggestion during the course of the next few months, the probationer will write home reporting her now more satisfactory way of life, decent job, good wages or comfortable lodgings. This letter is almost invariably answered by return of post with an encouraging reply. The tendency then is for the probationer to throw up the job, walk out of the lodgings, and without thought for references, clothes or ration cards, to go straight home, where a most touching reception awaits him or her. Then after sometimes only a very few days, history most sadly repeats itself. There are more rows, and out flounces the probationer as she did before, leaving angry misgivings and disappointment at home. The fact is that the probationer is still irresponsible ; dad still irascible maybe, or mum a nagger ; the respectable brothers and sisters at home still critical. In short, all the factors that made for quarrels before still exist unabated. Their urgent desire to get back home shows how deep is the need and capacity for affection. Homesick people, whether they be runaways, evacuees, or soldiers serving overseas, are all apt to glamorize home, to remember only the endearing aspects, and to forget the other side, the irritations and limitations of family life. Hence homecomings after long absences are apt to have a difficult aftermath of disillusionment following the first rapture of reunion. Add an element of instability, as in the case of so many probationers, and something of the sort is doubly certain. It is difficult for people who are in the throes of deep emotion to see cold reason, and hence preparation for reconciliation, as it were, should be begun before there is any suggestion of writing home. We have established that this probationer has a family and feels deeply about it, and later, that family life was difficult, and that relations, never too easy, came to an explosive end. This must be probed a bit further before any suggestion is made of writing home. What was it that exasperated the family so ? What was it that caused these rows ? What was it about the family that annoyed the probationer ? How could these things be avoided on any future occasion ? Incompatibility of temperament can exist side by side with deep affection, but it must not be ignored on that account. It must be allowed for, and reckoned with. Probably it would never do to try to live at home again. But a great deal of mutual satisfaction and comfort can be had from correspondence and occasional visits—short visits. It is better to go home for the day, or the week-end, and come away again leaving all parties pleased and warmed by the renewing of relations, than to make a longer stay and begin getting annoyed again. The probationer is more likely to be able to analyse the home situation objectively in this way *before* his emotions are aroused by a forgiving letter from home ; and he is much more likely to be able to make a success of any ensuing *rapprochement* if he is thus prepared. If a lasting reconciliation can be achieved in this way, a big step has been taken towards the recovery of such a delinquent. An abortive reconciliation makes this much more difficult.

There are many young people, however, who literally have

no homes or families. The great majority of these have been
brought up in institutions. It seems incredible that orphan-
ages should be the means of cutting children off from their
remaining relatives, yet this has happened. Gillian was
five years old when her mother died in the 1914-18 war. Her
father was given compassionate leave from the Army, and
came home to make arrangements for his children. The
three eldest were taken charge of by neighbours. Gillian
and a little sister were taken to a well-known orphanage.
The little sister was eventually adopted, and Gillian alleged
that she was never afterwards allowed to have anything to do
with her, though she often saw her playing in a neighbouring
well-to-do garden. When she was 16 she was found employment, and eventually had occasion to seek help from the
probation officer. Repeated efforts were made to trace her
father and older brothers and sisters. No record had
apparently been kept of their whereabouts, at any rate no
information or explanation was given to Gillian or the
probation officer, though it was divulged that her father had
been to see her once at the home, and that he was then running
a small business of his own. No record of his address had
apparently been kept. Thus Gillian found herself in the later
teens with all the need and capacity for personal affection,
and relatives existent, but where ? The probation officer's
job in these cases is to leave no stone unturned in search of
relatives and, if any are found, to contact them, preferably
himself personally, but if they live beyond his reach, then
through the good offices of a colleague. If they prove likely
to be sympathetic and interested they will help the probationer
a great deal, even if only by such indirect ways as occasional
letters, parcels and visits. One of these lonely probationers
approached her officer with considerable embarrassment as
Christmas drew near. She gave the officer 2s. 6d. and asked
if she would be so kind as to despatch her a little present of
some kind. She was working in a residential job, and found

it difficult to explain why nothing ever came for her when all
the others on the staff were getting letters and cards and
parcels. It is not only the hunger for affection which gnaws
at these people, but the hunger to be the same as other folk.
Such a girl has no one to write to when she has news to tell—
a rise in wages, a new boy friend, a row with her landlady.
One needs to share one's life with somebody. If the relatives
are not really interested, and unlikely to take much notice of
the probationer, little should be made of it, but efforts
redoubled to find satisfying friendships elsewhere. These
probationers are not children ; they should know that efforts
are being made to trace relatives and that relatives are not
always forthcoming or interested. It is unwise to suggest or
connive at the probationer going to live with newly-found
relatives in a hurry. It is better for the parties to get to know
each other gradually before attempting the exacting test of
living together.

Lodgings provide a much safer home for these lonely young
people. The danger here is that a good maternal landlady
is moved by the lonely plight of the probationer, goes all out
to give a real welcome and make a real home, and then is
disappointed at the cool, matter of fact way all this is accepted
and taken for granted. This is because the young people
concerned, by their institutional bringing-up, with its insecurity and lack of give and take in the normal relations of
affection, are unaccustomed to thinking of other people's
feelings. They accept what is pleasant as right and proper,
and resent what is unpleasant, not realizing that there is often
a personal element in both, and that other people are involved.
The parties therefore each need a bit of private coaching : the
young people in suggestions as to little services and courtesies
which would show their appreciation, and the landladies in
being prepared to find the young lodger less responsive than
perhaps their own children would have been to special efforts
to please. One woman worked hard and long with an

unresponsive youth of 17 or 18. She knew the drawbacks of his upbringing and tried to make allowances for them, but she found him very selfish, and she was annoyed that he never thanked her, or offered to help her, or expressed any appreciation at all. Then one day she had a surprise. It was her birthday. He pushed a pound note into her hand and said, " Here you are, Ma ; you never seem to have anything to spend on yourself. Go and buy yourself a new hat or something." This put a different complexion on matters. The tendency is, once the youngster has made an effort of this kind, he so much enjoys the glow of appreciation which results that he tries it again. This is the way small children learn to give.

There can be an element of permanence about placement in lodgings in the case of these wage earners. There is no reason to leave the lodgings if all parties are satisfied when the term of probation comes to an end. The probationer by now is presumably self-supporting, and no public grant is required to keep the arrangement going, as with a younger child still at school. Many such young people have really become one of the family and settled down happily with " Ma " and the others. Some have remained for four, five, even six years, possibly longer, until such time as marriage called them away to a home of their own, or the call-up to duties elsewhere. In such cases it was the home element, the maternal care, belonging somewhere, that called out their own affections and introduced a note of stability into their lives and that played the principal part in their recovery. There is an art in discovering and preparing these landladies, and this will be discussed in a later chapter.

Much the most difficult offenders to help are those whose capacity for affection has either never developed at all, or has been very badly damaged in early childhood, so that they have no sense of security, no belief in human nature or in goodness of any kind, and are resistant to it. " That's a child whom

nobody could love " said the Sister in charge of the toddlers'
ward in a big Public Assistance Institution. She pointed to a
little grim-faced two-year-old sitting eating her dinner with
thirty other children of the same age, at a low table. " None
of us can stand her." What chance had that child to grow
into a warm-hearted, amenable, out-going personality ?
This is the type of person who makes the really " hardened
criminal ", the person who is himself so hard and unfeeling
that he commits heartless, cruel crimes, thereby calling down
upon himself harsh treatment from an outraged public opinion.
These in turn only further arouse his natural enmity towards
society and authority. This state of things constitutes a
literally " vicious " circle, and there is little as yet in our penal
code with which to meet it.

The difficulty in dealing with these people is that ordinary
good-hearted kindness does not touch them at all ; they
exploit or abuse it, and pass on, leaving a trail of disillusionment and bitterness behind them, making it harder for those
good souls who tried to help them to do the like again.
Eleanor E., aged 17, was such a person. She was charged
with two cases of fraud. She had presented herself as a
woebegone, pathetic, sweet young thing, penniless and
stranded, at people's houses ; been welcomed in with open-
hearted hospitality and concern, and decamped next day,
taking their valuables with her. It appeared she was the
illegitimate child of a woman of the streets and a cultured
educated man, whose good looks, gentle manners and beautiful
poise she had no doubt inherited. She had been brought up
in circumstances of great insecurity. She was sent to an
Approved Probation Home for six months while various
relatives were being sought out, and eventually a young
married cousin on the maternal side, who knew about
Eleanor and the rough deal she had had, offered her a home.
It was a sweet little home, dainty, comfortable and loving.
The cousin found her some pretty clothes and a highly

suitable job in a neighbouring flower shop. Within a few weeks of going there Eleanor had defrauded both cousin and employer of money and valuables. The last news of her was that she had gone as maid to a family who did everything in their power to give her friendship and security, but the same thing happened. A nice young man who had been courting her and believing in her was similarly let down. Kindness failed over and over again to touch Eleanor ; so did punishment and repressive measures which were also tried. What is the right treatment for her and her like ? Effective treatment would consist in awakening and developing the normal emotions of love and trust. She is what is termed " emotionally retarded " ; that is to say that while physically and mentally she is her true age of 17, or 25, or whatever it may be, emotionally she has not developed beyond the stage of a normal child of 18 months. The normal baby of this age thinks only of itself, making for whatever it wants, without regard for the feelings of others. One does not expect consideration from a baby ; one does from a seventeen-year-old. The treatment really requires residence. The offenders need to be under the consistent care of skilled, affectionate people, the same people over a long period. It must be skilled care, by persons trained to understand the workings of abnormal minds, and the reactions to expect. It must be affectionate care, for the aim of treatment is to draw out and develop the capacity for affection in the delinquent. Penal methods do not elicit affection. I know of no institution which provides treatment of this kind for adolescents in this country, though there are some schools run by, or in close consultation with, psychiatrists, which cater for schoolchildren of this maladjusted type, and which are recognized by the Ministry of Education.[1] Readers who are interested in this matter are referred to Aichorn's book, *Wayward*

[1] For further discussion of institutional treatment in this country, and the gaps in our present penal code, see Chapter X.

Youth,[1] in which he describes a successful experiment on these lines with apparently incorrigible youths in the chapter entitled The Aggressive Group. Here he describes how he dealt with twelve violently delinquent youths who were sent to his establishment in Austria for correction. All of them, he says, had been deprived of "the affection necessary for their normal development". All of them had in the past been treated with harsh and even brutal severity. Aichorn was determined to try to cure them by affection, but knew that it would be a long and stormy job. He instructed his assistants to maintain an attitude of consistent friendship whatever happened, and to offer no force, however outrageous the conduct. They were only to intervene if bad behaviour seemed likely to lead to someone being hurt. With this unexpected relaxation of discipline, pandemonium reigned for nearly three months. The place was smashed to pieces. The boys behaved like unrestrained infants in a nursery—naturally, for they had not developed emotionally beyond this stage. Kindness was rewarded by more and more outrageous and studied aggression and provocation. But it worked itself out, as Aichorn believed it would do, and after three months the intervals of sanity and serenity lengthened, and the group were moved into a new comfortably furnished house, and this house was not ill-used. From that time the boys steadily developed normal emotions of reciprocal good feeling for their staff, and of comradeship and co-operation towards each other. Their later history is not described in the book, but all were subsequently successfully placed out into employment, and none had been in trouble again after a period of ten years. The moral of this story is that affection *does* pay, and is a satisfactory method of eliciting and developing better feelings and behaviour, provided it is in the hands of skilled and very unusually gifted and perceptive people, and provided a suitably isolated setting is available where the

[1] Pages 167-87.

abusive phase can be worked through without upsetting the general public. Marie Paneth in her book *Branch Street*[1] has shown us the disastrous results which can follow when untrained and unconvinced folk use Aichorn's methods without the proper setting.

Eleanor, as far as was known, like many delinquents in this class, had never been treated with physical brutality, nor were her offences of a violent nature. She was always gentle, demure and pleasing in her approach to people. But though the symptoms were different from those of Aichorn's boys, the inner malady was the same, emotional retardation; and treatment would have followed much the same pattern—consistent, gentle affection, ill-requited and exploited to saturation point, and then a dawning consciousness of the real abiding truth and strength of love; a wish to be and do the same, because of the satisfaction found in being so; and with practice a final acquiring of normal adult emotional give and take.

There are plenty of open-hearted, generous, good souls in this country, but not nearly enough of them who are trained to understand the workings of the human mind, to know what kind of reactions to expect and how to treat them. It is the combination of both that is needed for the Eleanors, and it is a very rare combination. So we maintain a Borstal population at ever-increasing cost—£378 odd per head per annum (1954 Report). But no Borstal treatment will convert a heartless girl like Eleanor into a young woman moved by the normal emotions of affection, loyalty and generosity.

4. *Courtship, Marriage, Parenthood and Adults*

" Falling in love " can be one of the deepest emotions of which the human spirit is capable, and a person may be

[1] See pp. 23 and 46 for accounts of discussions with her workers, and p. 124 where she states, " we . . . failed so often because intuition and imagination and understanding through pity and human contact are much, but are not good enough ".

literally transformed by it. It is therefore often somewhat lightly assumed that this experience will happily solve the behaviour problems of unsatisfactory young people— " Wait till she falls in love ", or " Marriage will settle him down ". The fact of the matter is that falling in love is the first stage only of a long and difficult process of adjustment of two minds and natures to each other, and unless the first rapturous stage is followed by the subsequent ones of constant accommodation each to the other, and growing powers of perception and understanding of one another, it may have a positively harmful instead of a beneficial effect on the parties concerned. An unsuccessful engagement or an unhappy marriage increases people's difficulties. The intimacies of home-making are more exacting than those of love-making. The normal ill-humour of people who have not breakfasted, or are out of sorts, and the ups and downs of worries and disappointments, of hopes and ambitions, all have to be shared all the time in married life. It is not possible to prepare oneself for each encounter beforehand, as in courtship. The process of adjustment each to the other is hard enough for the most poised and balanced people, and most married couples experience some difficulty in it. It is not, therefore, surprising that many of the undisciplined, unstable young people who come the probation officer's way, do not make a success of it.

Unfortunately young people are fed to-day with false notions about the art of love-making by the films and novelettes which are the only nation-wide propaganda on the subject with which they are provided. Here only the first stage is touched upon ; everything is glamorous, thrilling and passionate.

Many girls, particularly perhaps those who have been starved of physical tokens of affection, who have never been kissed or cuddled in childhood, are fascinated by the love-making which is presented to them on the films, and dwell in fantasy upon finding themselves wrapped in the arms of an ardent imaginary lover. This makes them easy prey to the first real man who puts his arm round them. And further, with films as their only guide to the business (since these things are rarely discussed with parents or adults) some are led to think that physical satisfaction is the be-all and end-all of marriage, and are dismayed and disappointed when they find that other things are involved in mutual happiness, or even that the physical relationship itself is unsatisfying.

Further, courtship in films and novelettes is usually accompanied by fearful storms and scenes, suspected unfaithfulness, and then by wonderful passionate reconciliations. Some girls seem to think this all part of the game, and deliberately work up some flame of jealousy to test their man's devotion or the better to establish their feminine ascendancy. The story of Mrs M. is only one example of many possible ones to illustrate this. She was a young married woman with two small children, whose husband was a deep-sea fisherman and therefore away from home for weeks at a time. She missed and needed him more, probably, than he did her. At any rate, when he came home, instead of spending his evenings with her, as she expected, he would go off to the public houses with his men friends, in a carefree, boyish kind of way, quite unperceptive of her loneliness. Mrs M. found this intolerable, and determined to test the strength of his feelings for her. She began going about with other men friends in his absence and, as she intended, the neighbours began to talk. Mr M. was madly angry, and nearly killed his wife. But she had achieved her purpose. " I never knew he cared so much about me," she said. This dangerous strategy is less often successful in real life than it is on the films. In married life it often leads to permanent estrangement ; in courtship to a broken engagement ; and in both to the engendering of a most confusing and insidious artificiality of mind and emotion.

Most girls feel a stigma if they are not successful in securing a boy. The married status for women is traditionally as well as biologically the only natural one. Hence much so-called falling in love with girls is in reality simply boy-catching, not love at all, emanating from insecurity, prompted by pride, ambition, and the fear of losing caste. It is all too possible to be in love with being loved, that is to say with the attentions, the flattery, the presents, the devotion, of the lover, rather than with the lover himself as a person, as he really is.

The time to talk to young people about courtship and marriage is before they begin to fall in love, and probation officers should make an opportunity of doing this. It is easy enough to drift into the subject whenever a film is discussed, for instance, since nearly all films turn on a love affair. No young person is prepared to listen to prosey old adults, especially unmarried ones, once their emotions are thoroughly aroused. Discussed impersonally and in cold blood, something can be done in the way of preparation. Young people of this age are both critical and observant. They see the mistakes their own parents make with each other. (Indeed, quite young children often know better how to handle their parents than the parents themselves do. " Oh, shut up, dad ; you'll only set her off again " said a five-year-old about his hysterical mother, and he was quite right.) Further, they have the adolescent's firm belief that happiness is a person's natural right, and they are determined to be happy. They are therefore receptive of suggestions to this end, and interested in the matter.

They should be told that happiness in married life demands that husband and wife should be friends as well as bedmates ; this means some degree of community of tastes and standards, of interests and outlook ; or alternatively that both parties should be endowed with very rare disinterested tolerance. They should know that the cultivation of intimate friendship like this demands time and trouble ; that is to say, they should reckon to give up a certain amount of time to each other, and take trouble to know about what interests or concerns the other. This sounds axiomatic, but in numberless marriages the husband and wife pursue their own avocations week in week out, and find on reflection that it is months or years since they spent any leisure together, and each in consequence knows very little about what is passing in the other's mind—Mr M. made this mistake. They must be prepared to forgo their own preferences occasionally, and that without drawing attention to the fact. They should each study the other, and learn the other's red lights, as it were, the times when he or she may always be expected to be dejected or irritable, or the things that particularly annoy or arouse the other, and take trouble to avoid or allow for these, as the case may be. They should know that there are bound to be difficulties, no matter how careful each of them tries to be, and that the only thing to do about difficulties is to keep one's nerve and try to overcome them. They should not think that one horrid quarrel is enough to disrupt a marriage. They should know that there are certain common pitfalls, which have caused, or contributed to, shipwreck in countless marriages, such, for instance, as living with in-laws. This seems sometimes inevitable in times of housing shortage, but it should be avoided wherever possible, and only attempted with the eyes of all parties wide open to the snags. The arrival of the first baby demands an emotional re-adjustment on the part of both parents, but particularly of the father. They should know that a doctor can often give helpful advice or treatment if physical intercourse is unsatisfying to either or both.

The probation officer has been called upon of recent years to undertake a whole new department of work over and above his probation duties, in the field of what is known as "matrimonial reconciliation". The Domestic Proceedings Act of 1937 made it part of his statutory duty to interview and try to assist, at the request of the magistrates, those married couples who come to the courts seeking legal separations or advice about their marital difficulties. Well-to-do persons who can afford to employ solicitors and to fix these things up privately without recourse to court seldom come the probation officer's way in this connection. In some adult courts the greater part of the officer's time is now taken up with this matrimonial work. It is a subject about which there has as yet been little research in this country, and there is therefore insufficient reliable data upon which to form an assessment of its value, actual or potential. The Marriage Guidance Council's work is growing rapidly, and should provide valuable data on this subject before long. It warrants an enquiry to itself. We are only concerned here with probation, and the kind of ways in which an officer can help delinquents to a more stable responsible outlook on life. As we have seen, the intimate relationships of family life have a tremendous effect on people's behaviour and mentality, and in many cases—both adult and juvenile—the officer discovers upon investigation that there is marital unhappiness in the home. Naturally, parental friction has a most upsetting effect upon the children of the family, and the juvenile court officer is bound to pay attention to it. Where there is severe friction between the parents, the children may be quite unnerved by it. It was the cause of persistent truanting in the case of one little girl who was terrified to leave her mother since overhearing her father threaten to kill his wife with the bread knife. Children become nervy and taut with the perpetual strain of expecting and trying to ward off outbursts and scenes between their parents. They lose sleep, and thereby often appetites and health, lying awake at nights listening to or anticipating the sounds of dissension. They find themselves taking sides, and thus sometimes come to hate the offending sex. If this state continues, a girl who has conceived a hatred for her father may shun the male sex so effectively that her own

chances of getting happily married are very slight ; and so it
may be with a boy who comes to despise his mother.   They
do not care to invite friends home, for fear of a row, and so
tend to lose chances of making friends.   Some children lose
all faith in adults, and hence in life and in human nature.
This kind of background of emotional insecurity lies behind
much delinquent or unsatisfactory behaviour.

Wherever the probation officer finds marital friction,
whether in his adult or his juvenile cases, he should always
have an eye to the welfare of the children of the family.
Where it exists it is a great mistake not to discuss it with the
children.   They always know of its existence, and are deeply
ashamed and troubled by it.   Children are taught that it is
wrong to criticize their parents, and also wrong to quarrel.
Hence when they see their parents quarrelling, or one being
patently unkind to the other, they know it must be wrong,
but are too ashamed to admit or mention it.   It will rankle
in the deep recesses of their minds, darkening their conception
of life and human nature unless it can be brought out,
recognized for what it is, and accepted as such.   Children
should never be questioned about this matter ;   no child
should be expected to " split on " his parents.   An officer
who knows or suspects that there is parental friction should
make an early opportunity of telling the child, without
referring specifically to his own home situation, that grown-ups
often quarrel, just as children do.   It is not at all unusual.
It is so hateful that people do not talk much about it, except
in novels and plays, where it is a favourite theme, but it is
quite common all the same.   It eases the child's sense of
shame to know that his parents are not really peculiar.   They
must also be told that people say a lot of wicked, hurtful
things when they are angry, but do not really mean half
they say.   This is true, as children themselves have reason
to know from their own paddies, and it is reassuring to them
to be reminded of it.   It may be that in some cases one can

say, " Dad only says these terrible things because he's ill ;
you know that, don't you ?   Dad is ill ".   There are mental
and emotional maladies as well as physical.

Children who are worrying should be told what to do about
it, even quite little ones.   " They're unhappy when they
quarrel.   What you need in your home is more happiness.
If you were happy, they would be pleased.   You ought to get
as much happiness as you can outside, at school, at work,
at the club, at Gran's, at swimming . . . and then when
you come home full of all the stories about what's been
happening they'll be pleased."   Fortunately, this is often true,
too.   There can be no standard pattern of how children
can be helped in this way.   What is said must always be
strictly related to the truth of the situation.   But whatever
the situation, it goes without saying that these unhappy
children, whether it is they or their parents who are actually
on probation, must be put in the way of as full, satisfying and
happy an outside life as possible.   One wants to build up
their belief in goodness, and this can only be done in these
cases by building up outside contacts.   Adolescents sometimes obtain much relief by pouring out their minds to some
outside friend like the officer who knows what is going on.
They should be allowed to do this.   Reassurances do not help.
The fact is, and the youngsters know this only too well, that
it is unlikely that much can be done to help their parents to a
more tolerant understanding of each other.   The attitude to
take when these young people pour out their hot resentment
or abject misery about conditions at home is, in effect, " It is
wretched.   It is a great handicap to you.   But it is *not* the
whole of your life.   Don't get it out of proportion.   Do not
let it colour the whole of your life.   It is a great handicap to
be born with bad eyesight or a dislocated hip, but people
surmount these handicaps, and get a good deal of happiness
and satisfaction in spite of them.   Most people have some
handicap to contend with, some more apparent than others.

N

Those that have none are liable to grow up soft and imper-
ceptive." The officer should avoid passing judgment or
criticizing either parent to the child, but rather offer such
excuses as he believes exist.

In the same kind of way, whether it is one of the parents
or one of the children who is on probation, the officer must do
what he can to ease the parental friction, and for the same
reason. These intimate relationships affect profoundly the
attitude and outlook of each member of the family. The
causes of marital friction lie deeply buried in the personalities
and past histories of both parties, and their ability to understand and manage each other better depends upon the degree
of perception which each can bring to the situation. The
wave of infidelity which is threatening family life just now in
this country is due as much to social trends as to individual
weakness. A generation or two have been reared in the cult
of extreme individualism, in which people think they must
do exactly as they feel inclined in the interests of self-expression
and sincerity, and then have been subjected to all the peculiar
exigencies of the war, with its special strains on both sexes.
Society as a whole will have to take the teaching of ethics
seriously before this tidal wave can be controlled within
socially acceptable bounds.

In the meantime, the probation officer's job is to endeavour
to get each party to understand both himself and the other
better. Apportionment of blame, so far from being helpful
to this end, merely exacerbates the situation ; for the party
condemned loses faith in the impartiality of the probation
officer, and the party justified is handicapped by the halo of
righteousness which thereafter accrues. Persuasion to do this
or refrain from doing that, insofar as this means trying to
make someone do what he does not want to do, has little
place in conciliation. As in probation, attention to the
immediate symptoms which bring matters to a head do not
go very deep or help matters for very long. If this man's

trouble is that he feels more secure with his mother than with his wife, moving away from his mother's house will not necessarily better the situation fundamentally. If a wife's invalidism or a husband's drinking habits are a form of escapism, and they often are, elaborate arrangements for convalescence or for coming straight home will not ease the tension fundamentally, or for long. To mend these states of mind people have to be helped to see for themselves what the inner motives that prompt their failings are, and to accept each other as they really are. This is not an easy thing to do, even for the most balanced. Marriage Guidance Clinics are now being set up in all the bigger towns where skilled help from doctors and psychologists may be available for these people, and officers would be well advised to use this. An easing of the tension at home can, however, sometimes be brought about by attention to the wider issues stressed in this book, a bettering of material standards of well-being and comfort ; the development of independent interests and hobbies ; the cultivation of friends and outside interests ; and, if it may be, a philosophy of life. All these things give a greater happiness and satisfaction in life, and happiness is healing. They divert people's minds a bit from brooding over the latest scene, and shift the focus of attention from the current exasperation. It must be remembered that the fact of severe friction does not necessarily mean that there is no affection. Some of the saddest cases are those in which there have been over and over again ample grounds for separation or divorce, or in which there is chronic incompatibility, but in which the bonds of dependent affection are so strong that neither can contemplate life without the other.

Parenthood in happy circumstances really does seem to bring out the best in both parents, but here again the probation officer often meets it in most untoward circumstances. With unstable, selfish or irresponsible parents the coming of a child may have a far from salutary effect, and with an unmarried mother this is more than ever liable. Motherhood is always supposed to " steady " a girl, give her deep emotional satisfaction, and develop her maturity of mind and heart. This being the commonly accepted belief, it is odd that so many Maternity Homes and homes for unmarried mothers seem to do everything in their power to defeat nature. The baby is taken away, kept often in a completely different room, looked after by another woman, and only brought to the mother at clockwork intervals for breast-feeding, then severely taken away again. The mothers are not allowed to worship their babies, to hold them, cuddle them, and gaze on them. They are spared all the fatigue and vexation of wakeful nights, and much routine tending during the day. The reason for this is that it is less trouble for one trained woman with a helper or two to take charge of a number of babies, than to supervise a roomful of often inept and foolish young mothers and to train them in the ways of wise handling of their children. It is easier and cheaper for the Home to go against nature, but whether it pays society in the long run to do so is a different matter. It is, further, quite common in the case of an unmarried mother for every effort then to be made to secure adoptive or foster parents for the child, and as soon as possible to release the mother from the last vestiges of maternal responsibility. Small wonder, then, that motherhood does not re-make many young women probationers. The experience instead has a very deleterious effect. They suffer all the discomfort of thwarted nature, as well as from the social stigma, and so tend to become more irresponsible and hard than they may have been before.

Girls are now sometimes taught " Mothercraft " in girls' clubs, senior schools or evening classes, but the idea of giving boys any kind of preparation or training for the responsibilities of fatherhood seems still to strike many club leaders and school teachers as comic, if not almost indecent. This is extraordinary, particularly at a time when there is mounting public concern at the figures of juvenile delinquency and when this is commonly ascribed to the mismanagement of children by their parents in the home.

Social workers have long been accustomed to the callousness of some fathers where the well-being of their children was concerned, but there is evidence that the indifference of mothers is growing. Whereas formerly in the case of a separation the mother almost always fought for the custody of her children, or even hesitated to go to the court at all for fear of losing them, now we are told that it is quite common for mothers to fight to be relieved of this responsibility. " Why should I have all the bother ? They're his children as well as mine, aren't they ? " is not an unusual attitude amongst women nowadays.

This brings the vicious circle back to where we started from, the unhappy and profound effects of being unwanted and unloved on the children, and to the ways and means, all too inadequate, of trying to mend this situation from their point of view.

Of the older adults, many are lonely folk with no relatives or friends. They live in tiny little confined worlds of their own, composed of memories and fantasies. Unlike the youngsters, they are not forward looking. They dwell in the past, hardly even sometimes in the present, going over and over the phases of their life that might have been different, picturing themselves in their triumphant moments, real or imagined. They have learned to take what comes with resignation rather than resentment. For this reason, contrary to common belief, older delinquents are usually easier to help than young ones. Young folk are self-willed ; these older ones much more open to suggestion. For one thing it is so long since anyone has been interested in them, has concerned themselves in their welfare, health, or personal feelings, that the probation officer's attentions are a novel and warming experience. It has been found that young probation officers are often successful with older probationers. Older people are flattered by the attentions of the young. Further, they do not demand or expect so much from life as young folk, and are content with much less. Recidivists and convicts who have spent many years in prison do not expect leniency, and are often completely taken aback if they are bound over on probation. Such really accept it as a new lease of life and are gratefully and humbly prepared to carry out suggestions, whereas a younger person is often secretly determined to pursue his own way. It is both harder to find outlets for close personal affection for older people, and perhaps less necessary to do so. They are prepared to find satisfaction in sublimation, that is to say in second best alternatives. By introducing them to a wider circle of friends, such as men's and women's fellowships attached to churches and chapels, where there are opportunities for service to others as well as of making friends, they find life more satisfying and diverse than in the old lonely days, and they often settle down to humble respectability and do well.

To sum up, then, it is the theme of this book, and of this chapter in particular, that for effective treatment the probation officer should give his main thought and attention to finding emotional satisfaction for his probationers on these deeper levels. Youngsters in particular need the emotional anchorage of assured continuing affection and home ties. Where the real home is either wanting altogether or inadequate, a substitute home must be found, and this leads us on to consider what the possibilities of removal from home are and entail.

X

Removal from Home

Sometimes an offender's home conditions are so appalling that the natural instinct of most people is to begin planning at once as to how he could be removed from it, but experience now provides ample evidence to show that the most obvious immediate remedies are not always the most satisfactory in the long run. To try to sever or weaken family ties, however bad or unhappy the home, is a hazardous undertaking. For one thing it rarely works. Alastair may be whipped off to an Approved School, or an ill-used child to foster-parents, but absence makes the heart grow fonder. So necessary to the human mind are home ties that where these are weak, fantasy often leaps in to strengthen them, and the child who is sent away broods in bed at night, or even about his business all day, of a dream home with his own parents, and this kind of thing militates against his being able to grow up and face life realistically, as well as against his developing any real sense of loyalty to the new home, however suitable this may seem to be. Again, the chances of building up an adequate substitute home, with full emotional security, are thin. An Approved School order always comes to an end after a few years, sometimes after only two or even less. Foster homes are by no means always permanent. The foster-parents' circumstances are liable to change ; their own children or grandchildren may come home to live with them ; death or illness may break up the home, making it no longer possible for them to keep a foster child. If, therefore, the aim of weaning the child's affections away from his own home standards and affections is achieved, he may be left after only a year or two emotionally stranded, his own home lost to him,

187

and nowhere else where he belongs. Where such a trans-
ference appears, on the other hand, to be successful, and the
youngster adopts the new standards as his own, he may come
to hate or despise his own family. He may become such a
" toff " in his smart clothes with his opening prospects, that
he is positively ashamed of his brothers and sisters or parents.
This is not a lovable trait, nor one which is likely to minimize
his emotional difficulties. " A bad home is better than no
home " is the modern slogan, and it deserves careful reflection
in every case where one is tempted to substitute another. If
removal from home is, despite these considerations, thought
to be unavoidable in the best and long-term interests of a
young delinquent, it should only be embarked upon with
these dangers in mind, and every possible effort made to
counteract them. On the other hand, the probation officer
also meets adolescent and adult offenders who literally have
no homes or near relatives with whom they are in touch, and
for whom a home of some kind must be found. And there
are, of course, many institutions, such as well-run boarding
schools or working girls' or boys' hostels, which do not aim
at severing home ties, but at widening the young people's
horizon and so developing maturer judgment. The officer
and the court[1] must then first decide whether removal from
home is indicated, and if so whether it should be a total and
final one or only partial or temporary. If it is the former
the probation provisions of the Act will not be used, for no
probation order may exceed the maximum of three years.

There is some provision in the Criminal Justice Act for
removal from home of a partial or temporary nature. A
requirement as to residence may be included in the order,
by which the offender agrees to go and live at some place
named by the court. This applies to any age and any place.

---

[1] The officer must decide what he thinks is best in order to know what
to suggest if his opinion is asked. The court, of course, is responsible for
making the final decision.

An adult probationer, for instance, may be asked to go and live with a married son or daughter ; or in some inebriate home ; or at a hospital or convalescent home where necessary treatment can be given. Young offenders may be asked to go and live with relatives, or in a specially chosen lodging with a family, in a hostel, training home, maternity home or special hospital. The magistrates have no power to order a person to any of these places under the Criminal Justice Act because the probation order is a voluntary undertaking and the offender can decline to be bound by any such condition. The alternatives divide themselves into two main groups, institutions and families, and we will examine each in turn.

1. Institutions

The institutions which merit most attention in this context are those which set out to train character. Hospitals and convalescent homes are normally only interested in their patients' return to reasonable physical health, and discharge or lose interest in them when this is supposed to be in train.

A " Home " normally implies a place of residence which gives purely institutional training. That is to say, the inmates live, work and play within the precincts, never leaving the place except with permission or under supervision. A " Hostel " is one in which the inmates sleep and live, but from which they go out to work or play, earning their living in the ordinary way, the amount of freedom allowed in leisure hours varying from one place to another. There are innumerable Homes and Hostels in this country, run by many different bodies, all avowedly setting out to train character. Some of them cater for delinquents only, others are intended for stranded young people, some for the highly respectable (but these may be persuaded to take a probationer if they know the full facts and are in sympathy with the plan of treatment). An " Approved " Home or Hostel is one which is not only inspected by the Secretary of State, but mainly financed by the Exchequer, or public funds. These institutions are approved for the reception and training of probationers and have to comply with a Home Office standard and to accept certain conditions before approval or financial grants are given. One important condition of approval relates to length of residence. Probation is intended to be a training in normal ways of living, in freedom and in society, and to require a person to live for long periods immured in an institution is to defeat this purpose. Probation treatment and institutional treatment are distinct and different methods. The Act therefore provides that a requirement as to residence in an institution may not extend for more than twelve months, and Approved Homes and Hostels may not keep anyone longer than this, even voluntarily. Other conditions relate to classifications of age and sex, and to standards of feeding, hygiene and daily programme.

Young people are never sent to institutions of these kinds unless their own homes are unsatisfactory in some way. Their own homes may be non-existent or unhappy ; vicious or lax in discipline ; over-protective or over-rigorous in control ; they may have failed in understanding the young-sters or in handling them wisely. Something has gone wrong, or removal from it would not be sought in these circumstances. The institutions should therefore aim at providing or compensating for what has hitherto been missing. Insofar as it aims at character training it should seek to provide fuller emotional satisfactions. That is to say, these institutions should aim at finding the young people full scope for their latent powers in profitable and legitimate interests ; happy, confident social relationships ; a wide circle of friends ; and some lasting bond of affection and loyalty—preferably with their own kith and kin. The

theory of the Approved Home has been that some young
people have been leading so wild a life, are so much out of the
way of normal conventions, that they are practically unem-
ployable. One could not recommend them to any employer
with any confidence at all, nor expect them to settle down to
regular work in their present condition. They must become
accustomed once again to the regular rhythm of life. They
need the regular routine of rising at a normal hour, washing
and dressing on rising, sitting down to table and using a
knife and fork at meals, and must learn the discipline of
concentration necessary to a good day's work. The employment provided by these homes is limited. It usually includes
domestic work, laundry, needlework, sometimes a little
gardening for the girls ; and domestic work, woodwork and
gardening for the boys, with evening classes in either case,
such as P.T., English, dramatics, organized games, and an
occasional social evening with dancing. At the end of the
time here the probationer is still on probation and under the
guidance of his officer, whose duty it is to advise and assist
him in further plans regarding his work and place of residence.
He may go to a hostel or to lodgings, or return to his relatives
if he has any. In some cases residence at a home of this kind
does help boys and girls to steady down. Their health
improves, and they are ready for the next step and do quite
well in regular employment and normal conditions of living
again. One has the feeling, however, that such young
people are the more promising ones, who might have done
equally well under wise guidance in a hostel or well-chosen
lodging. For the really tough customer, even twelve months
is not nearly long enough. The aggressive kind of person
finds the restrictions intolerable ; rebels against them ; runs
away ; breaks his probation and finds himself in worse trouble.
Others, like Eleanor (see page 171) submit demurely to the
routine, and leave at the end of their time with their characters
quite unchanged.

There is a curious gap here in our provisions for delinquents. There is still no provision for the compulsory long-term training of young people over the age of 17, except in the penal establishment of a Borstal Institution or prison. A youngster under the age of 17 who does not respond to treatment in the open as provided by probation can be sent, whether he likes it or not, to an Approved School for anything up to two or three years. A youngster over this age who needs residential treatment can decline to go to an Approved Probation Home, and the only alternatives are, under the Criminal Justice Act, a few months in a detention centre (which is not long-term residential training), a Borstal sentence, or a prison sentence. None of these establishments provide the type of training which would be likely to help Eleanor and those like her, and these are society's more dangerous menace. Penal conditions do not develop normal ways of living and thinking. They give little or no appeal to powers of initiative or judgment, no contact with the opposite sex, scarcely any training in the handling of money, and involve often long hours of solitary confinement.[1]

There is need here for revised provisions. The Approved Home might, for instance, be taken right out of the probation scheme and become an institution to which offenders over the age of 17 could be committed by the court for a maximum period of three or even four years. The Superintendent should have powers such as the headmaster of an Approved School has now, to license out the young people within this time to employment under continued supervision if he feels they are ready for it.

Unbecoming or ill-fitting uniforms are deeply damaging to self-respect, and are now being abandoned in our Borstals and prisons. The clothing provided in training homes should

[1] When meals are taken alone in a cell, and long evenings from 4.30 or 5 p.m. onwards spent there, this amounts to several hours of solitary confinement, whether or not it is officially so designated, and the results are just as deleterious to the mind.

be neat and attractive, and a high standard of personal appearance should be demanded. Care of the hair, hands and complexion should not be neglected. Personal appearance is intimately connected with personal hygiene, and offenders should be taught the connection. Good carriage and appearance are as much a matter of adequate vitamins in the diet, and happiness in the heart, as of P.T. in the daily programme.

It is not normal to eat one's meals in solitary confinement, nor is this the way to teach social adaptability. Meals should be taken in company with the adult staff as well as with the other inmates. This is the opportunity for teaching table manners and social conversation. The Ministry of Education has realized the value of communal meals as a factor in education. It should be made much more use of in these institutions for re-education.

It is not normal to live in segregation. True, these young people have proved themselves unfit to live freely on equal terms in society, but to fit them to do so it is necessary to let them see and meet, make friends with, and get interested in as many ordinary people as possible. It is not normal never to meet any of the opposite sex. Mismanagement of friendships with the opposite sex is a common cause of downfall. Surely, then, training should include opportunities of meeting the opposite sex in normal ways, of learning how to assess character, and how to manage the emotions and reactions which other people arouse in one. Something of this kind is done in good hostels and could be done in training homes, by means of a steady flow of outside visitors, the inmates inviting their own visitors freely, under some kind of supervision, and a constant stream of visitors and workers of both sexes being invited by the staff. This maintains contact with the outside world.

To develop the full use and appreciation of innate gifts, it is necessary not to curtail the activity of delinquents, but greatly to enlarge it, and to allow plenty of opportunity for trial and error. There should be scope for individual pursuits as well as organized games and sports. Organized games have a value : they teach team work and co-operation. But individual ploys are no less important. They develop initiative, imagination, self-reliance and persistence, as well as offering scope for self-expression.

Young people should learn that right living leads to happiness. Virtue should not be associated in their minds with grim clothing, idle thoughts and hands, boredom and loneliness. Life in training homes should awaken them to life's opportunities. They should be in close contact with people wiser than themselves, who understand them and for whom they have affection and respect. This means a regime not of rigid discipline of officers, warders, supervisors, but of friendship. There must be constant companionship and easy relations between inmates and staff, so that a girl or boy, wrestling with inner doubts or fears, moved by elation or despondency, can and will naturally confide in the staff, and thus be helped.

Those who believe in the deterrent effect of a sufficiently punitive regime should read that lamentable story, *The Natural History of a Delinquent Career*, by Clifford R. Shaw (University of Chicago Press). Every time this poor child was sent to one of the brutal institutions here described he made up his mind he would never return, he would always go straight, and yet he came to realize with miserable despondency that he could not help himself. He was bound to go back to the old gang. That was the only life he knew.[1] This is the core of the matter. If society wants delinquents to lead a better life, it must show them one. Punitive regimes may deter the general public from venturing into crime. It takes a re-educating regime to deter a criminal from returning to it.

[1] See pages 85, 92, 138.

Training of badly delinquent young people should be in the hands of specially trained persons. Ordinary club or teaching methods, assuming a degree of common sense and self-control and appealing to their reason and their finer natures, simply do not work. Those in charge should be trained in mental health and in the science of human behaviour so that they know what reactions to expect, understand the reasons for them, and get more interested rather than irritated when things go wrong. They should work under the guidance of and in close touch with qualified consultant psychiatrists, whose principal job it should be to meet and advise the staff in handling their difficult charges, rather than to treat the youngsters themselves (though there should be facilities for this when necessary). These specialists should be allowed a free hand. The managing committee of the home should be largely composed of similarly trained and qualified people. No doctor would permit a lay hospital committee to criticize the treatment he prescribed for his patients there. Time must be allowed before results are looked for. Individual and unconventional methods of handling behaviour problems must be encouraged and expected.

The hostel is much better suited to probation than the home, since it provides continual contact with the outside world. Probation is essentially treatment in the open, as opposed to institutional training. In the Approved Hostel, designed specially for delinquents, the young people go out to work, earning their living in the ordinary way, and meeting the outside world on terms of equality, while yet being under supervision in their leisure hours. The amount of freedom allowed in leisure hours varies from one hostel to another, and in the same hostel from one probationer to another according to their good behaviour and increasing reliability. There is always a degree of freedom to make outside friendships, and in the best hostels facilities for bringing in these outside friends, of either sex. The hostel offers scope for training the young people in the wise budgeting of their money. Unfortunately present financial regulations, designed no doubt for ease in administrative book-keeping, restrict full use of this opportunity. The probationers pay a weekly sum towards the cost of their board and lodging, this amount being calculated in relation to each one's wages, up to a pre-scribed maximum. They are allowed pocket money according to an agreed rate, and considerable freedom to spend this as they choose. Any surplus is banked for them. The young people are expected to maintain a high standard of personal appearance, and helped and advised in doing so. In the best hostels great attention is paid to social life. The youngsters are definitely taught such social activities as tennis, swimming, dancing, ping-pong, card games and the like, so that when they leave, knowing that these things are fun and that they can do them as well as anyone else and not disgrace themselves by poor performance, they are more likely to join a youth club where they can continue them, for proficiency gives natural confidence and provides incentive. Further, in the best hostels they learn manners from the staff, the gracious way of behaving at table or when visitors call. They learn what rational conversation is, and the interest and pleasure it can bring. Their love affairs are now not judged exclus-ively by the heat of their own emotions, but by the floodlight of public opinion, by the reactions of staff and fellows alike to the loved one. They begin to grow some capacity for judging character by comparison. They learn new ideas, new skills, new satisfactions. Most valuable of all, these young people who have hitherto proved so inept in managing their affairs and their life here find wise, affectionate guidance and sympathy from people experienced in handling their sort of dilemma and used to their kind of difficulty.

But Approved Hostels however good, and some are very good, suffer from two severe handicaps, inherent in the scheme. One is that the companionship is bound to be undesirable. Here is a house full of of delinquents, unstable and mischievous. Some run away ; some get dismissed from their jobs ; some play truant from their work ; some stay out too late ; some stay out all night. There are fights and quarrels and scenes. New probationers arrive, in tearful or rebellious mood. Old ones go, and whet the appetite of those who remain for a greater measure of freedom. The police call, enquiring about the runaways or following up clues of various crimes. There is a continual atmosphere of restless excitement, however well run the place may be, by reason of the very nature and history of the young people living there. Hence one is naturally hesitant to recommend a youngster from a respectable home to go to a Probation Hostel. He will certainly learn much more of evil than he knew before, and possibly meet deceit, dirty talk and restless excitability which he need not otherwise have met, at an impressionable stage of his career. The other inherent weakness is that the Approved Probation Hostel can only provide a temporary sojourn. It was never intended to provide a permanent home. No sooner, therefore, has the youngster begun to grow a few roots, to get attached to the place and loyal to the staff, to settle down into regular ways, than he has to be uprooted, and start all over again somewhere else. Some young people find in these hostels their first real taste of happiness and of home life. For the first time in their lives they meet someone who seems to call out all their best and to care about their happiness and success. Here is comfort, friendship, happiness, such as they had never envisaged before. But, no ; it is not to be theirs for long after all, it seems. However much they want to stay, go they must when their allotted time is up. This is, of course, right. An Approved Probation Hostel with all the drawbacks mentioned above is not a proper place for a permanent settlement. It is not a normal place to live in. But the

o

uprooting is a disadvantage, and a painful, delicate business.

James X. seemed a very suitable case for an Approved Hostel. He was charged with several cases of larceny at the age of 15. His father was a cowman. There were four children : an older brother who had for some years been the leader of a troublesome gang in the neighbourhood, but who had never been before the court ; James ; and two little sisters. He was an errand boy earning 30s. a week (at that time reckoned a fabulous sum for a juvenile), of which he gave his mother 10s. and kept the rest for himself as pocket money. His parents were both easy-going people. There were no suitable youth clubs in the little town, and James spent his time and his money in the cinemas and streets. This child needed discipline, he needed to learn the value of money and to have far more intelligent scope for his leisure. A six-months' sojourn at an Approved Hostel might help him very much. His home was not a vicious one, and there was no reason to contemplate a permanent rift. He was unlikely to learn much of evil that he did not know before from the other delinquents in the hostel. On the other hand, he would have the salutary experience of trying to pay his own way and discovering the value of money. He would be introduced to sports and games normal to his age, and be put on the road to better use of his leisure. He might be under the care of wise, firm men, and learn from them better standards and ideals than he had yet done. Further, absence makes the heart grow fonder. Instead of being the swaggering, moneyed, independent man of the world, he would discover himself in the big outside world as a homesick little boy who wanted his mother. This would be the opportunity to talk about his responsibilities to his home, how he might on his return make things easier there by contributing a more manly share to the household, by helping in the house and trying to give his mother a happy time. At the end of six or twelve months

he might either return to his own home with better ideas and
ideals in his head, or possibly, and this not infrequently
happens, having got used to town life, attached to a youth
club, and well embarked on a job with some prospects, he
might elect to remain in the hostel town and go into carefully
chosen lodgings. A temporary stay in cases like this thus
has a real value, and the Probation Hostel has a definite
function within the probation system.

But since, as we have seen, the Probation Hostel is not
the panacea for all undisciplined or homeless adolescent
offenders, the probation officer has to be aware of other
possibilities.

There are, of course, innumerable other homes and hostels
not specially designed for delinquents or court cases, run by all
kinds of societies and individuals. There are homes for
maladjusted children, and private and experimental schools
run by enthusiasts of one kind or another. There are hostels
run by the G.F.S., Church Army, Salvation Army, Y.W. or
Y.M.C.A., for working boys and girls and sometimes for
older folk, too. The probation officer must be acquainted
with all these possibilities, and know the type of training or
help which each can give. Some are very good, some are
very bad. Some are not approved by the Home Office for
Exchequer grant because they do not come up to the standard
of care which is required ; others because they prefer to work
unfettered by regulations as to length of stay, age or sex
groups. The probation officer learns a lot from his colleagues ;
enthusiasts who have met a progressive, helpful place, talk
about it. An officer with a particularly difficult probationer
in mind consults the nearest Child Guidance or Psychiatric
Clinic as to possible places. He keeps his eyes and ears open
for new places opening in or round his own district. If he
hears of a likely place he must make careful enquiries from
people qualified to know about it, those who have already
used it and those whose names appear on the prospectus as

supporting it. He must visit it if possible himself, to judge whether his probationer would be likely to fit in there. In this visit he will be guided principally, no doubt, by his impressions of the superintendent and staff, particularly by the way they talk about their charges and seem to size up their difficulties and characters. He will watch the staff and inmates together and observe the relationship between them. He will observe the inmates themselves and judge whether they seem to be happy, purposeful and friendly in their attitude. He will be interested in the programme provided, of both work and play, and in the rules of the place. It is important to ask about the recreation. Sometimes one sees a party of girls in their later teens, desultorily throwing a ball about in the garden ; it does not appear to be a recognized game like rounders or netball, and such a pastime seems derogatory to the dignity of their age and capabilities. Sometimes one is shown a bare room with benches all round the walls and a locked piano in the middle. No one is allowed to play the piano. Recreation here consists of having nothing to do. On the other hand, in some of the more progressive places one is shown a variety of pets, handiwork, collections of stamps, flowers or photographs by enthusiastic young people full of information, purpose and pride in their projects.

If the probation officer is impressed by what he sees, and believes it would meet the needs of some individual probationer, he reports to the magistrates and, if they are satisfied and the probationer is ready to go there, a requirement of residence can be made. The Home Office is notified of all such requirements,[1] and has the duty of inspecting all places which receive children or young people and are partly or wholly financed by voluntary subscriptions. This is an

---

[1] Except in the case of approved homes and hostels or under a requirement of mental treatment. See Criminal Justice Act, 1948, §§ 3 (7) and 74.

additional safeguard for the probationer, the officer and the magistrates. The responsibility of placing people in these homes where so much potential good or evil is involved is great.

It is sometimes difficult to persuade a hostel designed for respectable young people to take a probationer. The danger of a probationer contaminating other young people in such a hostel is over-estimated. It is much more likely that the probationer will feel miserably out of place in such an atmosphere and decline to stay there. The superintendents not unnaturally hesitate to undertake the special responsibility involved in the case of an unreliable or unstable young person. Nevertheless, they can sometimes be persuaded to try, and the scheme not infrequently works well, the probationer adapting himself to the standards he finds there, and benefiting from association with steadier young people. The advantage of such a placement is that if it is successful there is no need for it to come to an unnatural end. The youngster can stay on there long after his probation is over if he has found friends and is getting on well. But since even the best of these hostels rarely provide an adequate substitute for family affection, youngsters who go to them should be helped to patch up existing family relations or to find new friends with whom long-term relations of affection can be built up.

The probation officer is not technically concerned if the magistrates make an order committing a child or young person to an Approved School, since this is never combined with probation supervision—but he is indirectly involved if their decision to do so is largely based on his report or recommendation.

A child is committed to an Approved School by order of the court, neither his consent nor his parents' being necessary. The maximum term is three years, except in the case of children under the age of 12 years and 4 months on committal,

when it may be longer. The actual term is variable, for the
school has power to license youngsters out as it feels their
conduct and progress warrants this.

Children are only sent to these schools if their own homes
have badly broken down in discipline or understanding.
They have for the most part already defeated not only their
parents or guardians, but their trained day-school teachers,
and one or two trained probation officers as well. By what
magic then is it hoped that the approved school may succeed
where all these others have failed?

The curricula and policy of these schools were made known
to the general public in an attractively illustrated brochure
entitled *Making Citizens,* published by His Majesty's Stationery
Office in 1945. This showed photographs of bonny young
people happily and purposively engaged in well-equipped
workshops, classrooms and playing fields. It would appear
from the letter-press that great attention is paid to physical
health, sport and handwork, less to academic education.
What of character training? Is this regime of organized
activities, so satisfying to normal young people of school age,
going to transform the abnormal ones—our Eleanors, the
heartless, warped, emotionally retarded youngsters already
described, who constitute the real challenge to society? It is
difficult to see how, unless the staff are not only unusually
gifted and long-suffering, but also persons of specialized
training and experience.

Judging by current advertisements in the press of vacancies
on Approved School staffs, this would not appear to be the
case. There are usually two or three advertisements for such
posts every week in the *Times Educational Supplement.* A good
many of these demand professional teaching qualifications,
in general subjects, or woodwork, for instance; some demand
a diploma in domestic science, some even a diploma in social
science. Occasionally the advertisement states that "a sympathetic approach to adolescent problems" is required—a

very naïve understatement. A Mental Health qualification is but rarely asked for, and some simply advertise the post and salary arrangements, indicating no special requirements. There is therefore nothing here to suggest that any special training or preparation for this most perplexing and demanding of jobs is commonly either provided or called for.

Psychological help could be made available within the Approved School system in either or both of two ways. The youngster in question might be referred to a medical psychologist for regular and direct treatment while at the school. This is not often practicable. Successful psychotherapy demands a degree of intelligence and co-operation or responsiveness in the patient—by no means a common combination amongst young delinquents. Further, not all psychiatrists themselves are sufficiently in touch with criminal mentalities and ways of life to be able to make or maintain the necessary rapport. And finally it must always be remembered that a "maladjusted" person needs pre-eminently to be helped to "adjust" himself—to his family, his circumstances or his setting. Treatment to be effective must be related to his family and his setting. Close co-operation between delinquent, school and home, through psychiatric social workers, who have the confidence of all three, is required. It is a mistake to assume that psychiatric treatment can be "applied", like so much penicillin to certain types of infection, with the same sure and prompt results. All these factors combine to make this form of treatment rarely feasible, but it should not be, and is not, entirely ruled out. The indications are that with careful selection of appropriate cases by qualified persons it might be tried more extensively.

But psychological help might be, and sometimes has been, available in these schools in the way already described, the lay staff working under the guidance of a visiting specialist. The latter interviews the more difficult youngsters periodically, considers reports from teachers and home visitors, discusses with the staff possible causes of trouble, forewarns them of likely reactions to forthcoming situations, makes suggestions as to their handling, and reviews the case from time to time.

In the brochure *Making Citizens*, referred to above, the Home Office stated their belief that only 3% of the children committed to approved schools were "clinical cases for a psychiatrist", and that this was too small a number to warrant the appointment of psychiatrists on to the staffs. Quite so, but there the matter was dismissed. One was left wondering what help was given to these 3% of children, and to the unfortunate staffs, who were supposed to reform them, apparently unaided by specialist training or advice.

In a later Home Office publication, *Approved School Boys*, dated 1952, Mr John Gittins shows the great use now being made of psychological methods and experts at Aycliffe Classifying School, in diagnosing causes of behaviour problems, and prescribing the most suitable form of treatment within the admittedly narrow range of facilities offered by the various Approved Schools. This searching analysis has revealed a higher percentage of maladjusted young people, who would probably benefit from psychiatric treatment, in one or other of the ways outlined above, were it available or practicable. He states, on page 84, "The facilities for treatment of young people in custody are being developed, but they are quite inadequate, although experience in Prisons and Borstals is more extensive than in Approved Schools". The whole of his chapter eight is interesting in this connection.

One may therefore regard some of the best of these Approved Schools as likely to be helpful for the more or less normal, high-spirited youngster, who would never have got into trouble at all had he had proper supervision and outlets at home, but it is difficult to see how the régime outlined can assist those with real character defects. There must be long-term institutional treatment for some types of children and young people who have been mishandled or neglected in their own homes. Consistent handling in such cases is necessary. The youngsters need to be in the charge of the same or likeminded people continuously for a long time, under a stable régime, where a consistent code of behaviour is presented and demanded, which does not vary from day to day or from mood to mood or from one adult to another. Institutions can provide training in corporate living in a way that no private family can, and some young people need this invigorating and stimulating experience to find themselves. Only in such a setting can some of these undisciplined youngsters develop new habits of mind. An institution which employs trained and carefully selected staff, such as Aichorn's, described on page 173, is likely to be able to handle the abnormal or neurotic better than ordinary lay teachers and youth leaders. But what many of the most wayward youngsters most sorely need is emotional security, and this means the personal attention, recognition and love which institutions by their very nature cannot normally give in an individual way. So we are led to examine the possibilities of placing some of these youngsters in private families.

2. Families

There are three distinct schemes for removing a child or young person from its own parents into the care of another family. This can be done by an Adoption Order, a Fit Person Order, or a Probation Order with a requirement of residence. The probation officer is variously concerned in all three, but what concerns us here is the latter. There are, however, certain common factors in all three. Under whatever provision a long-term substitute home is being sought, the child in question will already have suffered severe emotional damage, and therefore, under whatever provision, the substitute home if it is to be beneficial must provide full

emotional satisfaction on all the levels we are here discussing.
Adoptions usually take place in early childhood before the
child is supposed to be of an age to appreciate what is happening.   But there is now ground for believing that even infants
in arms feel intuitively that they are unwanted or insecure
if this is the case, and adoptive parents should know this.
Children who are boarded out, and young people who go
into approved lodgings as a long-term settlement, are of an
age to know and understand what is involved, and to have
already suffered severe emotional shock from their previous
neglect or mishandling, and to be disturbed by the proposed
change with all its uncertainty.   Sometimes the reason for
the change is well-intentioned misunderstanding, or failing
health, physical or mental, of the parents.   Sometimes the
breakdown of their own home has been a violent one, caused
by death or adultery, depravity or insanity.   Sometimes the
child has suffered gross neglect or maltreatment.   Whatever
the cause, such a youngster will have sustained emotional
shock ; how much, depends upon his own temperament and
sensitivity, and upon the circumstances.   But in all cases
damage is done by the breakdown of family life.   Emotional
shock shows itself in many different ways.   People learnt
something about its diverse manifestations in the days of
evacuation—bed-wetting, skin complaints, digestive troubles,
nightmares, sleep-walking, openly aggressive behaviour, a shy,
retreating attitude to life.   As the latter is not so objectionable
to adults, in fact often very convenient, it does not attract
so much attention, but it is a poor attitude to life, and such
children need skilled help.   Children who have suffered
severe emotional shock (and this is usually the case when a
Fit Person Order is made, because these orders are only
decided upon when the child's own home is deemed so bad
that a permanent new arrangement is necessary) are apt to
lose faith in life, in people, and often in themselves.   Their
whole background has been swept away at least once already ;

if that happened once, why should it not happen again ? Why should any new arrangement work out better or last longer ? Nothing in this world is to be relied upon. Hence it is essential that anyone taking charge of these damaged children should know that they will be difficult and know why, should see how past experiences have contributed to their present outlook and be instructed in the best way of handling them. This factor is often overlooked. Children are usually placed in clean homes (not always), but whether the woman in charge knows what to expect and how to handle it is rarely taken into consideration. A loving, gentle home is not enough. There must be understanding as well as kind intentions. This is where the probation officer's special responsibilities come in, in selecting and vetting the prospective homes. It must be remembered that to make a mistake and place such a child in a home that does not after all prove to be the right one is to add to his distrust of himself and of life. He then has one more proof that nothing is safe in this world ; things never last ; it is clear that he belongs to no one ; no one understands him ; he is just hopelessly the odd man out. The more changes there are, the worse it is for the child.

Removal from home to approved lodgings can, of course, often be a very suitable solution of temporary difficulties in the home. A youngster may be sent for six months to a capable, kindly woman while his mother is having a new baby or his father undergoing an operation, or to secure a necessary change of air or convalescence for himself. In these cases where there is every intention of the child returning home, and he knows this, there is less likely to be emotional shock. It is still a great responsibility to choose or recommend a new, even if only a temporary, home for a child.

In adoption or Fit Person cases, the probation officer may or may not be involved in the choice or inspection of the substitute home, but in probation cases where a requirement of residence is to be made with a family, the officer is directly and solely responsible for all the arrangements and subsequent supervision. The lodgings have to be found and visited by the officer. If the court is satisfied with the officer's report, and the name and address of the proposed family is inserted in the probation order, Exchequer grant can be obtained where necessary, for a period up to twelve months.

The officer must begin by making up his mind what the child in question most needs. Where possible the advice of a Child Guidance Clinic should be sought. Does the child need stimulus or an easy-going vegetative existence for a while? Should he be the only one, or would he benefit more from companionship? If so, of what age? Youngsters in real difficulties do not normally hold their own with children of their own age; some do better with younger ones with whom they can assume a superior role without having it put to an ignominious test; others do best with older or even adult companionship, provided it is friendly and sympathetic. This draws out their best and may involve a bit of petting, which with neglected children is all to the good. With the youngster's special needs in mind, a search for a suitable foster-home begins.

What is needed is a public-spirited, intelligent, motherly woman, preferably in the forties or fifties, who has already successfully reared a family of her own; who is happily married; and who can manage to maintain her standard of living without anxiety or strain. A serene, confident personality is necessary, someone who is not easily upset or nonplussed. Where does one look for such treasures? The Women's Institutes and Women's Co-operative Guilds are fruitful hunting-grounds. Probation officers should contact these and similar bodies and be prepared to go and speak to them about probation work with special reference to the value and need of foster-homes for young people of all ages. In cities the Labour Exchange may have lists of lodgings recommended for older age groups, and in some areas the

children's officer may be prepared to help. Sometimes if
the story is written up in a sensational way in the local press,
offers of a home come from all sorts of families ; some of the
most successful have been found in this way. The health
visitor who is in and out of many homes may have suggestions
to make.

The next and much more difficult job is to investigate the
offers. This is delicate, because when people have been
moved to make a generous offer it may seem ungracious to
follow it up with a detailed enquiry. Yet nothing short of
this will suffice. The probation officer dare not risk submitting the child to another unfortunate experience or further
mishandling. Moreover, the right kind of woman appreciates
that thorough investigation and supervision of boarding out
is necessary, and it gives her confidence to know that high
standards are expected, and that someone who knows about
the business is in charge. Since the horrible cases of neglect
and cruelty discovered a few years ago all persons really concerned in child welfare appreciate the need for close investigation and supervision.

The necessary investigation falls under two heads : the
material setting, and the emotional atmosphere. It is easier
to take them in that order, for while one is discussing the
former one can be assessing the latter.

The initial visit must be paid with notice duly given
beforehand. This is only common courtesy. It must be
assumed that the place has been specially tidied up for the
occasion ; why not ? We all make preparations for expected
visitors. Even so, it is at once apparent whether the housewife is a fanatic for tidiness or an easy-going slut ; the
fundamental atmosphere and way of life of the family are
not disguised.

One begins with the living room. The parlour, if there is
one, is not of much importance, because it is reserved for
special occasions and is not the scene of everyday life. The

important thing to notice about the living room is, is it liveable in ? Is there comfort as well as cleanliness ? Could a child play happily here without constant threatenings and scoldings ? Could people make a mess here if they wanted to—cut out a dress, pull a wireless to pieces, get out the plasticine ? Would a jar of tadpoles or wild flowers, a roll of knitting or a bicycle lamp look incongruous on any of these shelves ? This is the opportunity to discuss these necessities with the woman, explaining that one of the chief needs of probationers is to learn new hobbies and emphasizing the importance of room to cultivate them. The paraphernalia involved, a half-finished meccano model, painting things, or collections of snail-shells, bus tickets and what-not, are often untidy ; the child needs a drawer or shelf of his own where he can keep his private possessions sacrosanct. There may be a back yard or garden admirable for pets or bicycles carpentry or gardening. The state of these adjuncts will also reveal something of the outlook of their owners.

Eyes and nose have to be alert in the kitchen to catch signs of food and cooking and to assess whether this woman understands food. A little feminine interest on the part of the visitor about the make of the cooking stove or the con-venience of the water supply may start up a housewifely discussion of these domesticities which reveals whether the prospective foster-mother is a good manager and knows this side of the job. This is the place to discuss the child's meals. She must be reminded that this youngster has suffered from neglect in the past (if he has, and most young people who have to leave their own homes in these circumstances have), and it is important that he should put on weight and be built up. He should have all his own meat, cheese and fat rations. Many people, oddly enough, in spite of the Ministry of Health's propaganda, think that children can manage without proteins, and all their share is consequently fed to the grown-ups. Milk, sweets and fruit are important items of diet, and the child should not be punished by being docked of these essential foods. It is important to find out what the woman's standards of feeding are, whether she reckons to give cooked breakfasts, and whether the evening meal is a high tea or a supper, and what constitutes either.

The bathing and lavatory arrangements should be inspected. This is important, partly to see if they are well kept, and partly as an opportunity to discuss the child's hygiene. Many excellent foster-homes have no bathroom or hot water system, and only an outside, sometimes an earth, closet. This does not matter. The important thing is that, whether the facilities are modern or Victorian, they should be well kept. It is essential to discuss the child's daily habits, particularly in the case of one who has been neglected. He will need daily reminders about the opening of the bowels. Some of the wartime surveys have revealed how grossly neglected is this fundamental rule of health. Many parents and foster-mothers are too embarrassed to mention it, even to small children, and leave it to chance. So a habit of chronic constipation is set up, with all its accompanying tendencies to piles, boils, mild tummy and backaches, irritability, general feeling of malaise, which play their part in the general attitude to life. The youngster will also almost undoubtedly need daily reminders about washing, and adequate facilities must be ensured. Where is he to keep his tooth brush, face flannel, towel, brush and comb ?

And so one reaches the bedrooms. Most reputable boarding-out authorities insist on a single bed, but in general it is only the well-to-do who can afford single beds for every-one. Very few probationers, unless they have been brought up in institutions, are accustomed to a bed to themselves, and some feel so lonely and cold without a bed-mate that they will creep into the next-door bed for company if there is anyone else in the room. To insist on a single bed is supposed to minimize the dangers of one youngster introducing another to masturbation or sexual play. It is doubtful if this is much protection. Plenty of this kind of thing goes on in school dormitories, we are told, where everyone has a bed to himself. It is much more important to know, if the bed or the room are to be shared, who the other person is and what he is like. It is necessary to strip the bed and examine the mattress, and to be prepared for shocks when doing so. The youngster's sleeping habits should be discussed. In the case of a child the time for going to bed should be agreed upon. Any tendency to sleepwalking or nightmares should be mentioned, and the possibilities of precautions such as a night light or the position of the bed and the window discussed. The possibility—or the certainty, as the case may be—of bed-wetting should be mentioned. If the probationer is known to be a bed-wetter the prospective foster-mother should, of course, be told, and given, if she has not got one already, a mackintosh sheet. This is not the bugbear to experienced women that it is sometimes supposed to be. No woman likes to be taken unprepared, and they naturally greatly resent not being told beforehand of the tendency, but if told many women take it with composure. "Oh, I understand about that. My Billie used to do that" or " My Doris took to doing that after she'd had the measles. I'll get my rubber sheet out again ". In the case of a persist-end bed-wetter a higher rate of pay should be offered, in view of the extra washing and trouble involved. Bed-wetters need warm beds. Plenty of blankets and even bed socks in cold weather should be provided. A mackintosh sheet is essential, but a thin flannelette blanket on top of it which can easily be washed takes the chill off. A chamber pot under the bed, easily accessible in the dark, is a necessity. Presumably the probation officer will have arranged for such a child to see a doctor, and the woman must be told what the prescribed treatment is. The probation officer should also ask to see where the probationer's clothes are to be kept ; adolescents need hanging space as well as drawers or shelves.

Next, the house and neighbourhood should be surveyed with a view to recreation, and this important item fully discussed. If the woman has brought up children of her own in the place where she is now living she will have suggestions to make as to the best youth organizations and the nearest open spaces for tennis or football, swimming pools and the like. It is important for the youngster to make friends, and one wants to know whether the household is prepared to allow him to bring boy and girl friends back to the house sometimes.

The youngster's religious training is important. The best setting is a family who themselves are active members of a go-ahead church or chapel, which contributes greatly to their happiness and satisfaction in life, and in which they find friendships and responsibilities. If the family seem otherwise likely to be helpful but do not take an active part in religious organizations, it is doubly important to find outside religious influences. It is useless to expect the youngster to become a regular attender at church or Sunday school if the family he is living with have no use for these things, unless his outside friends are enthusiastic and fire him with the interest and wish. The best thing to do in these circumstances is to seek the advice of someone knowledgable in the district, such as ·a progressive-minded minister of religion, who is known to be good with young people, or the local youth organizer, for suggestions as to the best clubs where religion is catered for.

So much for the material aspect of the prospective home, but the emotional atmosphere is more important still. Throughout all this interview, and while being shown over the house, the probation officer is in a position to sense the atmosphere of the house. A good deal is revealed by the way the woman talks about her own family. This may be in a possessive vein, or with a hard, unyielding attitude ; it may

P

show a tense or nervous anxiety, or a complete absence of perception or feeling. The way she reacts to the officer's points is important. Sometimes a woman will grow more and more remote, and begin to murmur that of course it all depends upon what Dad says. This is an indication that her spirit is failing, and she wishes to back out, and then the officer must back out, too. Others respond with alacrity, and forestall the officer with all the important points, volunteering suggestions which show considerable insight and feeling. A home that is totally unsuitable for most probationers might yet be just the place for one particular individual. A nervy, excitable atmosphere, or one tinged with a hard, dominating or bitter outlook is harmful for all. But an unimaginative, easy-going attitude, while hopeless for a youngster needing careful handling and affectionate guidance, may be admirable for a high-powered, forceful probationer in an older age group who can look after himself, or one who has been ruthlessly dominated in previous places.

Before any placement is definitely arranged it is imperative to see the husband, and to discover at first hand what he feels about the proposition. A lot of husbands simply indicate that it is up to the wife and she may do as she pleases. This may mean approval, or it may mean indifference. The latter is not good enough for a boy or girl who needs the active help and interest of a family man. It sometimes turns out that there is most unhappy friction between husband and wife, and the wife is seeking a lodger or foster-child to distract her mind and to ease her own unhappiness. Much as one may sympathize with this intention, the home is totally unsuitable for a probationer or any youngster in trouble. Sometimes the husband proves the biggest asset of the place, obviously suited to handling a difficult youngster, full of ideas and perception. Some authorities say that every member of the household must be seen by the officer before any child is placed in a home, and this is a wise precaution. Husband

and wife may be admirable people, but a neurotic granny, an imbecile son, or a not too particular lodger may vitiate the whole atmosphere, making the place unsuitable for the individual in mind.

If the place seems at all promising, both husband and wife should then be told about the prospective young person. It is well to begin with an outline of the story, emphasizing the factors that elicit sympathy and underlining all his potentially good points. One must then try to show how his background has affected his character ; how the insecurity of the constant changes, never knowing to whom he really belonged, and suspecting he belonged to nobody, have given him a cynical distrust of people and life ; or how constant bullying or beating have made him aggressive, sulky, or deceitful. The prospective foster-parents must understand what the young-ster's failings are, and, equally important, how they have arisen, in order to see the kind of handling now needed. They should clearly understand that there are bound to be difficulties. The way to recovery is a hard one for everybody concerned, and cannot be achieved without ups and downs, setbacks, and worries.

It has been found that there is a kind of stock pattern in the early stages of these placements. Sooner or later there is a stormy, difficult phase. At first all may go well. The new family go all out to please and to extend warm sympathy and welcome. The youngster is gratified and on his best behaviour. But after a week or two both parties begin to relapse back to their normal level. The foster-mother gets snappy perhaps, or begins to think the time has come to pull the youngster up (no doubt it has) ; the youngster is annoyed and disillusioned ; jumps to the conclusion that all this pleasantness was only veneer ; this place is at bottom no better than all the others ; everyone's hand is against him ; he is no good ; he never will be any good . . . and so on. The happy relations break down ; the youngster becomes sulky and defiant or openly provocative ; the householder is disappointed and recriminating. Unless carefully handled the whole thing blows up ; the family decide the youngster is a very ungrateful, disagreeable nuisance, a disturber of the family peace ; the youngster thinks it is a beastly place and nobody understands him there. Sometimes there is a variant to this pattern, and the stormy phase comes right at the beginning. Some children and young people who have been very badly damaged already and lost their faith in human nature cannot permit themselves to believe in this outward display of sympathy and goodwill. It is as though they needed it so badly, yearned so deeply for it, that they cannot face the shattering blow of again finding that it is not real and does not last, so they steel themselves against believing in it, and seem almost to try to prove to themselves that it is not real.[1] Thus from the moment of arrival their behaviour is outrageous. They are foully rude, throw the carefully prepared meal on the floor, mess the nice clean bed, deliberately spoil the poor woman's treasured possessions, and behave in an altogether appalling way. Generally, of course, they thus prove their point. They are quickly removed, and history repeats itself. They have one more proof that nobody wants them, and that the world is a hard, cruel place, and they become more and more difficult to help.

If people know beforehand that there is bound to be some trouble, and that a bout of bad behaviour does not mean that they have failed or that the child is incorrigible, they are more likely to handle it wisely and weather through to calmer waters. What is needed is inexhaustible patience and goodwill, and a matter-of-fact, commonsense, unruffled attitude. The less made of any scene that blows up the better. Discipline should be applied slowly and gradually but, when it is, with absolute consistency. The punishments threatened

[1] See *Forty-Four Juvenile Thieves*, by John Bowlby, p. 52.

should not be very severe ones, but should *always* be carried
out ; not, for example, " If you do that again I'll have you
sent away " ; rather, " . . . you'll have to go up to your
room ", or " Dad and I won't feel like taking you to the
pictures this evening ". It has been found that sensible
women who are prepared for trouble can take it in their
stride, objectively, so that it is minimized and diverted, and
the most outrageous things do not happen. The child,
instead of being angrily provoked to further defiance, is
mollified, and reacts itself to calm common sense. One such
woman, a wonderful creature with a large motherly heart,
took on a most tempestuous and badly mishandled little boy
of 8. She had been to the Child Guidance Clinic, heard his
story, seen how his previous mismanagement had developed
his outrageous behaviour, and decided to have a try. She
followed the doctor's instructions implicitly. On the day of
his arrival she cooked a beautiful dinner and called him to
table when it was ready. He responded with a flow of
obscene abuse and dived under the table, refusing to come out.
" Oh well," she replied calmly, " if you don't want your
dinner you need not eat it, Tommy. But you won't be able
to go out this afternoon if you don't have it." She said no
more, but sat down and began to eat the meal herself. By and
by he emerged, took his seat without more ado and ate his
dinner quietly. No further comment was made by either
party about the incident. Thus challenge number one was
successfully overcome, and the foster-mother had won the
first round. There were other incidents, but she met them
all with the same unruffled good humour ; and after a week
or two they reached calmer waters, only occasionally disturbed by a stormy outbreak. The woman's own older
children took a great interest in the boy, and their friendly
adult rational companionship helped him greatly. An
adolescent's reactions are always more difficult to tolerate
than those of a child of Tommy's age, although they are less

crude, because one expects more rational behaviour from an older child.

These very common reactions should be discussed with prospective foster-parents, together with any known weakness such as stealing, lying, showing off, moods, so that they may have some idea as to how they may be tackled.

It is important to know something of the motive of the family in offering a home. In many cases it is quite frankly a financial one : to have a lodger seems to the woman the most congenial method of raising a little extra money. This is not as despicable as some child-lovers would have us believe. If value is given for money, the motive is entirely natural and worthy. And, of course, a really good foster-home gives far more value than could ever possibly be paid for in money. Nobody makes much money out of this kind of lodger. Cheap labour is a possibility which should be watched out for. Families which offer a home for a boy or girl of 13 are sometimes found to have a large market garden behind the house, or a flock of small children within it, who need looking after. This state of things does not necessarily rule the family out, even if the boy or girl is expected to do their share of work in a busy menage, but it needs careful watching. Sometimes a man and wife offer a home to a youngster to meet an emotional need of their own. Perhaps their own children have grown up and left home, and the woman is lonely, and still has much maternal feeling in her. It is important that this maternal feeling should not be too possessive or protective, or a cloak hiding a desire to dominate others. Occasionally doctors and friends seem to advise a neurotic woman to get a child to look after, " to take her out of herself ". However excellent the material conditions of such a home, it is an unsuitable one for a child. No young person's budding personality should be sacrificed to patch up that of an adult. In some adoption cases the husband and wife have lost their own child and seek another to take its place. They must be warned not to allow their picture of their own child to colour their ideals for the adopted one. The adopted one will be quite different, and must be allowed and expected to develop differently. Sometimes such people can be advised to have the adopted child a different sex or colouring from the one that was lost. Had they been able to have a second child of their own, it would certainly not have been a replica of the first. Young married women who seek to by-pass the pains of childbirth may not always realize or be ready to go through with the pains and bother of motherhood.

Parents who are adopting a child should also be told of the extreme pain it gives older children to discover that their true parents are not the ones they know. There is abundant evidence now, from probation officers and Child Guidance Clinics, that children are emotionally damaged by this discovery or suspicion, and it is therefore kinder to let the child know as soon as possible the true position. As soon as he begins to ask, " Where did I come from ? "—normally about the age of 4 years—he should be told the simple straightforward truth. " Your real mummy and daddy couldn't look after you. They had not got a home, or were ill ", or whatever explanation can be given (there are sick-nesses of mind and heart as well as body), " and we *wanted* you, so you came to live with us, and now you belong to us ", or something of the sort. This simple matter-of-fact state-ment is accepted without question or distress by a four-year-old, just as the facts of sex are, but heard in adolescence for the first time both kinds of knowledge can give deep dismay and shock. The earlier the child can be told, the better. For this reason some adoptive parents begin as auntie and uncle from the beginning, so that there is never any question of the parental relationship in the child's mind.

Prospective foster-parents should be warned *never* to speak in a disparaging way of the child's own parents, however they may have behaved.   This serious mistake is frequently made.   Nothing is calculated to inflame the child's antagon-ism so quickly, or to fire a spark of such deep burning hatred against the speaker.   Such disparagement drives the unfortun-ate child back in his loyalties to his own parents, and where the parents are vicious or cruel this is the last thing one wishes to do.

If everything seems promising, and the home likely to be a good one, the question of references has to be considered. References are a further safeguard and should never be omitted.   However thorough the investigations, it is unwise to rely upon one's own impressions only.   Sometimes the recommendation has come from a recognized body or person, like the local Women's Institute or the health visitor, and this amounts to a reference if it is followed up and enquiries are made.   Otherwise references are sometimes rather a difficulty.   Many people who do not go to church and have had no occasion to call a doctor do not know a professional person who could act as reference.   An employer might do ; but many men might not want their employer to know about such a purely private matter, and many employers have no personal knowledge whatever of a man's private life.   If the family have reared children in the district, the school teacher may be able to help.   She is likely to know whether they were happy and well cared for.

Experience has shown that it is seldom successful to put two probationers together in the same lodging, even to place a second there after the first has had time to settle down. If the first has really settled down and begun to feel at home he is apt to resent the intrusion of a rival, and to regard him with furious jealousy.   Everything was so nice and safe before, now he feels his position challenged ; this newcomer may be preferred to him, or cleverer than he.   While the newcomer, feeling small beer because he is new, and from the other child's point of view clearly unwanted, in order to keep his end up begins the only kind of braggery he knows—about his misdeeds, real or imagined. More often than not, either number one is led astray or number two settles the matter by running away.

For somewhat similar reasons it is best to avoid homes where there are children of the family about the same age as the probationer or foster-child. This hardly ever works. It works very well when there is a disparity of ages. Many an adolescent girl has been greatly helped by the tiny grandchild of the woman with whom she has been put to lodge. This child is someone for her to love and fuss over, take out, sit on her knee, bath, put to bed, and so forth, and who in return will love her back in the openly affectionate way of small children. Jealousy does not come into it. Many a youngster has been greatly helped by the attentions of the older children of the family. From the family's point of view there is little risk of their own children being led astray if they are very much older or younger than the newcomers.

Some people are incredulous about all this. They do not believe that there are women so long-suffering, so devoted, so good. It sounds like an idealist's dream. But the fact is, there are. The story of Theresa told in Chapter XII is only one of many which might be given to prove their existence. Up and down the whole country probation officers who have taken the trouble to find and prepare foster-mothers in some such way as is here described, have been amazed at their patience, wisdom, goodwill and forgiveness, and the results which they ultimately obtain. The maternal instinct is an immensely strong one, and, once it is aroused, foster-mothers will put up with an incredible amount of trouble and disappointment. And because the good ones really do care, and are not prepared to get rid of the youngsters when things go wrong, they can work miracles. Hence it is a great mistake to suppose that boarding out is only a suitable disposal for the better behaved children, and that stormy, ill-behaved children are better sent to institutions. It should be the other way round. The better-behaved children, being more adaptable and amenable, will do quite nicely in a well-run boarding school. The stormy, passionate, unruly children urgently require this individual handling which only a long-suffering mother is prepared to give. But it is essential that the foster-mothers should be fully prepared and given expert advice and counsel.

Sir J. M. Barrie once said he thought a public statue should be erected to landladies. If this were ever done, magistrates and probation officers should be the first to subscribe to it. Landladies have done most wonderful work.

3. Essentials

Wherever the placement and whatever the age of the offender, there are certain essentials which are common to all cases where a change of residence is part of treatment.

It is of first importance when removal from home is proposed to secure not only the probationer's consent, but if possible his co-operative goodwill, in the scheme. If the officer has had an opportunity of discussing with the offender the best plans for recovery and has in any degree won his confidence, there may be no difficulty about this. More usually, perhaps the offender, still unwilling and apprehensive at heart, agrees to the suggestion because he is astute enough to realize that it is likely to be less objectionable than the probable alternative. One must consider his state of mind. He has been humiliated by failure and public exposure. His self-esteem and self-confidence have been damaged. A façade of defiance or contempt is often but the cloak to hide from himself as well as the public his inner state of extreme insecurity. His only course appears to be that of swallowing his pride, submitting himself to the supervision of a representative of Authority, Law and Order (that is how the probation officer often appears to him, for all he is termed " friend "). He has to agree to go and live at some place suggested by this officer. What is involved ? What will it be like ? He agrees to what is asked, feeling he cannot help himself, but is usually dubious, suspicious and, could he bear to admit it to himself, frightened.

This frame of mind is probably a right and proper one, at the time. He has undoubtedly made a mess of things ; he has every reason to distrust himself, for his powers of judgment have let him down badly ; he has lost any good opinion his family and friends may have had of him for good reason. Shattering as the whole experience is, it is probably salutary. But it is never salutary if it lasts too long. To remain in the valley of humiliation indefinitely is good for no one. At this point the probation officer should dwell on the delinquent's good points. Every offender is endowed with some gifts and abilities. He may have been a good son to his mother ; or have good intelligence ; he may be a leader and a strong character ; or versatile and many-sided. Every good point about him that can be discovered should now be emphasized. If he can be assured that the probation officer sees possibilities in him he is more likely to consider sympathetically the plans for his recovery, of which this business of leaving home seems to be the principal one to begin with.

Secondly, the officer should explain why he thinks it important to leave home and go to the place proposed. The probationer should see that the plans have a definite shape, relevant to his situation, and are not simply a means of punishment or a mark of disgrace. James X. gives us a good illustration of this. Here is a child who badly needs discipline; to tell him so in so many words is to send him to his hostel in a resentful, rebellious mood, determined to resist if he can, in self-defence, the influences he meets there. James should be told that things are difficult now at home ; the neighbours all know and are talking about what has happened ; he has lost his job ; it may be difficult to get another good one, for the employers in the district probably know he has been in trouble ; then there are his former pals ; they may make things difficult for him by expecting him to brag about what has happened, and jibing him if he doesn't. It would be better to leave home for a while, and try to get a really good job, with prospects, in a district where he is not known. If he can establish himself away from home, get a good reference, he could come home again later, and be much more likely to make a success of things. All this *is* discipline ; it is discipline to accept the unpleasant consequences of one's own misdoings ; it is discipline to take determined steps to live these down, and to redeem one's good name ; it is discipline to leave a home where one has been spoiled. One is not deceiving the child if one describes what the discipline will consist of instead of merely giving it its name.

Thirdly, the probationer is probably assailed by the horror of the unknown, and he must be prepared for what he will meet. This place he is asked to go to—what will it be like ? They will all be strangers there, there will be rules, almost certainly unacceptable discipline ; to whom can he turn there ? No one ; he knows no one there. Will he be punished for not wanting to eat greens, or laughed at for things he can't help ? No amount of assurances about football and woodwork, learning a trade, having a good time, will convince a timorous soul that the proposed change is desirable. If such talk ever does persuade a gullible delinquent that he is going to a paradise where everything is lovely, he will soon suffer disillusionment. For these reasons it is never wise or kind to be too reassuring. The truth is, it *will* be difficult ; life is difficult ; there is no getting away from difficulties. The best preparation for meeting difficulties is not to be told there are none, but to be told what they are and how they may be tackled. " You will feel strange at first . . ." is the line to take, with a description of the

regime, and how it comes to be run so, and how the newcomer
can best fit in and begin to feel at home.   He should be told
what is expected of him as far as possible, the most acceptable
mode of address (while in some homes the staff are addressed
as Sir or Madam, in others the Christian name is used ;
either may seem strange and take a lot of getting used to).
He should be told the arrangements for writing and receiving
letters and for seeing relatives and friends.   If the place is
out of the district he should know that a colleague of the
officer will be coming round to look him up.   In the case
of a home or a hostel he should know how long this regime is
to be endured and what arrangements are envisaged for
future plans.

   If by some such approach the officer wins the probationer's
genuine goodwill towards the scheme, it may be quite unnecessary, in fact sometimes a mistake, to make a condition of
residence in the order.   Mrs N., for instance, agreed with her
probation officer that her only hope of giving up her drinking
habits was to enter a voluntary inebriate home and undergo
definite treatment.   This being so, the officer suggested that
she should herself write and make all arrangements for her
admission, which she did.   Though the officer travelled with
her to the place on the appointed day for company's and
friendship's sake, she purposely did not escort her to the door
or go in with her.   Mrs N. had herself decided that this was
the right thing to do and the officer was determined that she
should have the satisfaction and self-respect of knowing that
she had herself taken the necessary steps, and not been under
any compulsion.

   Henry, described on page 161, is another example of this
same point.   Here is an intelligent, forceful young man, bent
on going his own way and of an age to earn his own living.
His officer might well be advised to discuss different possibilities with him, but to leave him to visit these, to write for the
necessary particulars and to do all the correspondence and

business himself. Such a procedure is educative, for one
thing, but for another he would be less likely to throw it all
up and leave the place if he had himself been responsible for
the arrangements. If it were a failure in these circumstances
it would be his failure, and he would feel sheepish. If, on
the other hand, the court had made residence at a particular
address chosen by the officer a condition of the probation
order, such a youth would probably feel the urge to resist
authority. Thus the officer's efforts would not only have
been in vain, but might actually contribute to the failure of
the plan. Even when change of residence is part of the
proposed probation treatment, therefore, it may not be either
necessary or desirable to make it a formal requirement of the
order.

Fourthly, since removal from home to an institution or to
another family is never recommended unless something has
gone wrong at the real home, or is missing from it, the question
of family ties must come in for careful consideration. It is
essential that the probationer's mind should be eased on this
issue. The whole question of a change, of saying goodbye to
his family or familiar circle, raises doubts and fears which are
not easily resolved, and most unnerving if left to fester.
" How do I stand at home ? I have made a mess of things
there. Will they get on better, or like it better, when I am
gone ? Whatever shall I do if I'm not wanted any more ?
How is this going to end ? " These haunting fears make a
background of insecurity which is a poor foundation upon
which to build up a new life. They must therefore be met.
If there is unpleasantness lurking about, it is always better
to meet it, size it up for what it is worth, and reckon with it,
than evade or be blind to it. With youngsters in particular,
it is important to discuss the family situation explicitly at this
juncture. Truth, even painful truth, can be strangely healing
at times—because there is something certain and bedrock
about it which is incontrovertible.

Rosalie R., aged 16, was charged with stealing jewellery from a store. She lived with her granny, who kept a very respectable boarding house for men. She shared her granny's bed-sitting room, and helped her to run the place. She was allowed out only one night a week, and was never allowed to bring any friends home—nothing must be allowed to disturb the lodgers in any way. No questions were asked and no interest was taken in what she did or where she went on her one evening of freedom. Rosalie had a mother and father and some much younger brothers living in the same town. She had been sent to live with her granny when the eldest of these was born, and never taken home again. She visited her parents on Sundays when her father was at home, but not when he was working on a Sunday shift. Here is a child, then, who has been rejected by her parents. Her granny only tolerates her for the help she gives in the house, and is not in the least concerned for her happiness. This girl badly needs adult affection and interest, as well as a wider scope of adolescent activities and friendships. An ordinary working girls' hostel or a well-chosen lodging, possibly in a different town, would probably help her most. But the thought that her family do not want her may haunt her mind and kill any real benefit or enjoyment she might get out of the new regime, unless it is brought into the picture somehow, and so recognized. " When you begin to meet people, Rosalie, and to know them well, it is quite surprising what a lot of people have had unhappiness at home one way or another. Quarrels and misunderstandings, people doing and saying hurtful things. It is very wretched, and a great handicap, for a girl to have an unhappy home. But it need not spoil your life. Don't let it. It does not mean that because you have had an unhappy childhood you have got to be unhappy all your life. You are old enough now to start a new chapter of your own choosing." Something of this sort, frankly recognizing the facts of the situation as they really are, but giving them some proportion in relation to life as a whole, may help such young people quite a lot. It gives the assurance that somebody else is aware of and is sharing their fears, but at the same time is not unduly appalled by them, and sees a way through. Most young people can take a straight recognition of their situation in this way, though probably few are able to discuss it further at this juncture.

Equally careful preparation of the parents or families, whenever there are any, is no less essential. Cases in which the family influence is thought to be so bad that complete severance from it is recommended are rare, and more rarely still come the way of the probation officer. When such a severance is envisaged it is usually in the case of young children, and they are put in the care of the local authority, not of the probation officer. If, therefore, there is any idea of maintaining relations with the family, or of building them up, as is usually the case in probation, it stands to reason that the family must come in for careful preparation and attention, too. In some probation cases, such as Henry's or Rosalie's, for example, the youngster is probably leaving home for good, but they are indelibly tinged with family feeling, and it matters to them and to the future development of their characters very much what kind of line the family takes.

The approach one makes to the parents depends upon the role one would like them to play hereafter, and this varies from case to case. The three cases we have so far discussed are sufficiently different to illustrate different approaches to parents.

Henry's parents (page 161) are probably feeling sore and angry at their own failure and at Henry for letting them down. Both set out meaning to do the right thing by him, and they have been defeated. Henry is a bad, ungrateful boy, but they feel somehow involved in the disgrace and humiliated. Henry must undoubtedly leave home, yet he needs his family badly, and a complete rupture would be harmful to him. The parents' own self-respect must therefore be bolstered up by the probation officer. In his dealings with them he should from the start recognize that they have done their best in providing a home. Deference must be paid to their parental concern for him ; they must be told what the plans are, and helped to see why it is wise to give this headstrong difficult boy a loose rein for a while. His good points must be emphasized, and as time goes on, if Henry does well, his progress must be duly reported to the parents. One wants them to begin to feel it was a good thing they did not put him away into an orphanage after all ; he may be an awkward customer, but he's got something in him. As, and if, their feelings begin to be mollified, it might be possible for them to see things more from his point of view.

In James's case it must be remembered that he is as yet only 15, and it is quite likely that he will return to his parents after his temporary residence at the Probation Hostel, so it is necessary to do a lot of work on them and on the home. The parents are easy-going people, who have never exercised discipline, and they may therefore hotly resist it. Though they would probably give their consent to the hostel plan in court, as being preferable to an Approved School, they probably feel, and say, at home that it is " a shame ; unfair ; hard on the poor little devil ". Such an attitude on their part is not likely to help James much. The same arguments that were given to James must therefore be used on the parents, and criticism left out of the picture. One wants first to play for their co-operation. If they can take the line, " Well, Jimmy boy, Mr So-and-So is quite right ; this'll work out best in the long run, and it won't be for long, sonny ", the probation officer has won the first round. The parents in such a case must be told all about the hostel : the food ; the sleeping arrangements ; the recreation ; the training it will give ; the kind of work he will have ; the arrangements for

Q

visiting and writing and so on. They should be visited regularly during James's stay away, and his progress reported upon. Not infrequently the parents' line then changes. "Coo! pays the hostel all that a week for his keep, do 'e? He never done that for his poor old mum." It is a real triumph if the parents themselves come to see how the ordered, disciplined life is helping their boy; it is in effect near to a recognition of their own shortcomings, and much more effective if they come to see it for themselves than if the probation officer tried to point it out. If they come to see this, as some do, the probation officer has won a second and most important round. If they visit James or he them, they are likely to be impressed at the change for the better. " Quite a little gentleman ", they murmur. James will splutter out how he paid for his new suit himself, and while he is gratified at their obvious pride, they will be at his improvement. This is a favourable stepping-stone to the next stage—future plans. If things worked out well, if James got attached to his new way of life and the extended interests and friendships, if employment prospects offered opening opportunities, he might well wish to stay away from home and settle in carefully chosen lodgings, and his parents, still easy-going, would be satisfied if he were. Alternatively, if at the end of his hostel stay he wanted to come back home, he would be imbued with different standards, and his parents, with continued encouragement and backing from the probation officer, more likely to expect a better standard of behaviour. Neither outcome would have been possible if the officer had left the family entirely out of his consideration.

Rosalie's case is different again. Her family would undoubtedly be angry and resentful with her. Granny obviously will miss her cheap labour, and did in fact begin to talk loudly about the child's ingratitude. Rosalie had never been *persona grata* with her parents, or they would not have rejected her and made her live out. Her offence will not improve the relationship. There seemed to be the closest bond with her father, and he might therefore suffer from an uncomfortable feeling that they were partly to blame for what had happened. Her father is probably the most hopeful member of the family, but it must be remembered that any attentions from him to Rosalie might arouse the mother's ill-will. It is unlikely that Rosalie would ever go back to live at either home, but if reasonably happy contact could be developed after a time, it would help her. To offer criticism to the parents or grandmother, or to point out how their treatment had contributed to Rosalie's offence, would be to inflame hostility. To point out the advantages of the new plan to Rosalie would hardly mollify them, either. " Why should she have all these advantages when she's brought so much trouble on us ? " Time is needed, and the approach here would be much slower. After the lapse of some months it might be possible to call on both granny and parents and report any satisfactory features of Rosalie's progress. The child herself should also be encouraged to write. The most one can hope for is that her father and granny would occasionally write letters and remember her at Christmas and birthdays.

The same rule applies to parents at this juncture as throughout probation in all its aspects : one must play for goodwill.

Fifthly, the actual introduction of the probationer to the new residence, and the manner of his reception there, is an important matter, often overlooked by both busy probation officers and superintendents of homes and hostels. Most probationers' spirits descend to their boots as they say goodbye to the familiar and approach the unknown. All but the most strong-minded and adventurous need to be personally escorted, and that by a familiar friend if possible, rather than a stranger. Students are sometimes despatched to escort probationers on these occasions. Provided they know the whole story, have been properly introduced, and have wit enough to understand in some measure how the probationer is feeling, and to enter into the experience, this may be quite all right. It is not an occasion for moralizing, but is nearly always one for a meal or some refreshment on the way. On arrival it is not uncommon for the officer or his deputy to be shown into the superintendent's private office, and for the probationer to be led away to humbler regions, to sit alone in a deserted well-polished recreation or waiting room for an interminable time, until all the other inmates come in for their evening meal. Such a reception is calculated to reduce what remains of his nerve or willpower to zero, and accounts for much absconding. In other places he is welcomed in by a warm shake of the hand and an immediate invitation to come and see over the place, or another youngster may be called up to do the honours and show him round. Sometimes he is invited into the kitchen by a friendly matron to lend a hand with making the toast for tea. In some places the officer and the probationer both sit down together as guests with the inmates and join in general conversation. This is far more likely to induce the desired reaction—" Not too bad for a start, anyway ". Before the officer leaves he should be assured that things seem happily in train for the time being, anyway.

Sixthly, something has already been said about the preparation of the landlady. The same thing applies to hostel wardens and superintendents of homes. It used to be thought that it was unfair on the delinquent for the story of his misdeeds to precede him ; that he should make a fresh start at the new place, the people in charge being unprejudiced by damaging reports of his past. This presumes that given a completely new setting, starting again at scratch, as it were, the delinquent *can* reform himself and remodel his character. This is now seen to be unlikely. However fresh the surroundings may be, the delinquent takes with him there his same old personality and failings ; his thoughts are bound to be coloured by his past mode of living and thinking, and it takes the injection of a new emotion, a new factor, to change them and their direction. If people are to give the right injection they must know something of the malady and how it has arisen. The more knowledge one has of the delinquent's past and present, the more intelligently and effectively can he be helped. The person taking charge should also know about the offender's family, the line the officer is taking with them, and the role he hopes they will play, so that he can work in the same direction. There must be the closest collaboration between the officer and the new guardian, or they may unconsciously pull in different directions, and give the probationer a chance to play one off against the other.

In cases where the placement is outside the officer's own area, a colleague has to be asked to take over—and he should, of course, be fully informed both as to the background and as to the future plans at present visualized. The fact that a colleague on the spot is visiting should not prevent the original officer from writing friendly encouraging letters giving family news and wishing him well, and so on.

Difficulties occur when the officer taking over develops a different point of view from the one who began the probation. The new officer is, of course, a person with a different temperament and approach, and is bound sometimes to take an opposite view of the probationer's needs and the way he should be handled. This is unfortunate for the probationer. The first officer may be right ; so may the second ; either might have been successful working on his own lines, but nobody can successfully work a plan which he does not believe in. A similar situation sometimes occurs in the medical world, where a patient under continuous treatment from one doctor leaves home for a while and is taken on by another. No one can expect the second doctor to go against his own judgment. The only thing to do is to discuss the whole thing frankly, possibly consult the magistrates of the court which is responsible, and if necessary make a different placement elsewhere. The great thing to remember is the effect on the probationer, and this means observing the common courtesies in the dispute.

Then there are financial details to be considered, when a removal from home is considered. The probation officer is responsible for seeing that the expenses of any scheme he sponsors can be met. This is not difficult nowdays. There is a good deal of public provision for widely varied needs. The Criminal Justice Act 1948 provides for payment from public funds towards the expenses of Approved Probation Homes and Hostels, and lays a duty on the Probation Committees to contribute in certain circumstances towards the maintenance of probationers required to live away from home. These Committees may also, with the prior consent of the Secretary of State, contribute towards the cost of probationers over the age of 21 who are sent for training to voluntary institutions. For instance, a pregnant girl, not eligible for help under National Health or National Assistance may be sent, with financial help from the Probation Committee, to a Mother and Baby Home; or a neglectful mother to a Home which gives training in child care and home management. These grants vary in amount from time to time with changing circumstances and are the subject of periodic Home Office circulars. The principle is that where the probationer is a wage earner, as in the case of an Approved Hostel or Lodging (but as is not the case in Approved Homes), the grant should be on a sliding scale, proportionate up to a stated maximum with his earnings. The local Education Authority has wide powers under the Education Act of 1944 to pay for the boarding out of maladjusted children of school age in specially suitable schools or private families. Where the probationer is destitute, and would in any case be a charge on public funds in one way or another, the Assistance Board has often been willing to contribute towards the expenses of residence.

These are the various public funds which may be available. Occasionally outside friends, or persons who have been contacted by the officer and interested in some one particular probationer, have contributed substantial sums of money to pay the fees or other expenses involved in some plan of this kind. Sometimes a fund subscribed by the public may be discovered which will help to meet the cost. In some cases no financial aid is required. Probationers in the older age groups are often self-supporting, and able and agreeable to pay their own way. Sometimes a relative is prepared to help, or parents to make a contribution.[1] Sometimes a home or hostel is prepared to take a free case, or to charge only nominal fees.

Clothing is another important factor in these cases. A probationer must have clothing up to the standard of those he is now to live and work with, or he will suffer embarrassment which might easily militate against the success of the plan. A young person going into lodgings with a respectable landlady, or a hostel with normal young people, is expected to have night clothes, a change of shoes, a tidy suit, and an overcoat—all things which a youth who has been roughing it or living in a very poor home does not normally possess. Clothes have a psychological effect on the wearer, and are now recognized as vital to the success of these placements away from home. Provision is made for a further Exchequer grant for the purchase of necessary clothing for any probationer going to reside at an Approved Home, Hostel or Lodging under a condition of residence. The probation officer is responsible for seeing that this money is laid out wisely. Sometimes, especially in the case of girls, the officer may go on a shopping expedition with the probationer, making a pleasurable little event of the business. Sometimes the

---

[1] The court has no power to order the parents to make a contribution under a probation order.

landlady is able to lay out the sum more economically, knowing the best local shops and being conversant with the kind of thing required.

Finally, when all the arrangements have been made, and the probationer settled in his new abode, it is essential to the success of the placement to maintain constant touch with all the parties concerned : the probationer, his family, and the persons with whom he is now living.

The necessity of contact with the probationer is obvious. The officer is in the role of adult ally ; he must not only take him to the new place and introduce him there, but write encouraging letters in the first few days, and make an early opportunity to see him again. Much running away and therefore many breaches of probation could be avoided if this were done. Not infrequently the officer is met by a very subdued probationer, and sometimes by a burst of tears. It is quite impossible to stay there ; it is so lonely ; the other girls and boys are so rough, or so stand-offish, or so wicked ; there is no justice in the place ; the probationer vows he could never get used to it, and he must be allowed to leave at once. All this must be listened to sympathetically ; the more that comes out the better ; it has the effect of what one might call emotional vomiting, and gives great relief. The mere coughing of it all up gives relief, and not until it has all come is it the slightest use beginning to reason, or to put another point of view, or even to call for time. If possible a cup of tea or a meal is then a very good diversion. In the case of lodgings or hostels it is not difficult to arrange to meet the youngster away from the place, in a teashop or at the office. The attitude to take is not one of reproach, or threats, or even exhortation, much less of giving way, but thoughtful consideration. " I'm sorry. I'm glad you have told me all this. We must think what is the best thing to do." Various factors in the situation can be brought to attention. " We don't want to make matters worse by acting in a hurry."

The officer has to do some hard thinking. If he does not know the place well—if it is a hostel he has not used before, or a new lodging—he must bear in mind the possibility that much that the probationer says may be true. It may be that he will never settle here ; that it is the wrong place for him ; that there is no justice in the place ; or that the others will do him no good. If the probationer is a headstrong type small good will come of trying to insist that he shall stay there. He would then almost certainly decamp, and have to be summoned for breach of probation.

It is perhaps best to leave the probationer in thoughtful serious mood, having discussed the whole situation and what is involved—including any undertaking given to the court— and promising to call again before long. Quite often the trouble then blows over, and on the probation officer's next visit the youngster has found his feet, weathered the worst, and is prepared to stay. Sometimes after the outburst, never until it has all come, one can appeal to some comic aspect of the story, and settle the matter with an involuntary laugh. It is dangerous to attempt laughing with a probationer who has no sense of humour, but mercifully some have, and after pouring out their pitiful and desperate tale they may suddenly see the funny side. Sometimes an apparent surrender on the officer's part has the desired effect. One officer, knowing her customer, an impulsive but lazy young woman in the early twenties, said, " Very well, Felicity ; if you don't want to stay here you need not. Find yourself somewhere better to your liking. Remember you are bound by your promise to let me know where you go " (there was no condition of residence). " You find me another place," said Felicity. " Oh, no," said the officer ; " you don't like the places I find for you. You had much better find yourself somewhere. Only be sure to let me know where it is. Meet me here next week, and tell me." They met again the following week at the appointed place and time. " Well, found a better place ? "   " No ; I decided the hostel wasn't so bad after all. I thought I might as well stay there."

In some few cases the officer may feel after further consideration and a serious talk with the landlady and her husband, or with the warden or superintendent, that the placement is unlikely to be successful, and that other arrangements should be made.   Where there is a condition of residence in the probation order this means that the magistrates making the order must be consulted, and possibly a summons issued to vary the order.   In such a case the purpose of the summons must be carefully explained, so that the probationer does not associate it with fresh trouble, but realizes it is in compliance with his own wishes and interests.   A change, especially an unexpected change like this, is always upsetting. The moral is, not to refuse to consider a change once a decision has been taken, but to make every effort to find a placement in the first instance which is suited to the individual's needs and temperament.

Contact must thereafter be regularly maintained in the usual way, normally rather more often in a lodging than in a hostel.   Those in homes or hostels far away from their families look for this contact with the officer, and appreciate it very much.   One has to live in such an institution for a while to realize how much regular attention from the probation officer counts.   Once the probationer has got over the initial difficulty of settling down, his next obsessing thought is the future.   Is he to return home or not ?   What sort of job should he go in for ?   Sometimes he yearns to get home again, and is counting the hours ; sometimes he dreads the day for leaving the hostel or home to which he has become so attached ; sometimes bleak uncertainty assails him as to what he should or should not do, and how things eventually will turn out.   Great confidence is reposed in officers who take these future plans seriously, who have suggestions to make, who are prepared to discuss every aspect over and over again, and who by eliciting the pros and cons of each scheme, and helping the probationer to weigh them up, assist him finally to make and carry out his own decision.

To leave a youngster alone until the last week or two of his allotted time with no discussion of what is to happen next, is not only inconsiderate but negligent of an opportunity for a highly educative experience. One wants to encourage them to reflect more, to exercise more foresight and judgment, to develop their capacity for weighing up different issues and looking ahead.

XI

Faith

We must now consider the weightiest factor of all in the formation of character—religious faith.

Faith is what you believe. One can believe in a code or a cause, or a person or in God, or in a combination of these things. One must not assume that because people do not live up to their faith or see all the implications of it, still less because they do not live up to ours, that they have none. In this matter delinquents represent a cross-section of society in general. Some are already devout and active members of a religious body ; some, while aggressively disputing religious creeds, show a higher regard for sincerity or common neighbourliness than others who profess the Christian faith ; some are found to be actively searching for a faith, and feeling the need for a greater sense of purpose in their lives ; others appear unconscious of any such need ; others again seem fully satisfied with dogmas which they have inherited, but apparently neither examined nor tested.

The human mind seems to be naturally attracted, as if by magnetism, to problems of right and wrong. Dr Macalister Brew in her survey of popular topics of conversation amongst young people in public houses, found that religion and the good life ranked second.[1] Food took first place (the survey was taken at a time of stringent rationing). In a hundred different visits to public houses food was 93 times the subject of spontaneous and sustained conversation, religion and how to lead the good life was 84 times so discussed. She found these young people " desperately interested in ethical values, in religious topics of all kinds, in the problem of leading a

[1] See *In the Service of Youth*, by J. Macalister Brew, p. 234

good life . . . it is astonishing how much notice they seem to take of occasional broadcasts on ethical topics . . . through it all there shines a sincere and yet pathetic desire to be good, that fundamental desire of every normal person ". This is convincing testimony. These young people were not church members, but those of whom our moralists despair—the frequenters of public houses.

And so it is with probationers of adolescent age and upwards. Ethical judgments crop up spontaneously in almost every conversation—films, education, the black market, the war, the Jews, family relationships, social happenings and industrial justice. It is not necessary for the probation officer to " direct " the conversation towards ethics. These questions arise naturally. Everyone is found to have some opinions about right and wrong, whether fully thought out or not. " I think so and so . . . " they constantly say, and they will expatiate on their view of the rights and wrongs of the subject under review. In this way it becomes apparent before long that they have a code : perhaps a hatred of hypocrisy or of unkindness are the commonest, which are the negative aspects of a belief that to be good you must be true or kind in your dealings with people. Pauline was a prostitute in the middle twenties, not a very successful or happy one. She spent most of her interviews with her probation officer describing herself as an atheist, and angrily denouncing religious people. They go to church, she said, and say their prayers, and come out as mean as they went in ; meaner than those who never go to church at all ; they're catty, you should hear the way they talk ; it's all hypocrisy . . . But once she had met some really good people ; really Christian they were ; they had brought a Christmas dinner to the house where she lived, and they *knew* the sort of place it was. That was what she called good, being decent to people no matter how bad they were. It came as a great surprise to her to be told eventually that she was talking pure Christianity : Christ denounced hypocrites with terrible ferocity (" ye generation of vipers "[1] is fairly strong language), and it was Christ who first taught men that God is kind to the unthankful and to the evil.[2] What she had been saying was not the whole of Christianity, but as far as it went it was pure Christianity.

Most people, it will be discovered, if they begin talking with any frankness, have a definite code. The difficulty is to live up to it. It is easy enough to notice when other people transgress our code and to criticize them for it, not so easy to see our own conduct in relation to it, still less to adapt our conduct to it. In this probationers are no different from anybody else. Few of us would claim to live up to what we believe to be right in every particular. Millicent, aged 18, held very strongly that unkindness was the wickedest sin of all. When she began going out with a married man from her office her probation officer asked her if she had changed her mind about this fundamental belief of hers, or merely forgotten it ? Was not this an unkind thing to do, to risk breaking up that home and bringing tragedy to that man's wife and family ? Millicent was troubled about this, but it was perhaps more through her charm than her moral preference that she soon picked up more eligible young men.

Two things appear to be necessary for true peace of mind in this life. One is to know what we ought to do, the other is to have strength of mind to do it. The latter is usually much the harder, and it is this that sets up an inner conflict which can be so devastating to true happiness. The role of the probation officer—or any other trusted confidant—in these circumstances is to help people to do their own thinking and deciding, not to do it for them. It is clarity of mind and understanding sympathy that one needs most in these times of searching decision, whether to do what one believes to be right at any cost, or to surrender to what one believes to be

[1] Matthew xxiii. 33.
[2] Luke vi. 35.

wrong. One needs to see clearly all the factors involved, for what they are worth, and the cogency of the analysis can be so painful and inexorable that one craves to have the situation shared by a non-critical, sympathetic, but equally clear-sighted friend. In short, this is one of the instances where the rational has to be backed up with the emotional.

Thus at times, if people are to be true to their code and to themselves, a certain amount of self-analysis may be involved. The amount of this that can profitably be introduced by a probation officer depends entirely upon the mentality of the probationer, and the relationship between them both. Self-analysis demands that the barriers are let down, and one's innermost thoughts and motives openly displayed to view and assessed for what they are. If there is any feeling of constraint the officer will probably do more harm than good in attempting to encourage this, for the probationer in that case would be on the defensive, determined to prevent this intrusion, and to hold his own, and in this endeavour to hide and protect his innermost feelings from the unwelcome intruder he may so cover them up that he loses sight of them himself, and in consequence will see things less rather than more clearly in the end.

Nevertheless some probationers may benefit from thinking out logically their own professed convictions, and seeing where it leads them. The process may be helpful to their self-respect—and everything that builds up self-respect is valuable in probation. Most probationers have far too low an opinion of themselves and their worth to be healthy. It comes as a gratifying and stimulating surprise to many of them to discover that they have a very high and demanding code of conduct.

But since we are members of a community it is not enough to have a personal code of our own ; we owe it to our fellows to study and pay some attention to theirs, and to be loyal to their expressed wishes as to what shall or shall not be done.

Probationers have transgressed the code of public opinion in most cases because they have never considered the matter, though sometimes, particularly in the case of sex offences, in spite of a strong personal preference for and belief in the conventional code, and abhorrence of their weakness ; comparatively few offenders deliberately mean to defy it. Law is the expression of public opinion on questions of morality. Persons who have never given much thought to it before become quite interested when their attention is directed to these questions. Valerie, an intelligent young woman of 17, was to go to an Approved Home. She was asked by her probation officer if she knew why she was going. " Discipline," she replied with a wry grin. And what did she think about discipline, had she any use for it ? " Oh yes, of course, there must be discipline." Why, what is discipline ? This caused some reflection, and in the end recourse was had to the dictionary definition, " Discipline is training, particularly in self-control, orderliness, obedience and capacity for co-operation ". This interested her. Which of all those things did she think was the most important ? There followed more reflection, then she said, " Capacity for co-operation, because to co-operate you need all the other things ; they are included in a capacity to co-operate." A belief in a capacity to co-operate is not a bad basis from which to begin a study of the claims of other people and one's own responsibilities towards them. Quite small children can be interested in how and why laws come to be made. Why do we have Rules of the Road ? Not for the gratuitous irritation of road users, but to make travelling more enjoyable and expeditious for everybody. It is the same with football and other games. The rules were devised because it was the considered opinion of the players themselves that a better game could be had by all if certain rules were observed. It is the same with all laws, at any rate in a democratic country. Children can be quite diverted by being made to work out for themselves the reasons for laws, and what would happen if everyone disregarded them. This makes perhaps a somewhat negative approach, emphasizing as it does why we should *not* do certain things, but it is important to realize that when one lives in a community, reference to one's personal code is not enough. One has to have clear reasons and to be sure that they are valid, before one is entitled to break the community's code. And if we do, then we must equally logically expect to suffer for it, as so many brave people did in Nazi Germany.

But to stop here, at a personal or social moral code, does not satisfy the human mind. Throughout all the ages it has sought for something more than this. It has sought for an Ultimate Purpose or an Ultimate Value, an Ultimate Being or Reality, or a God, without which life seems so insecure, so meaningless, fruitless and silly. Man seems to be endowed with a capacity for worship and for loyalty, and an urgent desire to reach beyond himself, to a reality which he senses but cannot fully apprehend, upon which to rely. Probationers are no exception to this general rule of mankind. They share with others, in varying degree, this feeling after Ultimate Reality.

Here all those, probation officers included, who have a strong personal faith in a living God, are in a difficulty. Naturally each thinks his own belief is the true one, otherwise it would not be a faith but only a line of thought. And because he believes he knows the road to Truth and finds it such a support and inspiration himself, he is naturally anxious to share it. It must be remembered that it was a religious society that originated the whole idea of probation. Probation is one of the many forms of social service which the State has now taken over from the Christian Church, which was the pioneer. The Church of England Temperance Society appointed the first Police Court Missionary in 1876, and from then until the present day, when public authority administers the probation service, numbers of persons have sought to

R

join it for no other reason than to introduce religion to those in trouble. But there is no matter about which people are touchier, or into which they more hotly resent intrusion, than their faith. This indicates the measure of its worth. The more precious the sphere, the less do we brook interference within it. We accept any amount of interference in the matter of what we eat, what clothes we wear, where we live, what work we must do, and so on (particularly in war), but none at all about whom we love or to whom or how we pray. Probation officers, representing as they do Authority in the public mind, are the last persons from whom direction or gratuitous suggestion on religious matters should be tolerated. This is not to say that people do not sometimes seek advice upon religious matters, of their own free will, from anyone who they feel may have something to offer, or whose opinions they have come to regard. If thus approached, officers like anyone else must give their own views as sincerely as they can, for what they are worth.

Further, the fact of the matter is that faith in a living God is not a thing which can be learnt from another like a mathematical table or a grammatical rule. " Here you are ; learn this, or do this, and then you will have got something precious which will stand you in good stead." There is more in faith than mere habit or rote. It is not to be acquired ready made, or cheap, or without much trouble. If God is real, then He is a living, dominating reality, to be reckoned with. If once His existence is admitted He takes command, issues His own terms, and makes His own demands. If God is real, He is not to be found nor yet served by an evasion, or a pose, or a subterfuge. The human soul who seeks Him finds an arduous, searching and demanding passage, from which the only road back is, in effect, a negation of God. And if God is real, immortal and omnipotent, then He will never be grasped in His entirety by any one mortal mind, and the mortal mind that seeks Him will always have fresh discoveries to make about Him. Thus we find that the road to Truth often lies through disillusionment[1]—finding that we were wrong—and the " atheist " who rejects a false conception of God, sometimes at terrific cost, may be nearer the truth, and therefore nearer to God, than a " believer " who dare not do so. And hence, too, many different conceptions may all be different aspects, and therefore tiny facets, of the one great majestic Truth which lies beyond our full comprehension. For all these reasons probation officers who hope to help their probationers to find God should go humbly and gently, only venturing on a direct approach by invitation, whether this be given by word or implication. It is easy for the ardent to assume an invitation, and so to force the pace or give offence.

Let us first consider those who seem unconscious of any spiritual need at all. Chief of these are the children. Children who are left without religious training are not free, as it is commonly supposed, to " choose for themselves " when they grow up. Unless you know what the alternatives are, there is no choice. Such children have simply been deprived of the choice, and start life with inadequate knowledge of its possibilities. Children, unlike adults, have an avid thirst for knowledge, and are not ashamed of it. They expect and demand instruction. Many adults are plagued by their ceaseless Whys ? and Hows ? Religious training falls under two heads : biblical instruction, particularly with reference to the historical facts of our Lord's life and teaching ; and training in worship. Small children have a natural sense of wonder and reverence. This, unfortunately, is all too often quickly knocked out of them. Few children now attend Sunday School, and as far as most probationers are concerned there is little religious training at home, so that school prayers and Scripture lessons, often conducted by those who do not themselves believe or understand either, may be the sum total of religious training that most of our children now get.

[1] Macmurray, *Reason and Emotion*, p. 22.

To enforce attendance at church or Sunday School by means
of a condition to that effect in the probation order is disastrous.
Religion then becomes associated in the child's mind with
humiliation, the Police, Authority, compulsion—all odious
things to be forgotten and escaped from as soon as possible,
and hated for their memory. A much better supplement
is that provided in some children's and youth clubs, where
these associations are run by people who are themselves
sincere Christians, or by individual persons of Christian faith
and practice who extend genuine friendship. Children,
certainly up to the age of 12 or 13, are sometimes fascinated
with pictures, such as Copping's or Hole's, depicting incidents
in our Lord's life. Left to themselves they will often return
to these again and again, poring over them, and then begin
to ask questions. So that probation officers who want to
help children in this way can secure a natural opportunity
to do so by providing such books, amongst others, in their
libraries for children at the office. (Some pictures of our Lord
do harm in representing Him as effeminate, vacant or pathetic,
and officers who use pictures must be prepared to discuss
them realistically.)

But there are other, more indirect ways of helping people,
both children and adults, to feel their need of God. If God
is Beauty, Goodness and Truth, or if these are aspects of
Godhead, as is commonly believed, then everything that
awakens a person's awareness and appreciation of Beauty,
or enlarges his experience and knowledge of Goodness, or
deepens his regard for Truth, is a step towards Him.

Beauty is a road which may turn men's minds to the
supernatural power that lies behind it. Scientists may
analyse the contents or processes of sunsets, starlit skies,
mountains, or seashores, but they do not thereby dispel or
belittle these mysteries for the seeing eye. Beauty has power
to grip a man, to change the whole tenor of his thoughts, to
hush him, and drive him to his knees. " The heavens declare

the glory of God," said the Psalmist, ". . . . There is no speech nor language where their voice is not understood."[1] It is true ; beauty is a language which speaks to all men, all over the world, of a power outside and beyond themselves. In so far, therefore, as probation officers can quicken the sensibilities of their probationers to beautiful things, introduce more beauty into their lives, develop an appreciation and perception of it, or even a dependence upon it for refreshment and repose of mind, they are leading them in the direction of a recognition of God.

And so it is with Goodness. Religion, when it is real, is an experience, not a theory. In so far, then, as a person's experience of goodness is enlarged, by deepening the bonds of affection, widening the circle of friendship, developing greater sensitivity and appreciation for what is good, his conception of God is being developed, as well as his conscious need of Him.

Truth is a third attribute of Godhead. Probation can be a real training to people, children as well as adults, in seeing, thinking and speaking truthfully. In the opening interview the aim is to help the offender to see for himself the true facts of his situation, and the sequence of events and trends which have led to this. In the subsequent interviews, as we have seen, sooner or later ethical questions are likely to arise spontaneously, and so he may come to see, perhaps for the first time, that he has a code, and because it is his own, and he arrived at it independently, and it is a self-respecting thing to have a code, there is some inducement to try, at any rate, to live up to it. If he does this, it will not be long before he finds himself defeated. " The good that I would, I do not ; but the evil, which I would not, that I do ", cried St Paul,[2] and many after him. And it is this truth, this discovery of self-insufficiency, that drives many people to God. We are

[1] Psalm xix.
[2] Romans vii.

back again at Millicent's dilemma. The finer the code, the more impossible of attainment it is. In short, without God high ideals may become a positive stumbling block. For instance, the pharisee may indulge in pride because he has so fine a code of conduct. The hypocrite pays lip service to one principle and acts on another, often unaware of his own self-deception. The sincere man may be driven to despair and even abandonment of his principles, by the evident impossibility of living up to them. And so we come to consider how a probation officer can help those who are conscious of spiritual need, or of their own insufficiency.

Probation officers are sometimes counselled to refer all such seekers to a minister of religion or to a church. The officer should know the ministers of religion in his area, if necessary by going around and personally introducing himself. It is important for him to know those of all the main religious denominations, for in the course of his work he will normally have to deal with people of all denominations. It is only by personally meeting and talking to these men that the officer can form an impression as to which are most likely to be able to help different kinds of person. There is a great chasm too often between the theological seminary and the factory or farm, between the vicarage study and the man in the street. Different experiences of life lead people in these different walks of life to express themselves in different terms, even the same words used sometimes have a different meaning. Some ministers of religion are better at explaining the Pentateuch or more interested in Q, the lost gospel, than in understanding the human needs and mental processes of inarticulate, diffident folk. This must necessarily be so. It is important that our religious leaders should be at home in the original Greek and Hebrew texts of the historical documents on which our religion is founded, and not dependent upon other people's translations. We are all differently endowed, and we need a wide range of differently endowed persons. We should not expect scholarship always to go hand in hand with strong human intuition and love of people. But for this same reason, it is unwise to recommend a probationer to go to any minister of religion. The officer should have sufficient acquaintance to be able to recommend a particular probationer to a particular minister, who he thinks is specially suited to help him.

In the same way, it is not always helpful to these probationers who are in spiritual perplexity or need to go to church. Our church services are for the most part conducted in Elizabethan language, which to inexperienced worshippers or to unlettered minds is unintelligible. " Prevent us . . . in all our doings " means to most people in 1955 " Stop us doing whatever we are doing ", and makes nonsense. Many of our hymns are couched in sentimental language, describing mystical experiences with which all but deeply spiritual people are totally unfamiliar. Intoning adds a further note of artificiality for many people. These hymns and prayers and Bible readings mean a great deal to many worshippers by reason of their associations and the affectionate memories to which they give rise. To such they bring a mood of reverent gratitude, love and aspiration, which is both stimulating to their finer natures and comforting in times of stress. As spiritual experience deepens, the mystical approach, which may at first be a barrier, comes to have more meaning. But to many an outsider, meeting these services for the first time, they are simply so much meaningless—and therefore to the desperate even infuriating—verbiage.

But Church is not the be-all and end-all of religion ; God is, and those who do not find Him there must look elsewhere. The Church is sometimes defined as the fellowship of all believers, and as such it is much more suited to meet the needs of people who have already found God, and who therefore all have something in common, and understand the language and ritual of corporate worship, than an outsider, one who as yet has not got this established belief and tradition.   Such a person needs much more individual help than is normally possible in a church service.   He needs the personal help and friendship, the personal spiritual hospitality one might almost call it, of another mind sharing with him his experience and knowledge, and the things which he has found helpful. We cannot get away from man's innate need of personal friendship and affection, the personal concern and interest of others in his life and his affairs.   This applies as much to the spiritual realm as to the social.

Thus perhaps the greatest service which a probation officer can render is to know people who have this generosity of mind and heart, in all walks of life, unlettered as well as learned, to whom he can from time to time introduce his probationers who are in spiritual need, and from whom they are more likely to get the personal testimony intimately related to their particular need.   But if such a contact does not help, there should not be undue disappointment or dismay, because, as already pointed out, one person's approach or experience is by no means necessarily the same as another's. If such contact is not helpful, others must be sought.

The natural thing to say to people who are in religious perplexity is, " Read for yourself the story of Christ, and what He had to say about this ".   The Bible is a vast compilation of legal, philosophical, historical and mystical works, written by different people, in very different circumstances, over the course of many centuries.   Scripture is for the most part so badly taught that few people have any idea of who wrote what, or why, or even where to look for what is most apt to their own situation.   Modern translations of the Gospels, printed like an ordinary book, in large print, without demarcations of verses and chapters, are useful here, and can help quite considerably those who want to re-read and form an adult impression of Christ's teaching.   Even so, one has to remember that many probationers are not natural readers, and will never get much out of the written word. Dramatic presentations like Dorothy Sayers' *Man Born to be King* have been found useful. The humble little Bible class meeting on a week night or a Sunday morning, at which the Bible is read out loud, explained and discussed, can be helpful, particularly as there is sometimes a bond of fellowship about these little gatherings. Men's and women's Bible classes of this sort are often attached to the smaller churches and chapels up and down the back streets, the less pretentious the better. Similar discussion groups, but in a more vigorous topical vein, often function for young people in those youth clubs which are run by practising Christians.

The more intellectual folk can, of course, be lent books, and will welcome this. They will also want to discuss the books, and pull them to pieces. Those who lend books must be prepared for this. The argument may be aggressive in tone, but this generally only indicates a desire for knowledge. It is a paradox that people often seek knowledge by presenting what looks like a closed mind. They try to make their view as impregnable as possible, by vehement and dogmatic assertions, to see whether it will hold against attack. The over-emphasis may really indicate inner insecurity, and the views put forward by no means always represent the speaker's real state of mind. The danger is that one is oneself tempted in the vigour of discussion to resort to the same technique, to overstate one's case, or to become heated in maintaining it ; and this, just as much in our case, may be to give a wrong impression, and so to damage it. People who demand a proof of God's existence must be asked what is their proof of the existence of powers like love or jealousy or ambition or fear. There are some things which cannot be scientifically analysed and proved. Experience is the only evidence upon which one can rely in the case of many realities which nobody would dream of writing off as fantasy.

All people searching for spiritual truth or light should be

encouraged to keep up the search. It is not likely that satisfactory answers to all their problems will drop into their laps without effort on their part. Religion is not like a ripe plum which can be had for the picking. People who give up the search live, as it were, only half a life, losing what those who have it deem to be the most worthwhile thing in life. Those who pursue the search have never done with it. A living faith must be a growing one. It must grow to meet every contingency which life brings, or it ceases to be a living thing and becomes a memory. Hence it is always being put to the test. There is always new light and new truth to be discovered, and often old to be discarded, about the Omnipotent.

Everyone who seeks spiritual enlightenment should be advised to pray, and prayer is the most effective way in which any probation officer who has himself a faith in the Living God can help his probationers. This is not the place for a discussion of prayer and the great variety of spiritual experience which has led men all down the ages to believe in its efficacy. Some people claim that they have never been disappointed in prayer, suggesting that all their requests have been granted. This is not common Christian experience.[1] Others say that prayer is not a matter of asking for things at all, but a state of spiritual communion with God, from which is derived quietude of spirit, greater courage, and further vision of where immediate duty lies. As spiritual maturity develops, if we are to believe the testimony and experience of saints and mystics, prayer becomes less and less utilitarian in purpose and content, and more and more an act of worship.[2]

In this matter of prayer, probation officers and their probationers are both in the same boat ; both are seekers ; both must approach God in the utmost integrity of mind and

[1] E.g. see 2 Corinthians xii. 8.
[2] See *The Little Flowers of St Francis*, Chapter II.

heart ; both have much to learn, and must be sufficiently courageous and open-minded to do so.

No one can give what he has not got. Probation officers who have no personal faith, or who do not practise such faith as they reckon to have, cannot help others to a religious faith. But one can give what one has ; and if an officer has a strong desire for faith, an honest seeking mind, a love of Truth, Beauty and Goodness, then he will probably impart these things to those of his probationers who are looking for them, quite unconsciously. And if one meets a believer, who lives consistently in humble awareness of the presence of God, seeking to align himself with His will, and praying about the people he does business with, it is impressive, even though religion as such may never be discussed at all. More people are seeking this inner conviction and assurance, this definition of God's love, than might be supposed, and when they meet it, they recognize it and respond to it.

XII

Results, Criticisms and Conclusions

There are no reliable figures by which the success or otherwise of probation methods can be accurately gauged. Probation officers are required to submit annual returns to the Home Office relating to those of their probationers who have completed their term of probation during the current year. Three categories are allowed for : satisfactory, unsatisfactory, and unknown. There are different interpretations of these classifications. " Satisfactory " may mean that the probationer in question kept the terms of his probation as far as was known, or that he has not since (within the current year of its termination) been found guilty of any further offence. In this case one who is known to be consorting regularly with thieves, or continually losing his jobs through unreliability, or quite regardless of the welfare of his children, but who has not actually been before the court again, will be marked up as satisfactory at the end of the year ; while another, who has made great efforts to pay back what he stole, is becoming much more amenable and reasonable at home or industrious at work, must go down as unsatisfactory if he became involved in a street fight on football or Derby night and was charged with disorderly behaviour. If, therefore, the strictly legal interpretation is abandoned as inadequate, the returns become a matter of personal opinion, and will vary from one officer or court to another, according to the point of view taken by persons of varying temperaments and outlooks. Returns which lend themselves to so many interpretations are worthless from any scientific point of view.

In any case an assessment of the value of probation based on only the year or two years of the actual order is bound to be inadequate. To get any real idea of its value one would need to have close personal knowledge of the parties concerned for five or even ten years after its completion. This is impossible. It would defeat the purpose of probation if the one-time offenders were followed around year after year. They would rightly feel that they could not regard the matter as over and done with if they were subjected to so long a period of subsequent official supervision. It would have the effect of making the probation five or ten years rather than the one or two envisaged as normal by the Criminal Justice Act. Officers who have served continuously for many years in the same district are often in a position to have continuing informal knowledge of some of their probationers, never of all. But many officers, particularly those attached to highly organized areas, are liable to be moved about from one district to another according to the exigencies of administration, and these lose touch with all but a very few of their former probationers.

Most probation officers who are really fitted for their work would, in any thoughtful review of it, have to confess to one or two miracles. This word is used advisedly. It indicates both that there has been a remarkable change for the better in the way of life of the offender concerned, and that the officer himself is unable to say what brought this about. To quote a few actual cases, the professional pickpocket with over thirty convictions against her name has, since her probation twelve years ago, lived as a respectable and hard-working woman. The prostitute who was charged with a gang of thieves eight or nine years ago has now completed her training as a hospital nurse and holds a responsible position as such. The young gangster of several years ago is now a happily married steady-going family man. In the very nature of things these are the stories one does not hear about. These people who have surmounted shameful chapters of their past do not want the matter advertised.

It would be damaging to them to publicize their story. So the general public hear only of the more sensational failures of probation which are written up by the press when offenders reappear before the courts. None the less there are miracles.

But candid officers, if questioned about the results of their efforts, would also confess to seeing little change in the majority of their probationers. This is natural. For one thing, many offenders are on the surface quite respectable people. Shoplifters are often devoted mothers and hard-working women. Many young people who get into trouble, sometimes for serious offences, come from good homes, and are on the face of it living orderly lives along the conventional lines. A change of heart is not always a spectacular thing. It is only a proportion of probationers whose outward way of life needs fundamental change of direction.

But even where spectacular change is needed, it is in the nature of things rare. The dice are too heavily loaded against people like the A.[1] or the J.[2] families, described elsewhere, for much outward and material change to be effected. Trained social workers can plan any amount of improvement on paper that looks quite feasible, and their minds must be continually moving on ways and means of amelioration, but in actual fact most would confess that their efforts make little visible difference.

The story of Letitia is perhaps typical of many probation cases in this matter. Letitia's probation officer was despondent at the close of the two-year probation period. She had seen the girl regularly, weekly or fortnightly, spending twenty to thirty minutes with her each time; she had suggested this and that; introduced her to more than one girls' club and to several hobbies; taken her out; discussed all sorts of issues; visited her mother; and racked her imagination as to how she could help this anæmic, purposeless

[1] Page 29.
[2] Page 53.

girl to a fuller, happier life, and thereby to greater stability
and contentment of mind. She thought she had failed.
Letitia could not bear company and would not go near the
clubs ; she had no eyesight for needlework ; she was bored
with knitting ; she had nothing to do but read an occasional
" fourpenny dreadful ". The family were obliged to spend
every evening in the local underground air raid shelter, which
was bad both from the point of view of her health and of
rational leisure interests, but seemed unavoidable at the time.
She took no pleasure in her monotonous unskilled work. As
far as the probation officer could see, Letitia and her circumstances were little different for these two years of probation.
To an outsider, however, hearing the story, it seemed otherwise. Here was a girl who up to two years ago had held
no job for longer than a week or fortnight, and who had
angered her family by her long spells of idling between each ;
throughout her probation she had been consistently at work,
and had only changed her job twice, in both cases for good
reasons and only after serious discussion with her probation
officer. Two years ago she had been without personal
standards, verminous and dishevelled ; now, always reasonably clean and tidy, she was beginning to experiment in hair
styles, and to take trouble about her appearance. Two years
ago she had run away from her family ; but throughout her
probation she had lived at home, being a stand-by to her
parents in perilous times, and was now getting real pleasure
as the self-appointed nurse to her sister's new baby. Quite
recently she had begun taking dancing lessons. Not much
to boast of, you may say ? No, not much ; and the probation
officer did not boast ; she thought she had failed. But
whereas this girl had been a misfit at home, at work and in
society, with nothing to live for and no interests in life, now
she had struck roots in all three spheres. She was a steady
worker ; she was reinstated in the family confidence, and had
grown fond of at least one tiny member of it ; and with

gathering self-confidence symbolized by her wakening
personal standards, she was beginning to look, of her own
volition, to a fuller social life. It is these things which make
a sound basis for a satisfactory life, but they may not be in
themselves spectacular.

Undoubtedly what had helped Letitia was the personal
concern and interest of her officer, wise enough not to dominate
her with her own ideas, but warm enough and genuine enough
to fire her with self-respect and self-confidence, and to elicit
aspirations.

Letitia's story typifies the slow rate of progress which really
fundamental change usually takes. It was so imperceptible
that her probation officer, seeing her regularly, missed it, as
parents see no difference in their children from day to day.
Indeed, speedy or spectacular results in probation should be
looked upon with scepticism. Many probationers are astute
enough to see the role that would be acceptable and to act it,
not with any deliberate attempt to deceive for the most part,
simply to oblige, to merit praise and to get through the
irksome period of supervision with as little fuss as possible.
Thus an inexperienced officer may feel things are going rather
well with So-and-So, " She seems so grateful " or " so
co-operative " or " such a hard worker ", when in reality the
fundamental factors which made for evil remain unchanged.

The public would like to think that the attractive and
lovable stories of bad boys being tamed by kindness and
understanding, such as that told in the popular French film,
" Une Cage de Rossignols ", are true. And so they are, but
it is only half the truth. The other half is ugly and dis-
illusioning, and the film portrayal is not a realistic one. The
truth is that the process takes years and years, as our story
of Clarissa showed. The first reaction of the deeply delinquent to kindness and understanding is to abuse and exploit it,
to test it and try to prove it false. Then moods of dog-like
devotion may alternate with recrudescences of mischief,

deception and spite. Probation officers and probation committees who look for any spectacular results in months will be disappointed.

One of the most difficult things for the social worker to learn is that there are some unhappy and unsatisfactory situations which *cannot* be rectified. They must be accepted, and taken into account, and efforts at amelioration built around them. Mrs F.'s[1] situation must be accepted. Her husband will remain in prison ; it is very unlikely that he will not constantly return there. She will remain under the care of the local authority, doing as she is told when the time comes, with no scope for her own initiative or enterprise. The J.[2] family are bound to continue having economic and domestic problems too great for their resources. Even if Mr J. procures—and manages with luck to keep—a more suitable job, his health has already been grievously impaired by years of unsuitable employment and consequent strain. Six children, even if they have no more, are a big responsibility and financial liability. They will all have illnesses and accidents to pull down any reviving family exchequer. Mrs J., feckless no doubt by nature, has now grown more so by force of habit, and such a habit clings. The most that " social work " can do, however skilled, in these circumstances is to bring about some temporary amelioration of the situation. This by itself is not enough to make any appreciable difference to their moral standards and values. What these people need is to be fired with some joy that makes life worth living, and ultimately only friendship and affection can do this. A true friend is not one who supplies the solution to all our difficulties, but one to whom we know we can turn for understanding, who enters into the situation with us, sharing its tragedy or comedy, and who we know is concerned about us and what happens to us in a personal way. With this kind of friend in

[1] Page 100.
[2] Page 83.

S

the circle, life takes on new meaning. Such a friend gives new standards of what we would and would not care to do, and takes us out of our confined little limited world into a larger one—his or hers as the case may be—and this gives us altogether better perspective. It is the element of friendship in probation or in any kind of social work that produces results, not " case work ".

But by every standard of computation all probation officers have to confess to some failures, and this, too, is natural and to be expected.

To begin with, as long as probation is not carried out as laid down by the Act, and offenders are dealt with without adequate preliminary enquiries, without understanding, or even agreeing to, the terms of their probation, one must expect a large proportion of failures. The system has so far hardly had a chance to show its merits, at any rate so far as the adult courts are concerned. It is not that probation officers if given an opportunity to express an opinion would only opt for the " easy " cases, those in which people have committed trivial offences, or where they are ready and anxious to make amends, nor that only those offenders who show genuine contrition are suitable for probation. Many of these would not be likely to offend again in any case, and absolute or conditional discharge, or a fine, might be a sufficient lesson to them, after all the anxiety and exposure of the court proceedings. The probation officer's job, if only he were allowed to do it, is to assess from what he can discover of each offender's present frame of mind, and the antecedents which have given rise to this, whether or no he might be expected, with help, to take a turn for the better. Hence it may be that a first offender charged with the theft of some petty little article or trifling sum of money may be quite unsuited to probation treatment, while somebody else with a long list of previous convictions for far more serious offences might respond very well. For want of proper

preliminary enquiry the nation is at present put to the
expense of maintaining large numbers of persons in prison
who need never have gone there, and who are certainly going
to be social liabilities in consequence for many a long day
when they are released ; while at the same time other persons
who are mentally deficient or deranged, or deeply anti-social
in mentality, and who need long-term institutional treatment
under trained specialists, both to protect the public and in
their own interests, are released on probation, and given
liberty to continue their spoliation of the public.

But the fact that there is a lapse, and that the probationer
does commit a further offence, must not be taken to mean that
probation has necessarily failed or is an unsuitable method of
treatment.   Theresa's story is a good example of this.

Theresa was a wayward young woman of 16 who had been
evicted from her own home by her stepmother, as well as
from a number of voluntary homes and shelters, on account
of her behaviour.   When she was placed on probation,
following the advice of a psychiatrist who had been consulted, her probation officer found her a highly suitable
approved lodging, and for some months there was a miraculous
change for the better.   The landlady had no fault to find ;
Theresa was a model girl.   Then came a multiple lapse.
She stole a watch from her employer ; left her lodgings
without warning or permission, and went to stay with a girl
friend without notifying her officer of change of address.   She
was missing for a couple of days, and finally, late one night,
rang up her officer in great distress.   Her girl friend had
turned her out, and she had nowhere to go.   The officer gave
her an address of a hostel for stranded girls, and went to see
her there next day.   The tale thereafter slowly and painfully
unravelled itself.   Theresa could give no explanation or
account of herself.   She had got fed up.

What was she going to do now ?

She had no idea.

What about the girl friend ?

Silence. . . . Ominous silence.

Couldn't Theresa go back to her ?

No, it seemed Theresa could not.

Why ?

More ominous silence, and then at last a burst of " She says I stole her gloves ".

" And did you ? "

Discomfort and embarrassment. " Well, yes ; I borrowed them."

" Well, why don't you give them back to her ? "

Another uncomfortable pause. " I can't. I pawned them. I had no money."

" Where did you pawn them, and where's the ticket ? If I lend you the money you can go and get them at once, and return them to her."

Theresa brightened up, went out and redeemed the gloves and returned them to their owner. Next day she and the officer met for another conference.

What was she going to do now ?

More discomfiture. It seemed that what poor Theresa wanted more then anything else was to return to her landlady, the happiest home she had ever had. The officer was dubious, and pointed out that Theresa had behaved very badly to the landlady in leaving without notice or explanation. She advised her to write a letter of apology. Theresa did this, and in a few days' time, as much to the officer's surprise as to anyone else's, was rewarded with an invitation to return if she wished. Theresa was delighted, and she and her officer set off together for the landlady's house. Theresa grew quieter and quieter and more and more uncomfortable. When they reached the house there was nothing for it but to say she was sorry the best way she could, and then sit down and cry. The landlady fetched some tea. She said she hoped Theresa would not go off like that again ; they were

all terribly anxious; and now they would say no more
about it. But Theresa's troubles and confessions were not
over. What was she going to do about work?

Now there were fresh tears, and finally the confession about
the watch. Once more Theresa set off to make what amends
she could, this time accompanied by her probation officer,
and again, miraculously enough, her apologies and explanations were accepted in good part, and she was reinstated and
forgiven. Theresa thereafter faithfully repaid all that she
had borrowed from her probation officer in weekly instalments.
The breaches of probation were duly reported to the magistrates (as Theresa was well aware they would be), who decided
that in view of her efforts to put matters right, no further
action would be taken.

This story could be used to illustrate many aspects of
probation. This officer believed in making her probationers
take full responsibility. Though she supplied the address of a
shelter, she did not take Theresa to it, and though as a friend
she went with her to the pawnbroker, the girl friend, the
landlady and the employer, she left her to make her own
explanations and write her own letters. Theresa obviously
regarded her officer as a real friend, one to turn to in a tight
corner and to whom she was not afraid to confess her misdeeds,
dismaying and multiple as these were. She might have been
expected in the circumstances to elude her probation officer,
and with an awe-inspiring person who believed in taking
" a stern line " this would undoubtedly have happened.
But our point is here that, even if there is a serious lapse or
breach of probation, and on that account it ranks as an
official failure, probation can still be an educative and
constructive business, in society's best interests. If a stern
line had been taken with Theresa, if she had been told that
she had had her chance and must now take her punishment,
and forthwith despatched to prison, Borstal or approved
school (she was already over-institutionalized, and these

places had no horrors for her), she would have been spared the discipline of meeting those whom she had wronged, and of trying to make amends for what she had done. She would not have been expected to do anything further about them, or given the chance to do so. In short, " justice " might have been done, but at the expense of her victims.

Much can be learnt from failures if they are objectively analysed. We do not expect a doctor to say, as one sometimes hears social workers, " Well, I've done my best ; if he can't get on now that's his responsibility ; I wash my hands of him ". We expect the doctor to re-examine the patient's condition and situation when his treatment does not seem to answer, to change the treatment, to get a second opinion. And if all fails and the patient dies, the doctor has a post-mortem examination, for he is humble enough to wish to learn. The point is not that all failures can be avoided by a really intelligent and conscientious officer, but that we can learn something more of human nature and its vagaries from unbiased consideration of our failures if we have a mind to.

But this counting up of supposed successes and failures is no sort of way in which to assess the merits of the probation system. In this respect probation is somewhat comparable to education. One does not calculate the worth of education by its results, but by its possibilities. One does not say " Is education a success or a failure ? " and seek figures to satisfy ourselves either way. We examine its possibilities, and strive by all means in our power to cultivate those factors which seem to contribute to desirable results, and to minimize those which seem to have the opposite effect.

But the probation system has to meet more serious criticism than that it fails. It is sometimes said that it is founded upon the wrong principles.

" Fancy, it seems if you do wrong these days instead of being punished you are allowed to do exactly as you please."

Freewill is the essence of morality.[1]   A child who is forced by an adult armed with a big stick or a lashing tongue to share his orange or sixpence with another is not on that account a generous child.   Similarly a boy who does not help himself to somebody else's tools because he knows his mentor is watching is not on that account an honest boy.   He is honest if, seeing the tools and wanting them very badly, perceiving that no one is about and he is unlikely to be found out, he reflects to himself that they are not his to take, and of his own preference refrains from touching them.   Goodness cannot be constrained ; its essence is freewill.

It is literally true that a person placed on probation can do as he pleases.   He cannot be so dealt with at all unless he pleases; he is at liberty to refuse to enter into the undertaking required.   If he chooses to do wrong, and this is discovered, he must take the consequences, but he is free to do as he will.   The only authority the probation officer has over him is that of applying to the magistrates for a summons for breach of probation if he discovers that a technical breach has been committed.   The object of probation is not to constrain the offender by superimposed authority to be good, much less to restrain him forcibly from doing wrong, but so to enlarge his experience and enjoyment of good that he comes to prefer it naturally, and so to seek it and choose it.   Probation is an educative process.

"But why should those who have damaged their fellows be let off so lightly, and have so much done for them?"   They have certainly injured their fellows, but perhaps society has unwittingly injured them.   We have said, and tried to show, that probation cannot be effective unless it takes into account the total situation of the offender, that is to say his family and his background, which have together contributed to his outlook on life.   But his family and background are

[1] See *Freedom in the Modern World*, by John Macmurray, particularly Chapters IX, X and XI.

conditioned by society. Crime always reflects the prevailing values of society. Thus in this country the crimes most heavily punished are those concerned with property, and thieves are more severely dealt with than persons who are convicted of cruelty to children, for instance, for we are property minded, and property stands high in our national scale of values. Russia is politically minded, and personal property is not a matter of importance there, so that Russia's criminals are her political opponents. If society as a whole, or large sections of it, live with money, pleasure or success as their goal in life, closing an eye to moral values where these interests are concerned, then we must not be surprised if large numbers of its individuals grow up without social responsibility. If life in this highly organized, highly industrialized country of ours is becoming more and more impersonal, by reason of its huge administrative units, then more and more individuals must be expected to lose the habit of personal responsibility for another's welfare. " Society gets the criminals it deserves " is a dictum worth considering.[1] If all this is true, then society is partly responsible for crime and therefore under some obligation to help those of its members who fall moral casualties to its trends.

" But are these people never to have it brought home to them that they have injured or damaged their fellows ? Is there to be no punishment or penalty ? "

This raises the whole question of the ethics and efficacy of punishment, about which much is constantly said and written. But whatever the arguments for and against punishment, the fact remains that probation is not a punishment and was never intended to be worked as such. To try to make it punitive is to defeat its purpose, for in the relationship of offender and probation officer severity has the effect

---

[1] See *The Criminals we Deserve*, by H. T. F. Rhodes, quotation on the title page from A. Lacassagne, *Congres d'Anthropologie Criminele de Rome*, 1886. " Les societes ont les criminels qu'elles meritent."

of antagonizing the former, so that he does not seek the help which it was intended he should have, even if it does not actually stimulate evil instincts rather than good ones, by eliciting rebellion, deception or hatred.

But the fact that probation is not a punishment and offers no constraint does not mean that the offender is left without discipline. Life itself provides this. All these people have difficulties to surmount, provided by their own situation, often exacerbated by their own wrong-doing. There is no need for authority to superimpose more. Probation is designed to help people to accept this natural discipline, and to learn from it rather than to run away from it. It does this by building up their self-respect, by helping them to understand themselves and their fellow creatures better ; by introducing them to a wider range of satisfying and legitimate outlets. It seeks, too, to instil a sense of responsibility for the welfare of others, by trying to deepen the offender's experience of friendship and of the comfort and stimulus which human companionship and loyalties can give. Punishment is negative : its aim is to teach people not to do something again. Probation is positive : its aim is to introduce a better way of life.

None of this can be done without the one great fundamental factor of love, or whatever other name is chosen for that warmth and strength of affection and fellow feeling, quite distinct from passion, which alone makes life worth living for any human being. Much has been said in this book about the value of psychiatry, but psychiatry alone cannot heal sick minds or reform wayward characters. As long as psychiatry remains a coldly objective analytical science it can do no more than show us or the patient what has gone wrong, and this, of course, is indispensable as a basis for treatment. What it has discovered by this means is that there can be no sanity or stability of character without love ; and that what delinquent characters need more than anything else is experience of this great emotion, experience of being loved, and, even more important, of loving. This much can be gathered from reading the psychological reports on young delinquents so often submitted to the courts. " . . . Above all he needs a wealth of adult affection ", they say, over and over again, in different words but always with the same sense. " Love is the effective agent in psychotherapy ", says Dr I. M. Suttie,[1] and whether it is given and elicited by the psychiatrist[2] or more commonly by a teacher, foster-mother, probation officer, friends or relatives matters little. The patient has to learn that love is unconditional, says Dr Suttie later in the same book.[3]

In this as in other respects psychiatry is re-stating in scientific terms truths which were first propounded by the Founder of Christianity. It was He who first taught men the profound truth that love is unconditional.[4] Christianity emphasizes man's need of forgiveness ; psychiatry does, too, but calls it " release from a guilt complex ". Christianity says, " The Truth shall make you free ", and speaks of the Spirit of Truth as the " Comforter ".[5] There is a rock-like comfort and assurance about knowing and accepting the truth, however unpalatable it may be, which can bring relief and healing to sick minds, and this recognition and acceptance of the truth is the basis of a psychological cure.

Good probation demands that its officers should be trained in psychology, that is to say in an understanding of the way the mind works, and that they should be persons of truly Christian magnanimity and discernment. (Some people who do not profess the Christian faith have these qualities.) A loving spirit of goodwill is not enough, neither is the enquiring, impersonal approach of the scientist. It is a

[1] See *The Origins of Love and Hate*, p. 215.
[2] Dr Suttie in the same book on p. 75 quotes a saying attributed to Ferenezi : " It is the physician's love that heals the patient."
[3] *The Origins of Love and Hate*, p. 252.
[4] See Luke vi. 35 : " . . . for He is kind unto the unthankful and the evil " ; or Romans v. 8 : " While we were yet sinners Christ died for us."
[5] See John viii. 32 and xiv. 16, 17.

combination of these two which is needed for probation to reach its highest efficacy. It is the merit of the probation system that it is consonant at once with modern psychiatric science, and with Christian faith and teaching. The theme of this book is that it is only effective when so conducted.

Appendix I

Individual Attention and the Time Factor

The Act and Probation Rules make it clear that there is to be close, regular, personal contact between the probation officer and the probationer. While no statutory minimum is laid down, most officers would normally expect to see their probationers at least once a week during the first month, and once a fortnight for the next six months of probation. Wide discretionary powers are allowed the officer, but obviously he would be expected to have good reasons for seeing less of a probationer than this, or for not seeing more of him if the circumstances demanded more—as of course they often do.

It is also clear that there can be no effective treatment without close, regular, personal attention and thought on the officer's part, directed on to the probationer and his situation. Contact alone without previous preparatory thought and subsequent reflection serve little purpose. Time and leisure of mind are essential factors in probation.

With the best will and the toughest physique in the world, it is not possible for one full-time officer to give more than forty or fifty people the kind of close attention which effective probation demands (less if there are other extraneous duties), and officers who have been grossly overloaded have been faced with a choice of giving all their probationers insufficient attention, or of concentrating on a few to the neglect of the others. One cannot assess the merits or possibilities of the probation system while such patently unsatisfactory conditions obtain. The techniques put forward here are based on the assumed case load of forty to fifty cases, exclusive of other duties.

The gross overloading of officers from the early years of operating the Probation Act until the present time has given rise to the most unfortunate practice of wholesale " reporting ". The word " reporting " is a lamentable one to apply to the personal contact between officer and probationer. It savours of the police station—a presentation of oneself, the exchange of official and, to the client, meaningless and unnecessary formalities, and then thankful departure—an irritating performance of an irksome obligation. If the word as applied to probation is unfortunate, the practice has been more so.

It has not been uncommon for one overworked officer to see as many as twenty, thirty, sometimes many more probationers all on one evening at the office. The amount of individual attention he can give in these circumstances to each depends upon the urgency of the affairs of any particular probationer, the number of others waiting their turn in the waiting room or passage, and the orderliness of this " queue ". The officer in these circumstances is obliged to keep one ear on the sounds coming from the waiting room, and hence has only divided attention to give to the probationer he is interviewing. There is little doubt that much harm is often done in the waiting room itself. One can take it for granted that if a crowd of unruly youths or gossiping women are sitting around there will be much bragging, the telling of unsavoury stories, mimicry of the officer's mannerisms by the wits of the party, and occasional open ragging, with consequent damage to the furniture and equipment. The whole procedure is damaging to the personal dignity and self-respect of the individual probationers, which it is the object of probation to build up. " If you knew the kind of talk which goes on in that room out there, Miss," said one outspoken woman, " you would never ask us all to come and sit there." One must further bear in mind the type of office which many officers are still expected to work in. They are often subjected to constant interruption by telephone calls and colleagues. Numbers of officers still have to share offices with colleagues of either or both sexes. Interviews conducted in these circumstances tend to remain at the superficial level, and to serve little useful purpose. Those who have appalling offices sometimes do all their contacting elsewhere. There are many alternatives. The officer can see his probationers at their own homes, or borrow the use of a room from an interested friend or fellow social worker, or a minister of religion perhaps ; he can chat to a probationer privately sitting in the car a few hundred yards or a turning or two away from the home or place of employment ; he may make an appointment at a teashop on the probationer's way home from work or in the lunch hour. Sometimes he goes with him to the Labour Exchange or hospital, sometimes to a show or concert of some kind. Some officers use their own homes for seeing probationers.

The art of securing that each of fifty different probationers gets the kind of undivided attention he needs is the art of planning one's work, of classifying outstanding needs, and staggering appointments for interviews.

All the probationers on the officer's register should be surveyed, say at fortnightly intervals. There will be some, probably not more than three or four out of fifty at any one survey, who are having special difficulties and who should be seen several times a week for a time, or have a special appointment for a long talk. These are worked in as occasion permits. One might be taken off in the car for an afternoon while the officer does his more distant visits ; one might be invited to a sandwich lunch at the office ; one to the officer's own home over the week-end, or he may hope to drop in at their homes during the week as he passes that way. There will be others nearing the end of their probation whom the officer would not normally expect to see more than once a month. One might roughly estimate that 25 per cent. would be in their last three months of probation ; 25 per cent. of fifty is twelve or thirteen, making three or four interviews a week during each month. A further three or four persons would probably be away, on holiday perhaps, or off on some temporary job away from home. There remain of the fifty some thirty probationers, half of whom should probably be seen weekly, half fortnightly ; that is to say, forty-five interviews must be arranged during the ensuing fortnight, for these, together with three or four of the monthly ones ; say forty-eight in all, or twenty-four each week. Three sessions of two hours each would give twenty-four fifteen-minute interviews each week, and no more than eight in each session. Each probationer is given his appointed time : A comes at 6 p.m., B at 6.15, C at 6.30, and so on. Some will come late and some early, which allows for a certain elasticity in the length of the interviews, but at no time under this system are there more than one or two waiting in the waiting room simultaneously. For regular contact this amount of time is probably sufficient. When any probationer begins to open up and a long story of perplexities or difficulties emerges, he must be put down for special time in the next survey, and given a longer period or an easier setting in which to pursue the matters so raised.

Eight consecutive interviews, each demanding individual preparation, memory, thought and judgment, constitute a considerable strain, and for most people two to two and a half hours of this kind of interviewing at a stretch is as much as can be managed efficiently without a break. All probation officers expect to do a lot of evening work. Probably one evening has to be set aside for evening visiting, and at least one from 7 to 9 p.m. for evening probation interviews. The other interviewing times can often be fitted in at different times ; 5 to 7 p.m. catches workers on their way home from work, 12 to 2 p.m. on a Saturday afternoon may be a convenient time for others or 2 to 4 p.m. on the local early closing

day ; women like an afternoon time, before the children
come out of school ; children can be fitted in on a Saturday
morning or from 4 to 6 p.m. on a school day.   It is essential
to secure that each is seen while the officer's mind is fresh
and alert.   This means that numbers must be broken up.
Breaking up the numbers in this way also enables some
classification of offenders to be arranged, where this is thought
to be desirable.   Schoolchildren and wage earners should
never be mixed at the same reporting time.   Particularly
tough customers, or probationers whose good faith the officer
may have reason to doubt can be asked to come on one day,
others on another ; boys at one time, men at another, and
so on.

   In most probation cases there comes what might be called
a " peak time ", a time when the officer's special attention
and imagination are called upon and great inroads on his
time must be expected.   It may come at the beginning.   For
instance, the offender may have lost his job and his prospects,
and be utterly down.   There is much to be done at once.
There must be long interviews, discussing this, that or the
other possibility ; the officer must be easily accessible, ready
with attentive consideration or further suggestions if the first
plans fail.   If he can see the probationer on to his feet again,
the peak time has passed, and periodic contact thereafter
need be of a less searching nature.   Or the probation begins
with the offender reserved and on his guard.   The officer
has no idea how his client's mind is working ; there seems no
clue, and consequently nothing effective seems to be happening.   Then there comes an explosion : a man gets the sack ;
a boy is turned out of his home ; a girl in floods of tears
breaks the news that she is going to have a baby, or fears she
has contracted V.D. ; a woman suddenly opens out about
her matrimonial troubles ; one of the family meets with a
terrible accident ;—the reserves are down, the officer suddenly
becomes the trusted confidante.   For a week or two he will

have to devote special time to the probationer and his immediate problems, and then, when calmer waters have been reached, less frequent contact will again suffice. Occasionally the peak time comes at the very end of probation, even after its completion. " Now that it's all over, Miss, I don't mind telling you . . ." Sometimes the whole probation passes with no peak, and then the officer may feel that he has never really got to know the probationer, and that he must therefore have failed to help him in any way whatever. But such a conclusion is by no means always true. The story of Letitia (page 258) is an example of this.

It is a good plan to keep a register of all one's probationers, on the plan of a school register, each vertical column representing a week instead of a day. The probationers' names have to be added as new cases are bound over, and hence will appear in chronological instead of in alphabetical order. Each week, or at least each fortnight, the officer goes through the names, ticking those whom he has seen, and making a note of those whom he has not, and must therefore do something about during the next fortnight. The object is to ensure that everyone is being kept track of. The symbols can be varied : H can be put for a home visit, O for an office interview, L for a letter received, and L for a letter answered, T for a telephone conversation and so on. But to complicate the symbols and the book-keeping is to defeat their purpose, which is the simplification of arrangements.

These regular interviews, wherever they may take place, constitute probation " treatment ". The time one normally has to give to each probationer measured in hours looks pitiful. Fortnightly interviews of fifteen minutes each add up to only six and a half hours in a year. Add an extra hour or two for the initial interview and any additional time one may have been able to give, and one still barely reaches ten hours a year. There is much ground to be covered in these few hours. Immediate problems have to be discussed,

T

new values suggested, family relationships sorted out. It is important, therefore, to make the best use of such short time as one can give to each. This means careful preparation for every interview. After each interview, before calling in the next client it is a good plan to make a note of how the conversation went, how it could be followed up next time, what other aspects of the same subject might well be raised, and so on. Each day the officer should refresh his memory of the probationers he is due to see, get out these notes, re-read them, and come to each interview with a clear idea of what he hopes to achieve to-day, of the way he hopes to turn the conversation. It may be his deliberate intention to-day is to leave the whole initiative to the probationer, and see what happens ; it may be that he himself has something definite he wants to raise. The important thing is that the officer should come to the interview with his mind geared into the problems and situation of this particular individual, clearly remembering what has gone before, and able to relate this interview with other previous ones. In this way the regular contacts form some sequence. The probationer is flattered and encouraged that the officer remembers so clearly and has obviously thought about things that were discussed before, and consequently becomes himself more reflective and interested, and may even begin to look forward to the meetings as stimulating. The same technique of careful preparation is necessary if contact is maintained by visiting the probationer at his own home. It is important to keep in touch with the probationer's home and family, as has been stressed throughout this book, but nothing takes the place of the regular undivided attention to the individual himself which only a private interview can give.

Appendix II

Records

Before one can consider the type of records which are desirable, one must know their purpose. Different people keep records with different purposes in mind, and some who see no purpose, fail to keep any. As far as probation officers are concerned there would appear to be at least three functions to be served by record keeping. The officer will want to record the week-to-week contacts, with a view to refreshing his own memory and as a basis for periodic assessment of his probationers' progress ; the magistrates and the Probation Committee want records kept of what is being and has been done in case the officer concerned is suddenly run over or taken ill, so that someone else could pick up the threads quickly, and also precise and accurate details of dates and court decisions in case a probationer is summoned for breach of probation or charged with another offence ; and finally, anyone interested in crime, its prevention and cure, wants reliable data on which to form and test theories. The last, though in many ways the most important, is the one most frequently neglected. This is because there has been comparatively little scientific research into crime in this country. Until officers are given some clear idea of the kind of data required, and are trained to understand how it may be collected and tabulated, their contributions to the scientific treatment of delinquency, which could be so weighty, will remain negligible. Some research has already been done on the peak times and ages of crime.[1] Individual probation officers have supplied data as to black spots of crime in their areas.

[1] See *The Young Delinquent*, by Cyril Burt, pp. 158-76.

The records at present handled by probation officers fall
into four main categories : face sheets, narrative records,
special reports, and correspondence.

The face sheet contains all the information which the court
is likely to want in a hurry : the name, age, address, offence,
date of hearing, the court's decision, dates and particulars
of any previous or subsequent offences, possibly a child's
school or a wage earner's occupation.

There are two types of narrative sheet.   One is the chronological entry, the most usual ; the other is the periodic survey.
The best records contain both.   The chronological entry
should record briefly the date of every contact between the
officer and the probationer, and the gist of what transpired
at it.   It is important to indicate the line taken by both
probationer and officer so that anyone else taking over
unexpectedly may be saved the embarrassment of inadver-
tently taking a contradictory line.   The chronological entry
should be accurate about dates, and show any failure of the
probationer to keep appointments which may have been made,
since these particulars might be required as evidence given
on oath in a summons for breach of probation.   It should
record the dates of Case Committees, the report given by the
officer, and any comment or direction given by the magistrates.

The quarterly summary surveys the probationer's progress
up to date ; the main happenings since the last ; any new
developments or factors in the situation which have arisen ;
the aspects upon which the officer thinks attention should now
be directed ; the plan proposed for the ensuing period, and
so on.   A closing summary surveys briefly the whole probation
effort, the various aims the officer has had, and any supposed
improvement or deterioration in the probationer's circumstances or condition which may have resulted ; and finally
the officer's own assessment of the factors which contributed
to this result.   It should in short be a frank and thoughtful
analysis of the whole business.

The chief value of these summaries is to the officer himself. To undertake them means that once a quarter at least he studies the whole progress of each of his probationers. He must read each record from the opening enquiries and findings with which probation began. From this over-all survey he is in a much better position to assess the trend, to see the direction in which things seem to be moving, to pick up earlier clues, the significance of which may have escaped him at the time, and to form a judgment as to the most profitable line to pursue now. From the closing summary, if it is an unbiased and frank one, he can learn something for the future. The summaries are also invaluable to anyone taking over the supervision, as a basis for a report to a Case Committee, and as subject matter for students to read.

All entries, whether chronological or summarized, should be initialled by the person making them. This is specially necessary now that records are commonly typed and there is not even a change of handwriting to indicate that someone else's opinion or action is now being recorded. Apart from knowing that a second or possibly third person has had a hand in the matter, it is as well to know who this somebody is. Some people's judgment is sounder than others.

Special reports are those written for a doctor or psychologist or Social Agency, whose help may be from time to time invoked ; for a colleague, if the supervision is being transferred ; or to a court, if a report is called for. They generally summarize the case up to date, with special reference to the matter in hand, and are useful for the officer to read when he comes to make his own quarterly survey. Copies of all such should be filed with the record, dated of course.

Correspondence may become very bulky, and letters are probably best kept clipped up in a separate bundle, in chronological order, inside the folder. It is not necessary to keep every incoming letter, nor yet copies of every outgoing one, and the bulk should be kept as reduced as possible.

Letters relating to the time and place of proposed appointments can be destroyed once the appointment has been kept. All letters that are important enough to keep should be dated on receipt. An undated letter is pretty well worthless as a reference afterwards.

The most important thing to remember about letters is to answer them. This is an undisputed maxim, but it is doubly important with probationers. To many probationers the writing of a letter is quite an undertaking. First, a purpose journey to the stores may be involved for the purchase of writing paper, envelopes, and possibly even a pen and ink. People who do not normally write letters do not keep these things in supply. Then a long, slow business ensues of writing, tearing up and re-writing, with accompanying misgivings. Finally, another journey has to be made to the post office for a stamp. People who have gone to all this trouble to write and post a letter not unnaturally hope for an answer. If one comes promptly it enhances their prestige and self-respect. So much is this the case that exchanging letters can become quite a constructive factor in probation, and some officers make a feature of it with good results. There is a snag about the business which has to be borne in mind. If the arrival of a letter for the probationer is an unusual occurrence, it will undoubtedly arouse the curiosity of neighbours, landladies and lodgers. " The postman ! Now who's he got a letter for ? George ? That's funny. Hi ! Mrs Jones, a letter for George ! Now what do you make of that ? . . ." The letter is well pawed over and scrutinized before George comes home from work to claim it. It may, of course, even be lost or torn by the ill-disciplined children of the place. For these reasons it is most important that the address of the court, or even the probation officer's address or calling, should not appear on the letter. It is not necessary to put it. The probationer knows the address well enough. It is better to write on unheaded blank paper. If economy labels are used over old envelopes, care should be taken to see that these incriminating addresses are not visible underneath. Postcards should never be sent—unless it is the cheery holiday picture postcard, of the " Having a lovely time. We had a picnic here on Wednesday " variety which have much to commend them. Some probationers are not alive to these embarrassments themselves until the mischief is done. A wardmaid sharing a bedroom with another girl leaves her letter on the dressing table, and is then rudely challenged—" Are you on probation, then ? " Girls have felt so badly that their shady secret has been discovered that they have walked right out of the job there and then, thus creating fresh difficulties for themselves. As probationers are inexperienced, therefore, probation officers should be doubly careful. Letters about appointments can be quite briefly informal, while at the same time conveying the necessary information in a friendly way. " Dear Nora, Don't come on Wednesday. I have got to be out after all. Come on Monday if you can, at 6 p.m. All good wishes. E.R.G." This is all that is required, and if anyone picks it up it does not at once give the show away, if it has no address on it.

The other question which crops up over letters is whether or not they should be typed. There are two reasons for typing letters. One is in order that an identical copy may be kept for future possible reference ; the other is in order that it may be legible. Handwritten letters are much less formal and more friendly and, provided the handwriting is legible, are on that account to be preferred to typed ones. Copies of letters giving detailed instructions or arrangements should be kept. If there is any subsequent misunderstanding the copy will show whether correct instructions were given. Some children like typed letters, they look so important. Officers have to be sensitive to all these points, and adapt their practice to the individual circumstances of their people.

The problem of confidences is an ever recurring one in

this question of records. A probationer may open out to a probation officer and tell him many of his intimate aspirations and incidents in his past life, simply because he feels drawn to do so, has confidence in his officer's judgment and good faith, and appreciates his comments, but they were never meant for circulation, and the probationer would be mortified beyond measure if he discovered that they had been passed on. Yet many of these confidences may be very relevant to an understanding of the probationer's outlook, and to withhold them from a colleague taking over supervision, for instance, would be a serious matter on that account. People's ideas on confidences vary. One finds confidential matter being bandied about in some offices amongst officers, students and clerical assistants to an astonishing degree. Even in courts one can see medical reports clearly labelled " Confidential " going the rounds, or left lying exposed to view on some table. If once a confidence is committed to paper one has no further control over it, over who may read it, or what they may do with its knowledge. Each must do what seems to him right in the circumstances in this matter. But officers should be meticulously careful not to leave records, letters and reports lying about in the filing trays of their offices. These private papers should be stored in drawers or cupboards while awaiting attention, and none of them should be exposed to view for any chance caller or waiting client to peruse.

All probation officers should keep a card index of all the clients with whom they have dealings, whether they came to court on a charge, or seeking advice, whether they were matrimonial, adult or juvenile court, probation or supervision cases. The cards should be filed alphabetically under the surname, and give details of the full name, address, date, and occasion of their coming to court, together with a brief note as to the action taken—"Probation order made"; "Dismissed with a caution"; "Referred to the Assistance Board"; and a reference to any fuller record of subsequent dealings. These record cards are valuable in several different ways. The question, " Now where have I seen this face before ? " is quickly answered. By reference to the card index the officer discovers with minimum delay that this woman was in arrears with her rent two years ago, and by ringing up the housing authority now he may be able to get accurate information as to what has transpired since, which may be helpful. Or the officer discovers that the mother of the girl before the court this morning was herself summoned by a neighbour a few months ago for brawling. Where there are a team of officers working a district together, it becomes more than ever important to keep a central index on these lines, otherwise they might all be visiting the same family unbeknownst to each other—the senior man concerning a matrimonial case, the woman officer about the daughter's bastardy case, and another officer in connection with the small boy on probation.

Bibliography

The following books have contributed greatly to my thought on this subject :

Aichorn, A. *Wayward Youth*. Putnam.

Badley, J. H. *The Will to Fuller Life*. Allen & Unwin.
Benney, M. U. R. *Low Company*.
—— *Gaol Delivery*.
Bowlby, E. J. *Forty-Four Juvenile Thieves, their Characters and Home Life*. Bailliere, Tindall & Cox.
Boyd-Orr, Sir John. *Food, Health and Income*. Macmillan & Co.
Brew, J. Macalister. *In the Service of Youth*. Faber.
Burbery, W. B., and others. *Child Guidance*. Macmillan.
Burt, Cyril. *The Backward Child*. University of London Press.
—— *The Young Delinquent*. University of London Press.

Clarke Hall and Morrison's Law relating to Children and Young Persons.
Coster, Geraldine. *Psycho-analysis for Normal People*.

Fleming, C. M. *The Social Psychology of Education*. Routledge & Kegan Paul.
Friedlander, Kate. *The Psycho-analytical Approach to Juvenile Delinquency*. Routledge & Kegan Paul.

Gillespie, R. D. *The Psychological Effects of War on Citizen and Soldier*. Chapman & Hall, 1942.
Gittins, John. *Approved School Boys*. H. M. Stationery Office.
Glueck, S. and E. *After-Conduct of Discharged Offenders*. Macmillan.

Hadfield, J. A. *Psychology and Morals*. Methuen.
Hale, S. and M. *Social Therapy*.
Hamilton, —. *Social Case Recording*.
—— *Theory and Practice of Social Case Work*.
Hayward and Wright. *The Office of Magistrate*.
Healy and Bronner. *Delinquents and Criminals, their Making and Unmaking*. Macmillan.
—— *New Light on Delinquency*.
—— *Reconstructing Behaviour in Youth*.
Howe, E. Graham. *Time and the Child or Morality and Reality*.

Hutton, Laura. *The Single Woman and her Emotional Needs*. Bailliére, Tindall & Cox.

Jephcott, P. *Girls Growing Up*.

MacMurray, John. *Freedom in the Modern World*. Faber.
—— *Reason and Emotion*. Faber.
Mannheim, Karl. *Diagnosis of our Time*. Routledge & Kegan Paul.
McCall, Cicely. *They Always Come Back*. Methuen.
Mead, —. *Coming of Age in Samoa*. Penguin.
—— *Sex and Temperament in Three Primitive Societies*. Routledge & Kegan Paul.
Mess, H. A. *Social Structure*.
Miller, Dr Emmanuel, and others. *The Growing Child and his Emotional Needs*. Kegan Paul.
Mowrer, E. R. *Domestic Discord*.
Mowrer, H. *Personality Adjustment in Domestic Discord*.

Paneth, M. *Branch Street*.
Pearse and Crocker. *The Peckham Experiment*. Allen & Unwin.

Reaveley, C., and Winnington, J. *Democracy and Industry*. Chatto & Windus.
Rhodes, H. T. F. *The Criminal in Society*. Lindsay Drummond Ltd.
—— *The Criminals we Deserve*. Methuen.
Rowntree, B. Seebohm. *Poverty and Progress*. Longmans.

Shaw, Clifford. *The Natural History of a Delinquent Career*. University of Chicago Press.
Suttie, I. D. *The Origins of Love and Hate*. Kegan Paul.

Thrasher, F. M. *The Gang*. University of Chicago Press.
Trenaman, J. *Out of Step*. Methuen.

Watson, J. *The Child and the Magistrate*. Cape.
Wills, W. D. *The Barns Experiment*. Allen & Unwin.

Index

Index 289

Index

For Product Safety Concerns and Information please contact our EU
representative GPSR@taylorandfrancis.com
Taylor & Francis Verlag GmbH, Kaufingerstraße 24, 80331 München, Germany

www.ingramcontent.com/pod-product-compliance
Lightning Source LLC
Chambersburg PA
CBHW070717280326
41926CB00087B/2403